LEADERSHIP
in Context

ENDORSEMENTS

Leadership is not a static concept, especially in a disruptive and connected world. It is complex and multi-dimensional. It needs to be understood and applied at contextual, operational and micro levels. Certainly it is much more than a set of competencies.

More has probably been written and spoken about leadership than almost any other topic throughout history. However, to understand leadership is to understand the concept from multiple perspectives. That is what this very comprehensive book provides. There is no single approach to leadership and the variety of perspectives provided in this book will further enhance our understanding and practice of leadership.

An important book with highly qualified and insightful contributors which will add to the conversations about leadership for a long time to come. An essential read for leaders and those responsible for leadership in their organisations now and in the future.

Terry Meyer, Strategy & Leadership Consultant, Leadership SA

Truly a standout book that packs a real punch in the sea of books on leadership. This extraordinary book has to be the most updated, and most comprehensive and definitive compendium on leaders and leadership, written by an impressive array of prominent and respected experts in the field.

Understanding the "what" and "how" of leadership is something that most organisations continue to grapple with in these volatile, complex, uncertain and ambiguous times. This book offers advice on the toughest challenges leaders are facing in business today.

This is compulsory reading for anyone seeking to understand and distil powerful perspectives on leadership and how to become a better leader.

The book provides robust perspectives on leadership fundamentals ranging from leadership theory, models and frameworks on leadership, leadership principles and philosophy, and, in addition, offers authentic, actionable examples. It is bursting with great tips and advice that are immediately applicable and anchored in research.

An indispensable and essential resource for leaders and aspiring leaders at all levels.

Shirley Zinn, Professor Shirley Zinn, Group HR Director, Woolworths

This book is rooted in the challenges facing leaders today, and offers current and future leaders a perspective to help them lead in a VUCA world. The authors take a unique view of leadership from a "value chain" perspective. They provide executives and those in the leadership development business a framework and insight into both being and building better leaders for tomorrow. I believe this book – a product of frontline leaders – will prove to be a great handbook for those who regard leadership as both an interest and a passion.

Paul Norman, MTN Group: Group Human Resources and Corporate Affairs Officer

I have read dozens of books on leadership but none of them has tackled this complex topic in the way that *Leadership in Context* has done. This book tackles the real issues of leadership from understanding the foundations of leadership to examining leadership within its unfolding context; to leadership identification, growth and development; to issues of leadership transitions and leadership wellbeing. The insights and models are based on research and on real experiences and I particularly enjoyed the section on leadership articles and stories – real-life leadership experiences as told by the leaders themselves.

This book is that rare mix of a treasure house of up-to-date knowledge about every aspect of leadership and at the same time full of insights and suggestions for practical implementation. It is both thought-provoking and enlightening, and a must-read for anyone trying to understand the complex issues surrounding leadership. This is one of the best books on the topic of leadership I have been privileged to read.

Italia Boninelli, HR Strategist, Executive Coach and Author, (recent past Executive Vice-president: People and Organizational Development, AngloGold Ashanti)

The seminal guide to the kind of transformational leadership required in the 21st century and beyond.

S'ne Mkhize, Senior Vice President, Human Resources – Sasol

What a phenomenal work!

This is the most comprehensive, insightful and well-grounded work on leadership ever published in South Africa.

It unpacks leadership in its many facets and perspectives – from individual to organisational and global leadership.

The authors are thought leaders, scientists and subject-matter experts; they ask the difficult questions and reveal the essence of leadership as an art and science.

This book is a must for everybody in leadership positions – be it the business sector, public sector, religious organisations, education, or community organisations.

An ideal reference work for the consultant or business science practitioner.

Dr Johan de Beer, Human Capital Executive, Africa Division, Imperial Logistics

Leadership in Context is a feast for scholars, students and practitioners alike who will find a comprehensive reference book on leadership theories a diversity of the schools of thought that have influenced and continue to shape the evolution of leadership as a fully fledged discipline that is applied to complex and changing contexts. As someone trying to master the leadership discipline and as an aspirant leadership expert myself, I was pleasantly surprised at how much there is still to know and learn about this enthralling subject called leadership.

Dudu Msomi, Chief Executive Officer, Busara Leadership Partners

Given the plethora of books on Leadership, one is tempted to think, "What else can be written about leadership?"

This masterful creation crushes that thought. It is a call to choose to be a different and better leader, to stand up and … lead.

I recommend that current and future leaders, young and old, study this gem and weave the learnings into their approach to leading our most precious asset, people.

Leon Steyn, Group Human Resources Executive, Bidvest

Copyright © KR Publishing, Theo H Veldsman and Andrew J Johnson

All reasonable steps have been taken to ensure that the contents of this book do not, directly or indirectly, infringe any existing copyright of any third person and, further, that all quotations or extracts taken from any other publication or work have been appropriately acknowledged and referenced. The publisher, editors and printers take no responsibility for any copyright infringement committed by an author of this work.

Copyright subsists in this work. No part of this work may be reproduced in any form or by any means without the written consent of the publisher or the authors.

While the publisher, editors and printers have taken all reasonable steps to ensure the accuracy of the contents of this work, they take no responsibility for any loss or damage suffered by any person as a result of that person relying on the information contained in this work.

All cases are for illustrative purposes only and the intent is not to evaluate the performance of an organisation.

First published in 2017

ISBN: 978-1-86922-688-6 (Printed)
ISBN: 978-1-86922-689-3 (ePDF)

Published by KR Publishing
P O Box 3954
Randburg
2125
Republic of South Africa

Tel: (011) 706-6009
Fax: (011) 706-1127
E-mail: orders@knowres.co.za
Website: www.kr.co.za

Printed and bound: HartWood Digital Printing, 243 Alexandra Avenue, Halfway House, Midrand
Typesetting, layout and design: Cia Joubert, cia@knowres.co.za
Cover design: Marlene de'Lorme, marlene@knowres.co.za and Cia Joubert, cia@knowres.co.za
Editing: Adrienne Pretorius, pretorii@mweb.co.za
Proofreading: Valda Strauss: valda@global.co.za
Project management: Cia Joubert, cia@knowres.co.za

LEADERSHIP
in Context

Edited by
Andrew J Johnson and Theo H Veldsman

2017

ACKNOWLEDGEMENTS

What a pleasure to work with authors who see the unquestionable criticality of leadership, and are passionate about the difference leadership must make in assuring a desirable, sustainable future for all. It was wonderful to have worked with each and every one of our 69 authors over such an extended period of time. Your wisdom, expertise, suggestions and time willingly shared in crafting your invaluable contribution in making *Leadership in Context* the outstanding and trend-setting Thought Leadership Book it has turned out to be is gratefully acknowledged.

A warm word of thanks is due to:

- All of our Peer Reviewers for your valuable input and time.
- To all our Endorsees for your time given, to offer our book the cachet it deserves.
- Wilhelm Crous, Managing Director of KR, for your constant stretch and guidance; constructive criticism; ongoing encouragement; infectious enthusiasm; and advice and help in working around and through barriers, that made it such a pleasure to work on our book.
- Joann Hill for organising the peer reviews and endorsements.
- Cia Joubert, for your excellent project management of our book that was mission critical in ensuring that the right things happened at the right time and in the right way so that our book became a reality.
- Adrienne Pretorius, our technical editor, for ensuring the technical quality excellence of our book.
- Valda Strauss, for the excellent proofreading of our book after layout.

Last but not least, a warm, appreciative "Thank you" to our families for their understanding, support and sacrifices throughout the painful birth process of the book which took two years from initiation, through conceptualisation and production, to final delivery.

TABLE OF CONTENTS

FOREWORD BY *DR MORNÉ MOSTERT*	ii
ABOUT THE EDITORS	v
ABOUT THE CONTRIBUTORS	vi

SECTION 1: SETTING THE SCENE   1
1. Leadership as strategic organisational capability and intervention by *Theo H Veldsman and Andrew J Johnson*   2

SECTION 2: WORLD OF TOMORROW
2. The world of tomorrow: leadership challenges, demands, and requirements by *Theo H Veldsman*   10

SECTION 3: SECTORIAL CONTEXTS
3. School leadership by *Louise van Rhyn, Gail McMillan and James Ndlebe*   31
4. Leading in South African higher education by *Crain Soudien*   49
5. Public sector leadership by *Vain Jarbandhan*   65
6. Community leadership by *R Bricks Mokolo with Mokesh K Morar*   79
7. Sports leadership by *Wim Hollander*   93
8. Leading professional firms by *Jenny Greyling* in association with *Ajen Sita*   105
9. Business leadership by *Hixonia Nyasulu*   119
10. Political leadership by *Chris Landsberg*   129
11. Religion, spirituality and leadership by *Anthony Egan*   145
12. Ecologically embedded leadership by *Jess Schulschenk*   159

SECTION 4: LEADERSHIP CONTEXTUAL ENGAGEMENT   **168**
13. Leadership engagement with the context by *Theo H Veldsman*   169

SECTION 5: LEADERSHIP STORIES   **185**
14. *Bridgette Gasa*: Good leaders unite people from *Sakebeeld*   188
    Cheryl Carolus: Leaders must lead by example from *Sakebeeld*   190
    Ali Bacher: Captaining on and off the field by *Wilhelm Crous*   192
    Shameel Joosub: Creating movement as a leader in a constantly evolving and changing environment by *Adriaan Groenewald*   199
    Herman Mashaba: Good leaders are guided by reality, not wishful thinking by *Adriaan Groenewald* and from *Sakebeeld*   201
    Pfungwa Serima: Head in the Clouds and feet on the ground from *Sakebeeld*   203

SECTION 6: LOOKING AHEAD
15. The future of leadership by *Andrew J Johnson and Theo H Veldsman*   205

Index   217

FOREWORD BY DR MORNÉ MOSTERT

Leadership is an emerging property of the intangible constituent parts of its context; it does not belong to any of the rapidly dematerialising parts of its agents or context, but is nevertheless exhibited as the result of their dynamic interactivity. Leadership, then, is not mere text. Its fissure-fusion dynamics render it both the producer and product of *con*text, i.e. what is *with, behind* and *ahead of* the text. There is perhaps no subject of our time more prone to the characteristic of multiplicity of perspective than the study of leadership in both government and business. This is especially true when leadership is studied not as a whimsical ideal but, as it is in this book, positioned within its inescapable social milieu.

The book illustrates elegantly that leadership context is not only conceptual, organisational and sectoral, but also temporal – its unique interpretational elements sit as much within the span of time and history as they do within the reality of its unique era. Simultaneously, contextual expectations position leadership within its implications for a time yet to come – a time that will inevitably judge it for its capacity to produce more meaningful alternatives than its own time seems to allow. It must therefore not only embrace its own interval in the spectrum of history, but also transcend it for preferred futures.

Thus leadership is woven inextricably into context. And, in a classical meta- (and para-meta) perspective, leadership also produces its own context. A dynamic reinforcing loop therefore exists between leadership and its multiple immediate and extended environments. Consequently, positional leadership, while aspirational, is simply the beginning. Leadership must transcend positionality and pro-positionality to become *dis*positional, i.e. constantly in relation to its multiple containing systems.

One risk is to treat leadership in a utilitarian manner in which it must simply fit its context. To say that the world is in flux is to observe the glaringly obvious. One meta-perspective offers the insight that leadership itself is in flux as its context is shifting; not only as a product of the context, but also as a discrete field of practice and study. Society creates its leaders while leaders co-create society. Far more valuable is the vantage point that leadership has the potential, even obligation, to shape its context and indeed its future contextual reality. Such systemic complexity places enormous cognitive and other demands on leaders who already appear to be struggling with current challenges. One explanation may be that too many leaders are clinging to a paradigm of mechano-social engineering rather than embracing anthropogenic approaches for which the global context is in such dire need.

In the same way that leaders both create and are created by their context, they also exist in and create the narrative of their organisational and social context. This book shows the power of the personal narrative through the deep reflection of successful leaders who have long since stepped across the boundaries of traditional leadership paradigms. It demonstrates the opportunity for leaders to use the power of ethnographic allegory both to synthesise their own experience and penetrate the fabric of their context.

Leadership is both a real-time paradigm producer and future-time paradigm designer. In the cognitive restructuring demanded by future societies, the sensing and anticipation of leadership as defined by the evolving context is a requisite competence of leaders of our epoch. The rapid acceleration of leadership excellence is desperately needed in the world of today and the multiple possible futures that leaders have the power to create. The authors of this book have demonstrated tremendous conceptual agility in articulating immensely conceptual dimensions which will, despite their intangibility, nevertheless impact significantly on our collective futures.

Dr Morné Mostert is Director of the Institute for Futures Research, a strategic foresight research unit at Stellenbosch University.

ABOUT THE EDITORS

Dr Andrew J Johnson

Andrew is the Chief Learning Officer at Eskom's Academy of Learning. An Industrial Psychologist by profession, he holds an MSc in Occupational Psychology (Nottingham) and a PhD in Industrial Psychology from the University of Johannesburg (UJ). He has also completed formal philosophical, theological and exegetical studies at Sts. Peter & John Vianney Seminaries and St Joseph's Scholasticate.

A seasoned HR executive, his special interests are HR strategy consulting, leadership development, talent and succession management, organisational transformation, and change management. His career in Organisational Effectiveness in the private sector has seen him working for Edcon, MTN, Avmin, JSE and Liberty in senior positions, and he has consulted to other state-owned entities, private companies, and African and BRICS (Brazil, Russia, India, China and South Africa) utilities.

He held non-executive roles in FASSET, the NEF, the COJ Property Company, Transparency SA, NSFAS, & King II; currently he serves on the Advisory Committee of the Industrial Psychology Department of UJ (where he is an occasional lecturer), and the HR (Staffing) Committee of the University of KwaZulu-Natal (UKZN). Andrew is involved in the Society for Industrial & Organisational Psychology of South Africa (SIOPSA) (president in 2011/12), and the Global Forum on Executive Development and Business Driven Action Learning. He is the winner of the prestigious IPM HR Director of the Year (2014), and the recipient of the SABPP Lifetime Achievement Award (2014) and of SIOPSA's Honorary Life Membership (2012).

He is in high demand as a speaker, coach and mentor. At his core he is a deeply passionate student of human behaviour in the context of work, and how this can create a better self, team, organisation and society.

Prof Theo H Veldsman

Theo, who is regarded as a thought leader in South Africa with respect to people management and the psychology of work, has demonstrated his ability to proactively identify emerging people and leadership needs and arrive at fit-for-purpose, innovative solutions that are theoretically and practically sound.

Theo holds a PhD in Industrial Psychology and is a registered Industrial Psychologist and Research Psychologist and accredited HRM Practitioner. He prefers to call himself a Work Psychologist. He has extensive research and development, as well as consulting experience gained over the past 35 years in strategy formulation and implementation; strategic organisational change; organisational (re)design; team building; leadership/management and strategic people/talent management. He consults with many leading South African companies as well as organisations overseas, in the roles of advisor, expert and coach/mentor.

In addition to being the author of nearly 200 technical/consulting reports/articles, he has done numerous management and professional presentations and attended seminars at a national and international level. He is the author of two books, and has contributed nine book chapters.

Up to the end of 2016, when he retired, he was Professor and Head of the Department of Industrial Psychology and People Management, Faculty of Management, University of Johannesburg. Since the beginning of 2017 he is a Visiting Professor at the sam eDepartment. He has led the profession of Psychology and Industrial Psychology nationally as president on several occasions. He has been awarded fellowship status by the Society of Industrial and Organisational Psychology of South Africa (SIOPSA), and is the 2012 recipient of a Life-Long Achievement Award from the South African Board for People Practices (SABPP).

ABOUT THE CONTRIBUTORS

Anthony Egan

Anthony is a Jesuit priest based in Johannesburg. His PhD (University of the Witwatersrand [Wits]) was in Political Studies, having previously studied History at the University of Cape Town. He studied Philosophy and Theology in London and Cambridge, Massachusetts. He has written three books and numerous book chapters, academic and popular articles in the areas of history, theology and ethics. Based at the Jesuit Institute South Africa, he lectures part time at the Steve Biko Centre for Bioethics, at Wits.

Jenny Greyling

Jenny, who is the Talent Development and Reward Leader for the Africa region at EY, qualified as a Chartered Accountant and specialised in the Retail and Consumer Products Industry. She holds an MPhil from the University of Johannesburg (UJ) in Personal and Professional Leadership. Over the past 20 years she has worked in the HR field, specialising in leadership development, performance, career and talent management in professional services firms. She was fortunate to gain experience working with EY in the USA and the UK. Her achievements include setting up a centralised recruitment function, designing a coaching and mentoring framework, developing a diversity culture change initiative, using the leadership pipeline, talent management and succession planning principles, as well as designing EY's Africa Leadership Development Centres.

She is passionate about her own growth and development, and is interested in giving EY employees meaningful career experiences, as well as learning and development opportunities. Her role includes driving EY's world-class learning practices, performance development, career management and the development of high potentials. A trained Life Line counsellor, she uses these skills to coach professionals.

EY received external recognition from FASSET by winning the "Making Best Practice Count" Award five years in a row for its leading practices in the area of learning and development. EY South Africa has ranked in the top ten across all companies in South Africa for the past ten years; it was Certified Top Employer Kenya, Nigeria, South Africa and Zimbabwe; and is the only professional services firm to be certified as Top Employer Africa across the continent.

Jenny, who is married with two children, enjoys swimming, spinning, walking and Pilates. She has a keen interest in child education and giving back to the community through a programme called Brain Boosters.

Wim Hollander

Wim holds a BSc in Botany and Zoology, a postgraduate teacher's diploma, a BEd (Educational Management) (Hons) (cum laude), an MEd (Didactics) and two doctorates: in Education (Didactics) and Commerce (Sport Management).

He has supervised and co-supervised 31 Master's and five doctoral students and published more than 35 articles in refereed journals. He also acts as moderator and external examiner for various higher education institutions in South Africa. He has presented more than 40 papers at national and international conferences and published in excess of 44 reports on international, national and local impact studies. He is subject editor of the *South African Journal of Research in Sport, Physical Education and Recreation* (SAJSPER).

Wim played provincial rugby at various levels, including for the South-Eastern Transvaal Craven Week school team, Transvaal u/20 and Senior Curry Cup teams. He was coach, manager, convenor of the selection committees and selector of the Rand Afrikaans University, Transvaal,

Golden Lions and South African Universities u/20 and u/21 rugby teams for several years; selector and coach of the South African u/21 rugby team for four years; and he coached the Golden Lions Currie Cup team for two seasons.

Vain Jarbandhan

Vain, who is a senior lecturer and Head of Department: Public Management and Governance at the University of Johannesburg (UJ), has been involved in education throughout his career. He started out as a teacher and acting head of department in various schools. Thereafter, he was appointed as lecturer at the former Vista University (East Rand Campus) in the Faculty of Economic and Management Sciences where he taught Public Administration at both under- and postgraduate levels. Following the higher education merger, he was transferred to the former Rand Afrikaans University (now UJ) where he still lectures and supervises students at the honours, Master's and doctoral levels.

His industry-related activities include training senior government employees in the Public Leadership and Management Academy (PALAMA) Executive Development Programme (EDP) and facilitating South African Local Government Academy (SALGA) programmes for both councillors and executive employees. He has also participated in and acted as session chair for numerous conferences.

Vain has published 16 articles in peer-reviewed accredited journals. He is Editor-in-Chief of *Administratio Publica*. He has delivered a number of papers at conferences, both nationally and internationally. In March 2013 he was part of a SALGA delegation invited by SKL (Swedish local government) to uplift local government skills. He has received numerous accolades, including the Faculty Prize for doctoral candidates (2013) and the Golden Key award of the International Honours Society.

Chris Landsberg

Chris is Professor of International Relations, specialising in diplomacy, foreign policy and African political leadership. He is South African National Research Chair in African Diplomacy and Foreign Policy at the University of Johannesburg (UJ), Acting Director of the Institute for Pan-African Thought and Conversation at UJ, and Senior Associate in the School of Leadership.

He holds a BA in Social Science and a BA (Hons) in Development Studies, as well as an MA in International Studies from Rhodes University. In 1993 he completed an MPhil in International Relations at the University of Oxford and a DPhil in International Relations (1997–2001), focusing on the international politics of South Africa's democratic transition.

Chris, who is a former Director of the Centre for Policy Studies (CPS), previously taught at the University of the Witwatersrand (Wits), and co-founded and co-directed the Centre for Africa's International Relations (CAIR). He is a former Hamburg Fellow at Stanford University and Visiting Professor in the Cadet Programme of the Department of Foreign Affairs. He has published and edited several books, including *The diplomacy of transformation* (Macmillan), and numerous articles and book chapters.

Gail McMillan

Gail, who is Symphonia's Monitoring and Evaluation Lead and Operations Manager for the Cape Region, has over 15 years' experience in social development programmes in Africa, Europe and the Middle East. She has led and managed teams in a variety of focus areas, including homelessness, education and legal advice.

Gail holds a BA in Psychology from the University of South Africa and a Master's in Management from the University of Winchester. In her MSc dissertation, Gail contributed to the field of knowledge on how leaders in non-profit organisations inspire followership. Her contribution to *Leadership – perspectives from the coal face* is her first published work. E-mail: gail@symphonia.net

Richard Bricks Mokolo

Richard is a paralegal and activist who provides general advice to Orange Farm and the surrounding community. He is also a mediator and counsellor who facilitates workshops and seminars, and promotes access to justice by taking part in community radio station programmes. He is Chairperson of the Association of Gauteng Advice Office and served on the National Council of the Association of Community Advice Offices SA. He is active in social movements aimed at protecting social justice issues in communities, dealing with cases such as housing and eviction, labour disputes, land claims, domestic violence, racism and xenophobia.

His paralegal work mainly focuses on disadvantaged and vulnerable groups within the community. He works hard to make people aware of their human and legal rights.

Mokesh Morar

Mokesh works as Chaplain at Holy Family College in Parktown and as organiser of Young Christian Students based in Johannesburg. He served as Director of Sekwele Centre for Social Reflection (Social Academy) in Bethlehem, South Africa (March 2000–November 2012), and before that as Parish Priest in Noupoort and Hopetown, as well as in the former Transkei area of Sterkspruit (1989–1999).

Mokesh holds a Master's of Divinity (Milwaukee, Wisconsin, 1988) and an MA from the University of the Free State (2002) as well as a BA from the University of South Africa (1987). He has been active on the ground in social justice ministry in different regions of South Africa, including the Karoo/Northern and Eastern Cape and the Free State, working extensively with community leaders both in and outside the religious sector, with a strong focus on agrarian reform.

Having researched the unique cooperation between the Roman Catholic Church and the Communist Party (India) Marxists and how they were able to eradicate poverty and inequality in Kerala, India, he published a book entitled *Christianity and socialism today – possibilities and lessons from Kerala*. Mokesh also served as a rapporteur at a symposium in May 2000, organised by the Bethlehem Catholic Social Academy (Sekwele) and edited the report *Bridging the gap between the rich and the poor in South Africa* (2000) for the Konrad Adenauer Foundation. E-mail: mokeshm@gmail.com

James Ndlebe

James is Director of Education Management and Governance Development at the Department of Basic Education (DBE). He began his career as a teacher in Soweto, Johannesburg, and progressed through the ranks as Head of Department, Deputy Principal and Principal before joining the Johannesburg South District as Circuit Manager. He subsequently took up the position of Chief Education Specialist at Ekurhuleni South and Johannesburg, leading to his current role at the DBE.

James holds a Secondary Teacher's Diploma, a BA and a BEd degree from the University of South Africa, an HR Management diploma and is a graduate of the Leaders in Education

International programme conducted in Singapore. He is the author of several policies and guidelines in the fields of district and school management and governance. E-mail: Ndlebe.j@dbe.gov.za.

Hixonia Nyasulu

Regarded as one of the most influential women in business in South Africa by *Financial Mail*, Hixonia is rapidly developing an international reputation for her integrity and drive.

Hixonia is Chairman of the women-controlled Ayavuna Women's Investments (Pty) Ltd. She previously ran T.H. Nyasulu & Associates – a strategy, marketing and research company she started in 1984. Her clients included retail, manufacturing, FMCG and tourism companies, as well as municipalities.

An experienced non-executive director, Hixonia has served on the board of blue-chip companies such as McCarthy Group Ltd, Anglo Platinum Ltd, Nedbank Ltd (as Deputy Chairman) and Tongaat Hulett Ltd. and on the JP Morgan Advisory Board. Attending the International Programme for Board Members at the renowned Institute of Management Development (IMD) in Lausanne exposed her to corporate governance models in various countries.

Hixonia holds an Honours in Psychology and an Executive Leadership Development Programme Certificate from the Arthur D Little Management Education Institute.

She served on the Banking Enquiry Panel, appointed by the South African Competition Commission to investigate charges in the retail banking sector, access to the national payment system and competition in the banking sector. She was a founder member of the WEF Advisory Group to set up a community of global chairmen, and design a programme and agenda for the first Gathering of Chairmen in Megève, in April 2013, where she led one of the discussion topics.

As Director of Sasol Ltd, she led the company as Chairman (2008–2013). By April 2016, she had served for nine years on the board of Unilever PLC and NV. She is also Chairman of Nyasulu Holdings, and owner and Executive Producer of "H to the power of You", a leadership and talent development TV show currently broadcasting to 48 African countries.

Jess Schulschenk

Jess is Director of the Sustainability Institute and an Extraordinary Lecturer with the School of Public Leadership at Stellenbosch University, coordinating the Corporate Governance and Sustainability module for the MPhil programme. She is Research Director for South Africa for the Embedding Project – a joint research initiative of Simon Fraser University and the Graduate School of Business (GSB) at the University of Cape Town (UCT).

A PhD candidate with GSB, Jess holds an MPhil in Sustainable Development from Stellenbosch University and a BSc in Ocean and Environmental Sciences (UCT). Previously, she led teaching and consulting programmes in corporate governance, sustainability and community development for the public and private sectors.

Ajen Sita

Ajen is a home-grown talent of EY, having started as a trainee accountant in 1993. He was made a partner in 1999 and subsequently became Head of Entrepreneurial Services, lead Audit Partner on Telkom and Head of Assurance, before becoming CEO of EY Africa in 2010. Ajen is part of EY's EMEIA (Europe, Middle East, India and Africa) Board and Global Emerging Markets Forum.

In 2008, EY set a new standard in the professional services industry when it integrated all its country practices across the EMEIA region. EY's operating model, used in 33 countries, brings a borderless approach to clients, and provides additional growth and development opportunities for staff. Africa is a particular passion and focus for Ajen, who has led the integration of EY across the continent.

In 2011 he commissioned EY's first highly acclaimed Africa Attractiveness Survey, which investigates the trends, FDI and relative attractiveness of various African markets. With this annual report having become a benchmark in the industry, Ajen is a regular commentator at conferences and in the media on investing in Africa.

Ajen's other passion is the transformation of the accounting and auditing profession. As Chairman of the Thuthuka Education Upliftment Fund, he helps drive the race and gender transformation of the profession. During his tenure as Head of Assurance, EY came first in the final qualifying exam for Chartered Accountants in South Africa, in four out of five years, and substantially closed the gap between the pass rates of white and black candidates.

During his tenure as CEO, EY Africa was recognised as "Top Employer" in eight African countries. EY SA also took third position overall in the Top 10 rankings for Top Employers South Africa, and came first in industry ranking in the Professional Services category.

Crain Soudien

Crain is Chief Executive Officer of the Human Sciences Research Council (HSRC), former Director of the School of Education at the University of Cape Town (UCT) and former Deputy Vice-Chancellor at the same university. He is Emeritus Joint Professor in Education and African Studies at UCT, a Distinguished Honorary Professor at the University of Pretoria and a Visiting Professor at the Nelson Mandela Metropolitan University. He has published over 190 articles, reviews, reports, and book chapters in the areas of social difference, culture, education policy, comparative education, educational change, public history and popular culture. He is the author of *Youth identity in contemporary South Africa: Race, culture and schooling* and *Realising the dream: Unlearning the logic of race in the South African school* and the co-author of *Education exclusion and inclusion: Policy and implementation in South Africa and India*, and co-editor of four books.

Crain was educated at UCT and the University of South Africa, and holds a PhD from the State University of New York at Buffalo. He is involved in a number of local, national and international social and cultural organisations and is the Chairperson of the Independent Examinations Board, the former Chairperson of the District Six Museum Foundation, a former President of the World Council of Comparative Education Societies and was Chair of the Ministerial Committee on Transformation in Higher Education. He is a fellow of a number of local and international academies and serves on the boards of a number of cultural, heritage, education and civil society structures.

Louise van Rhyn

Louise, the CEO and founder of the Symphonia group of companies, holds a PhD in Management (DMAN) from the Centre for Management and Complexity at the University of Hertfordshire, an MBA from the University of Stellenbosch and has worked as an Organisational Development Practitioner for the past 25 years. She believes that highly complex and intractable social challenges can be solved through cross-sectoral collaboration and an understanding of complex social change. This has led to the creation of the Partners for Possibility programme, which unites South African business leaders and school principals of resource-constrained schools in a reciprocal co-learning and co-action partnership to strengthen leadership and management capacity in schools. The process has also been recognised for its contribution to nation-building and reconciliation in South Africa. E-mail: louise@symphonia.net

SECTION 1
SETTING THE SCENE

Chapter 1

ORIENTATION

Theo H Veldsman and Andrew J Johnson

On many fronts, and in many ways, our insight into and the exercise of leadership is under severe scrutiny because of a radically changing and significantly different world; reinventing organisations; and working persons with significantly different, or significantly shifting, needs, expectations and aspirations. Without doubt, leadership is in the overheating crucible of a reframed/reframing world that is in the throes of fundamental and radical transformation.

The current fierce debate about leadership and leadership excellence (or lack thereof) may be one of the most important issues of our present time, alongside issues such as demographic shifts, the distribution of economic prosperity, food and water security, world peace, global warming, and sustainability. It could even be argued that these issues in and of themselves are but symptomatic of poor leadership; or, at worst, of the inability and/or a lack in the commitment to lead.

The clarion call is clear and unequivocal. At this critical juncture in our history, the search is on for better *and* different leadership. Leaders and leadership have to reinvent themselves if they wish to be successful in the unfolding world of tomorrow. Old recipes and conventional ways of leading will no longer suffice. They may even be detrimental and destructive. It can be argued that those nations, societies, communities and organisations that are able to demonstrate leadership excellence consistently will dominate and inherit the future, in particular in the case of emerging countries in Africa. Our very future is predicated on the quality of our current and future leadership who will either make us architects or victims of the future.

Without any doubt leadership is *the* critical strategic capability of nations, societies, communities and organisations, making them sustainably future-fit. The primary trigger for *Leadership in Context* is therefore to be found in the snowballing crisis around leadership, and the consequential imperative for better and different leadership.

The Strategic Leadership Value Chain Perspective: A Meta-framework From Which to View Leadership

Leadership is a critical organisational capability and intervention. To the best of our knowledge no overall, systemic, integrated and holistic perspective is available in the literature viewing leadership from a Strategic Leadership Value Chain perspective. Such a perspective would provide a meta-framework from which to look at leadership systemically and holistically as an organisational intervention. Such a perspective would assist one not only in bringing order to the overwhelming, exploding leadership literature, but also serve as an overall, integrative map for organisations in engaging with leadership. At best numerous, piecemeal treatises are available dealing with specialised leadership intervention topics, e.g. leadership assessment, leadership development, or leadership well-being but no overarching meta-framework exists.

Figure 1.1 provides our take on the make-up of the Strategic Leadership Value Chain in terms of which leadership as a mission-critical, strategic organisational capability and intervention can be viewed.

Chapter 1: Orientation

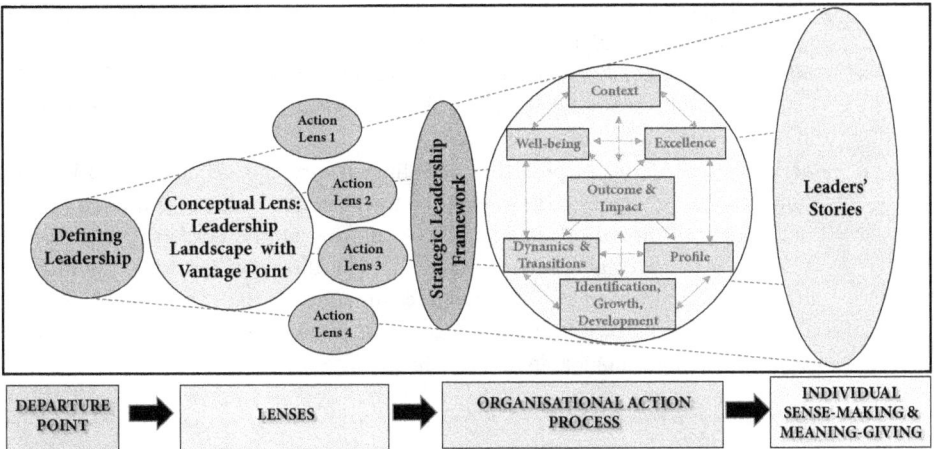

Figure 1.1 A Strategic Leadership Value Chain Perspective on leadership as an organisational capability and intervention

The make-up of the Strategic Leadership Value Chain

With reference to Figure 1.1, the Strategic Leadership Value Chain is composed of the following elements:

- *Departure point: Defining leadership*

   In crafting an organisation-specific leadership thinking framework, the organisation as a starting point must formulate explicitly and intentionally what they understand "leadership" as a phenomenon to be conceptually, in order to correctly demarcate the territory called "leadership". An incorrect definition of leadership can delineate the phenomenon either too narrowly, consequently excluding essential elements of leadership; or too broadly, resulting in the inclusion of unrelated elements ("noise") in its definition.

- *Lenses*

   Having demarcated the territory called "leadership" by defining it, the organisation must next construct and/or select the lenses it will use to map, make sense of, and give meaning to the demarcated leadership territory. The lenses represent the "toolbox" the organisation will use in engaging with the leadership territory. Three types of lenses can be discerned:

   o *Conceptual lens:* This represents the organisation's meta-view – its "Google map" - of what building blocks (= "towns with their suburbs") with their interdependencies (= "roads") make up the demarcated leadership territory. We call this meta-conceptual view the "Leadership Landscape".

   The value of the Leadership Landscape as meta-conceptual view of the leadership territory is three-fold:
   - to *simplify*, organise and integrate at a meta-level the complexity of the field of leadership with its ever-expanding and overwhelming literature;
   - to *provide* a common meta-language for an all-inclusive, coherent leadership dialogue about leadership, for example in teaching, or in an organisation; and
   - to *structure* an organisation's conversation about leadership, enabling it to arrive at a customised Strategic Leadership Framework (see below) for the organisation that

3

will direct and guide its thinking, decisions and actions regarding leadership as a strategic organisational capability and intervention.
- *Interpretative Lens:* A Vantage Point next must be chosen by which the Leadership Landscape with its building blocks will be interpreted. For example, Appreciative Inquiry or Critical Management Theory.
- *Action Lenses:* Having mapped the leadership territory, and having chosen a Vantage Point, the Action Lenses serve as enabling tools selected by the organisation to deal and work with the various building blocks making up the Leadership Landscape. Action tools represent various disciplines and theoretical/practical approaches that can be used to engage with the leadership territory in order to make sense of it. Examples of such action tools are neuroscience, action science, psychodynamics, narratives, and psychobiographical profiling.

- *Strategic leadership framework*

In proceeding along the Strategic Leadership Value Chain (see Figure 1.1), the organisation next has to make choices regarding its specific position on each of the building blocks making up the Leadership Landscape as Conceptual Lens, based on how it strategically wants to position leadership in its organisation.

For example with respect to some of the building blocks of the Leadership Landscape, the choices are:

- Its chosen *Leadership Stance* regarding leadership for the organisation: Does leadership need to be task- and/or people-centric? Must leadership be present and/or future focused?
- Its desired *Leadership Style(s)*: Tell, Consultative, Co-determination and/or Self-Governance?
- Its repertoire of expected *Leadership Roles*: Resources, Coach, Guide, Networker?
- *Leadership Talent Management*: its make-up; strategic talent timeframe; and talent pools.

The Strategic Leadership Framework therefore forms the reference point and basis regarding all the organisation's decisions and actions with respect to leadership. Its sits as a bridge between the organisation's Leadership Thinking Framework on the one hand, being part of the Thinking Framework itself. And, on the other hand, the Framework directs and guides how "things" must happen in the organisation with respect to leadership.

- *Organisational action processes*

The organisational action process refers to the frontline decisions and actions the organisation has to take on a daily basis regarding leadership. This process is made up of an integrated, reciprocally interdependent, set of organisational actions, embedded in an organisational change navigation process (represented in Figure 1.1 by the circle in which these actions are contained). The actions are as follows:

- *Action 1:* Understanding the unfolding *Leadership Context* with its leadership challenges, demands and requirements;
- *Action 2:* Formulating a context-relevant *Leadership Excellence* model;
- *Action 3:* Generating a future-fit *Leadership Brand and Profile*;
- *Action 4: Identifying, Growing and Developing* the organisation's leadership talent;

- o   **Action 5:** Managing the ongoing, everyday *Leadership Dynamics and Transitions* in the organisation;
- o   **Action 6:** Ensuring and enhancing *Leadership Well-being* (and countering leadership mal-being); and
- o   **Action 7:** Monitoring and tracking *Leadership Outcomes and Impact*

- *Individual sense-making and meaning-giving: Leadership stories*

    In the final instance, leaders have to be prolific, enticing storytellers. Through the stories they construct and share, leaders make sense of and give meaning to their leadership experiences, for themselves and others. Hopefully and ideally speaking, leadership experiences are transformed into information; information into knowledge; and knowledge into wisdom. In turn, the distilled wisdom can be applied to ground, enhance and enrich in a recursive fashion the preceding Strategic Leadership Value Chain elements as elucidated above.

This book – *Leadership in Context* – forms part of a five book series covering the respective elements of the Strategic Leadership Value Chain. The accompanying box gives a list of the books in the series, and what portion of the Strategic Value Chain they address.

Book	Portion of Strategic Leadership Value Chain Addressed (Refer back to Figure 1.1)
Book 1: Understanding Leadership	Departure Point: Defining Leadership Lenses: Conceptual, Interpretive, Action Strategic Leadership Framework
Book 2: Leadership in Context (This book)	Organisational Action Process • *Action 1: Understanding the unfolding Leadership Context with its leadership challenges, demands and requirements*
Book 3: Leadership Excellence	Organisational Action Process • *Action 2: Formulating a context relevant, Leadership Excellence Model* • *Action 3: Generating a future-fit, Leadership Brand and Profile* • *Action 7: Monitoring and tracking Leadership Outcomes and Impact*
Book 4: Building Leadership Talent	Organisational Action Process • *Action 4: Identifying, growing and developing the organisation's leadership talent*
Book 5: Leadership Dynamics and Well Being	Organisational Action Process • *Action 5: Managing the ongoing, everyday Leadership Dynamics and Transitions in the organisation* • *Action 6: Ensuring and enhancing leadership well-being (and countering leadership mal-being)*

Book	Portion of Strategic Leadership Value Chain Addressed (Refer back to Figure 1.1)
Leadership Stories	Throughout the above five books stories by prominent SA leaders are given to illustrate how they have made sense of and given meaning to leadership

Purpose and Structure of *Leadership in Context*

The purpose of *Leadership in Context* is to explore and discuss the *Leadership Context* as part of the Strategic Leadership Value Chain. The location of the Organisational Action Process within the Value Chain, and the *Leadership Context*, are indicated by arrows in Figure 1.2. (To note: all of the actions making up the Organisational Action Process are encapsulated in an organisational change navigation process, represented in Figure 1.2 by the circle enclosing these actions). As reflected in the Figure 1.2 the Leadership Context is the point at which the organisational action process regarding leadership as strategic organisational capability and intervention commences.

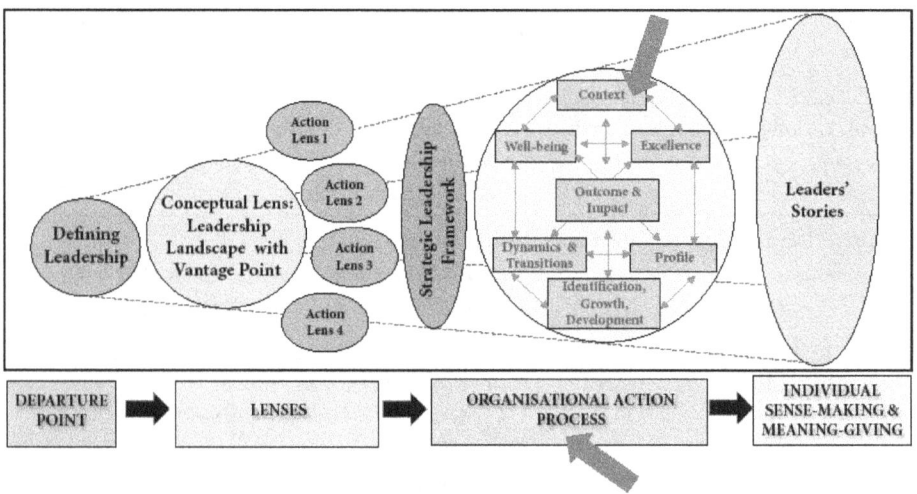

Figure 1.2 Strategic Leadership Value Chain: Thinking Framework

Leadership and their organisations are always embedded in a certain Context with its commensurate unfolding leadership challenges, demands and requirements with which their leadership must be able to engage constructively in order to be effective. Excellent leadership is a function of the correct understanding of, and appropriate engagement with the unfolding Leadership Context, in the present and going into the future. Figure 1.3 depicts the make-up of the Leadership Context.

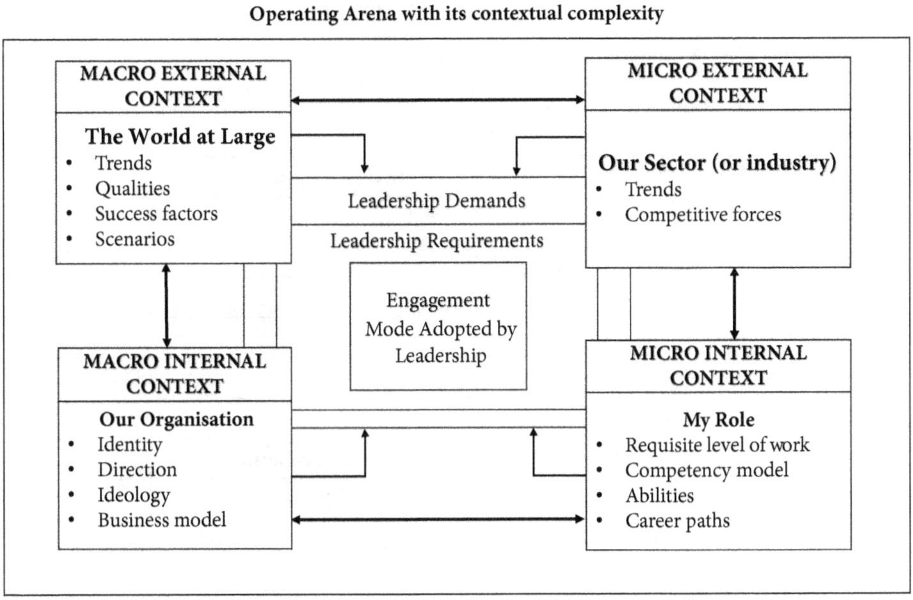

Chapter 1: Orientation

Operating Arena with its contextual complexity

MACRO EXTERNAL CONTEXT	MICRO EXTERNAL CONTEXT
The World at Large • Trends • Qualities • Success factors • Scenarios	**Our Sector (or industry)** • Trends • Competitive forces

Leadership Demands
Leadership Requirements

Engagement Mode Adopted by Leadership

MACRO INTERNAL CONTEXT	MICRO INTERNAL CONTEXT
Our Organisation • Identity • Direction • Ideology • Business model	**My Role** • Requisite level of work • Competency model • Abilities • Career paths

Figure 1.3 The Leadership Context

According to Figure 1.3 the Leadership Context in the first instance consists of the all-embracing chosen Operating Arena of the organisation with its commensurate contextual complexity. In turn, the Operating Arena is made up of four interacting, interdependent and reciprocally influencing contextual dimensions:

- the world at large;
- the sector/industry in which the organisation is active;
- the organisation itself; and
- the role of the leader.

Jointly and individually, all of these contextual elements invoke certain leadership challenges, demands and requirements. Leadership needs to adopt an appropriate contextual engagement mode: a chosen set of glasses leadership uses to look at, interpret, and take actions with respect to the Context (given in the centre of Figure 1.3).

Leadership in Context is organised around four broad themes:

- The *Operating Arena* of the organisation with its contextual complexity and four Contextual Dimensions: Macro/Micro, External/Internal with their unfolding leadership challenges, demands and requirements informed by the imperative of a good Leadership-Context fit.
- Unfolding *Sectorial leadership challenges*, demands and requirements. The Sectors addressed in Leadership in Context were chosen in terms of the central role they play in society. Chapter wise, they are addressed from foundational, micro to enfolding macro Sectors.
- Possible *Leadership Contextual Engagement Modes* consisting of different World Views, Decision Making Frameworks and Value Orientations.

Based on the above discussion of the pertinent Action Process Step, and using Figure 1.3 as an organising framework, the topics addressed in Leadership in Context are given in the accompanying box.

SECTION	TOPICS ADDRESSED	CHAPTER
Section 2: World of Tomorrow	The world of tomorrow: leadership challenges, demands, and requirements	2
Section 3: Sectorial Contexts	South African Schools	3
	South African Higher Education	4
	Public Sector	5
	Communities	6
	Sports	7
	Professional Firms	8
	Business	9
	Politics	10
	Ecologically Embedded Leadership	11
	Religion and Spirituality	12
Section 4: Leadership Contextual Engagement	Leadership engagement with the context	13

Leadership Stories (Section 5: Chapter 14)

In this section prominent leaders express their personal views on leadership from the front line where it is happening for them, illustrating many of the topics discussed in *Leadership in Context*.

The future of leadership (Section 6: Chapter 15)

In this chapter we would like to gaze into the crystal ball by answering the question: Is there a need for better and different leadership going into the future? If yes, what would it look like with the conditions attached to such future-fit leadership?

Our intention with and aspirations for *Leadership in Context* – ambitious and bold, but humble

Our intention with and aspiration for *Leadership in Context* is for the book to be a thought leadership book on the current and future expected Contexts leadership is will be embedded in and have to engage with. *Firstly,* by providing cutting edge, present-into-the-future, and future-into-the-present, thinking with respect to the Leadership Context, leveraged from the best currently available insights and informed views about the expected probable futures to be faced by leadership within different contexts. *Secondly,* by providing actionable knowledge and theory-informed practice about Leadership Contexts where it matters at the organisational front line.

Both in our intention and aspiration we realise we may be overly ambitious and bold by deciding what we believe are some of the more important Contexts in which leadership is embedded. Simultaneously, however, we are fortuitously humbled by the depth, richness and diversity of the overwhelming, exploding body of knowledge regarding different Leadership Contexts. In no way can we claim, or wish to claim, that we therefore have covered all of the possible/potential Leadership Contexts. That would be arrogant.

The Intended Audience of *Leadership in Context*

In the first place, *Leadership in Context* intends to assist executives and leadership specialists within organisations, whether public or private, to direct, guide and build – confidently and with well-grounded insight – leadership as a mission critical organisational capability and intervention in their organisations, using a Strategic Leadership Value Chain perspective. In this way we hope that they will be able to ensure a future-fit organisation and leadership who are able and willing to be architects of the future they so ardently desire.

In the second place, *Leadership in Context* aims to assist academics and their students in the teaching and studying of leadership as a critically important subject. In the third place, the topics covered in *Leadership in Context* may also provide creative triggers to future leadership research.

The Intended Use of *Leadership in Context*

The intended use of *Leadership in Context* is to serve as a handy daily "desktop" reference book on leadership lenses to our intended audience:

- for ongoing referral as and when ways of understanding leadership matters arise in an organisation, and
- where input from a thought leadership source is desired and necessary on available leadership lenses.

Thus *Leadership in Context* is not intended to "Rest in Peace" on the bookshelf but to be a "Working Manual" by being an ever-present companion for continuous, daily consulting, referral and advice. Also in a similar fashion assist as a reference for teaching on and research into leadership.

The Expected Value-add of *Leadership in Context*

We hope *Leadership in Context* will provide you as the reader with four overriding insights (or Lessons-to-be-Learnt):

- Leadership Contexts are *changing radically and fundamentally*, consequently shifting leadership challenges, demands and requirements in trend-breaking ways.
- Without an in-depth insight into unfolding Contexts with their associated leadership challenges, demands, requirements, and the choice of an appropriate engagement mode, the likelihood of *a good fit between Leadership and the Context*, and hence Leadership Excellence, would be slim.
- Organisations that make it their *ongoing business to gain pro-actively insights and intuitive feels for expected contextual trend breaks, and translate them into future-fit leadership capabilities* to be nurtured, will have a significantly higher likelihood to be architects of the future they desire.
- Even more strategically, *organisations that envision desirable futures by visiting the future – with the corresponding, needed leadership capabilities – and then return to the present to realise those futures*, will dominate the world of tomorrow within their chosen Operating Arenas.

We wish you a stimulating, enriching and capacitating journey through *Leadership in Context*

SECTION 2
WORLD OF TOMORROW

Chapter 2

THE WORLD OF TOMORROW: LEADERSHIP CHALLENGES, DEMANDS AND REQUIREMENTS
Theo H Veldsman

Leadership and their organisations are always embedded in a certain Context. Context, Organisation and Leadership need to be seen as an inseparable, seamless, holographic, dynamic whole. The one cannot be understood without the other, also as they reciprocally co-evolve and unfold.[1] Masterful leadership requires, *firstly,* an in depth understanding of the Context with its accompanying leadership challenges, demands and requirements; *secondly,* how to attain a good fit between leadership and the Context in which they are embedded;[2] and, *thirdly,* how to engage appropriately with the Context. This chapter deals with the first two topics: contextual understanding and fit.

The purpose of this chapter is to discuss the world of tomorrow with its accompanying leadership challenges, demands and requirements. The chapter will cover the following themes with respect to the Leadership Context *in general*: choosing a contextual vantage point; the Operating Arena with its contextual complexity and stakeholders; the contextual dimensions and facets informing the Operating Arena; contextual fit; and future-fit leadership requirements for the world of tomorrow.

Choosing a Contextual Vantage Point

From an organisational perspective, the leadership of an organisation has to choose a contextual vantage point. In choosing a vantage point, leadership can adopt different Frames in viewing the Context. Conceptual Frames are made up of two dimensions in terms of which leadership can position expected contextual shifts:

- *Degree of contextual change*: Recreate/Transform versus Maintain/Enhance; and
- *Time orientation*: Present-directed versus Future-directed

The four options related to each dimension give four possible contextual Frames in terms of which leadership can engage with the Context, as depicted in Figure 2.1. The choice of a specific Frame is a function of the Strategic Posture adopted by the organisation: a Reactive, taker of change, versus a Proactive, instigator of change, regarding the Context (given in the middle block of the figure). In the first instance the organisation is a follower and merely adapts to contextual shifts: Maintain/Enhance, being mostly Present-directed with extrapolation into the Future. In the latter case, the organisation takes the lead as a source of the contextual changes and shifts: Transform/Recreate, being mostly Future-directed, even in dealing with the Present. The choice of a Frame, with its accompanying Strategic Posture, has direct bearing on the leadership challenges, demands and requirements faced by the organisation since it delineates in a fundamental sense the Context with which leadership has to engage.

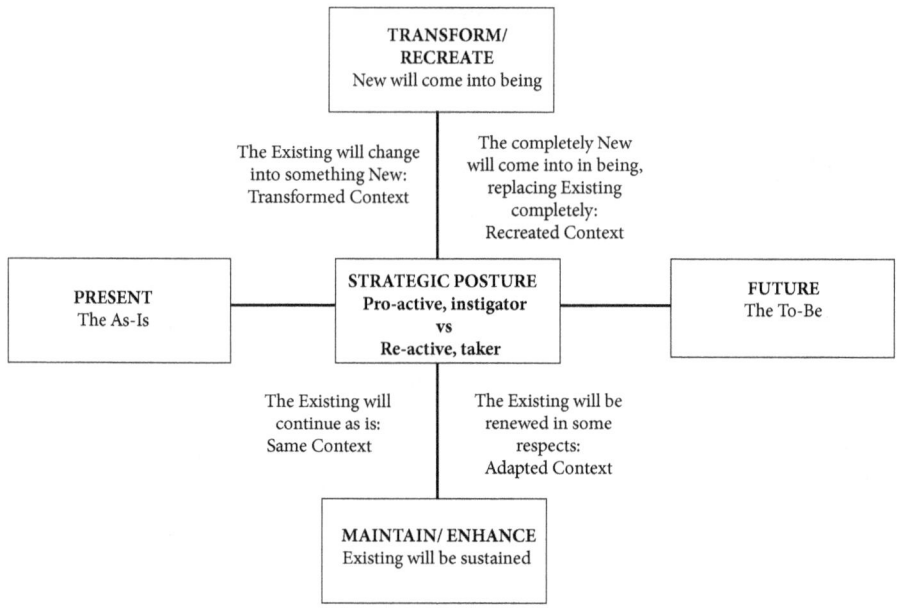

Figure 2.1: Strategic postures and contextual frames

For the sake of this chapter I will assume that the organisation's leadership has chosen a contextual vantage point that is predominantly a Transform/Recreate Frame, from a Future perspective, leveraged from a Strategic Posture of being a Proactive, instigator of change. Given the features of the emerging world of tomorrow to be elucidated below, this vantage point appears to be the most appropriate assumption on which to base this chapter.

The Operating Arena with its Contextual Complexity and Stakeholders

Within the context at large, leadership choose an Operating Arena for their organisation, and by implication for themselves as leadership: its theatre of action and influence. To use a sports analogy: the Operating Arena forms the Outer Context of the organisation, the "playing field" of the organisation and its leadership. For the purpose of this chapter two aspects of the Operating Arena will be discussed affecting leadership challenges, demands and requirements, namely contextual complexity and stakeholders.

The Operating Arena with its contextual complexity

Each Operating Arena comes with a corresponding contextual complexity. To continue with the sports analogy, contextual complexity defines the "league" in which the organisation and its leadership want to play: 1st, 2nd or 3rd. Both the playing field, the Operating Arena, and the league, contextual complexity, are predominantly a function of the chosen strategic intent of the organisation. Contextual complexity – low, medium or high – affects the "pitch" of the leadership challenges, demands and requirements faced by the organisation in its Operating Arena.

Leadership needs to understand, *firstly,* the requisite level of contextual complexity they have to deal with within their Operating Arena, now and going into the future, as directed by the organisation's strategic intent; and *secondly,* the degree to which leadership fits the requisite contextual complexity in their endeavour to demonstrate masterful leadership within their Operating Arena.

Contextual complexity is a function of five complexity variables, as depicted in Table 2.1.

Table 2.1: Contextual complexity variables

CONTEXTUAL COMPLEXITY VARIABLE	DEGREE OF CONTEXTUAL COMPLEXITY			
	1: Low	2: Reasonable	3: High	4: Very High
Space Boundaries, *the location in which we operate*	Local (Single location)	National (Multiple locations, but one country)	Multi-national (Locations in multiple countries with high local autonomy)	Global (Fully integrated global organisation)
Time Boundaries *for thinking about world, industry and own organisation*	2 to 3 years	3 to 5 years	5 to 10 years	10 years plus
Scope of organisation *in terms of Markets, Customers, Products/ Services*	Single	Multiple but related	Multiple, related and unrelated	Multiple, unrelated
Variety within organisation *in terms of strategic intent, policies and standards, work processes and practices, outputs delivered required to lead organisation*	Uniform	Diverse but similar	Diverse but similar and dissimilar	Dissimilar
Degree and rate of change in context	Slow, incremental	Evolutionary: Predictable trend shifts	Trend breaks	Revolutionary: Re-creative

The degree of complexity increases significantly as the above complexity variables shift from left to right (see Table 2.1) because one moves: from a limited set of similar variables to many, diverse variables; from tangible, visible to intangible, invisible variables; from the predictable, certain to the unpredictable, ambiguous; from known facts to estimated probabilities; from the simple, ordered to the complex, chaotic; from linear causality to systemic patterns; from single to multi-dimensionality; and from a Past/Present-into-Future to a Future-into-Present orientation.

Two contrasting examples of different degrees of contextual complexity are given in Table 2.2, below.

Table 2.2: Examples of different degrees of contextual complexity

SIMPLE CONTEXT	COMPLEX CONTEXT
The leader is heading up local (= a within country) organisation requiring a two to three years' time thinking framework; has a single market, type of customer and product/service; can lead the organisation with a single strategic intent, set of policies and standards, work processes and practices, and outputs delivered; and faces slow, incremental, predictable change	The leader is heading up a global organization requiring a 10 years'-plus time thinking framework; has dissimilar markets, types of customer and products/ services (the typical diversified corporation); has to lead the organisation with a portfolio of diverse strategic intents, set of policies and standards, work processes and practices, and outputs delivered; and faces revolutionary, recreative change

As the contextual complexity of an organisation increases/decreases, organisational and leadership challenges, demands and requirements will look significantly different.[3] For example, a shift in the space boundary from local to global sets the leadership fitness requirements of a "global mindset" and "intercultural sensitivity". An expansion in the scope and variety of the organisation imposes the fitness requirement of "systemic thinking". A shift from incremental to revolutionary change makes "real time, large-scale organisational change" an essential leadership fitness requirement.

The Operating Arena with its stakeholders

Included within and surrounding the chosen Operating Arena is a set of stakeholders. Elsewhere in *Leadership in Context* stakeholders have been described as anyone (in other words, an individual, individuals, groups, institutions) that can affect and/or are affected by the direction and actions of the organisation, intended or real, and consequentially having an impact on its image and reputation.[4]

Regardless of their "remoteness", all stakeholders have to buy-in and own the desired future pursued by the leadership of the organisation, in this way becoming followers. Diverse stakeholders with multiple needs/interests are the heartbeat of the emerging global order, the fountain head of sustainability. In the newly emerging order, not only has the range of stakeholders expanded, but their needs/interests have become manifold and widespread. Figure 2.2 depicts the typical set of diverse stakeholders in the emerging world of tomorrow.

Chapter 2: The world of tomorrow: leadership challenges, demands and requirements

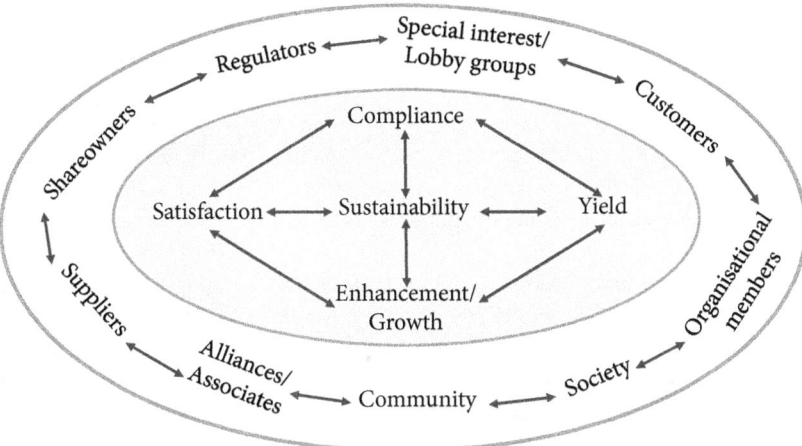

Figure 2.2: Diverse stakeholders with multiple needs/interests

According to Figure 2.2, each and every stakeholder (given in the outer circle of Figure 2.2) has a range of diverse needs/interests (given in the inner circle of Figure 2.2), which must be fused dynamically not only for the specific stakeholder concerned, but also simultaneously across all stakeholders. For example, for shareowners' compliance (in other words, sound corporate governance), return on investment (in other words, an attractive, recurring dividend pay-out), and sustainability (in other words, assuring the organisation as a future going concern) must be balanced. For organisational members (employees), however, these very same needs/interests take on another form: compliance in their case pertains to the meeting of an agreed-upon employment contract(s); return on investment to a favourable effort/performance to reward ratio; and sustainability to job security and employability. Needs/interests are therefore in a dynamic tension not only for a given stakeholder but also across stakeholders. In the emerging world order, stakeholders' power to mobilise for or against the organisation and its leadership has also grown exponentially through the use of the social media.

Jointly the diverse stakeholders of the organisation with their multiple needs/interests, form an action community with respect to the organisation concerned. This action community is tied together by their shared stake in and shared destiny with the organisation, affecting and being affected by the organisation's actions and reputation. If stakeholders are seen as an action community, and are located centrally as the primary focus of leadership, relationships become the core focal point of the organisation with regard to its future and wealth creation. From this perspective the organisation equates to a complex web (or connectivity) of relationships which need to be set up, nourished, grown and terminated. It is argued in many quarters that the relationship (or social) capital (that is, goodwill of an organisation and its leadership) has become the most important asset of the organisation.[5]

The leadership challenge and demand in this case is to understand and meet the diverse needs/interests of multiple, diverse stakeholders in a balanced, fair and equitable manner, such that leadership is able to put goodwill as the manifestation of social capital in the "bank", allowing them to pursue a longer-term vision. Consequentially leadership are trusted and empowered to take greater calculated risks as they journey into the future in pursuit of greater dreams and legacies. The burning issues are: how and by whom does legitimate and credible leadership emerge? How is it sustained among stakeholders as a powerful action community?

The Contextual Dimensions and Facets Informing the Operating Arena

The previous section essentially dealt with the demarcation of the organisation's Operating Arena with its resultant requisite contextual complexity and multiple, diverse stakeholders that impose certain leadership challenges, demands and requirements. This section deals with the "content" of the Operating Arena, its make-up, which forms the ecosystem within which leadership has to be exercised.

It can be argued that in terms of the make-up of an Operating Arena, an organisation must decide on the "breadth" and "depth" of the Context it will take into consideration in its thinking, decisions and actions with respect to the Arena. "Breadth" refers of the range of contextual dimensions to include, for example, the world at large, the organisation's sector (or industry). "Depth" pertains to the contextual characteristics to be considered: from "superficial" characteristics – the tangible, concrete features of the Context, such as the infrastructure of a country – to "deep" characteristics – the intangible, invisible features, such as the cultural orientations of a country. Each is discussed in turn, first breadth, followed by depth.

The contextual dimensions of the Operating Arena: The breadth of the context

The Operating Arena is made up of four interacting, interdependent and reciprocally influencing contextual dimensions as depicted in Figure 2.3: Macro/Micro; Internal/External.

Operating Arena with its contextual complexity

MACRO EXTERNAL CONTEXT	MICRO EXTERNAL CONTEXT
The world at large • Trends • Qualities • Success factors • Scenarios	**Our Sector (or industry)** • Trends • Competitive forces

Leadership Demands
Leadership Requirements

Engagement Mode adopted by leadership

MACRO INTERNAL CONTEXT	MICRO INTERNAL CONTEXT
Our organization • Identity • Direction • Ideology • Business model	**My Role** • Requisite Level of Work • Competency model • Abilities • Career paths

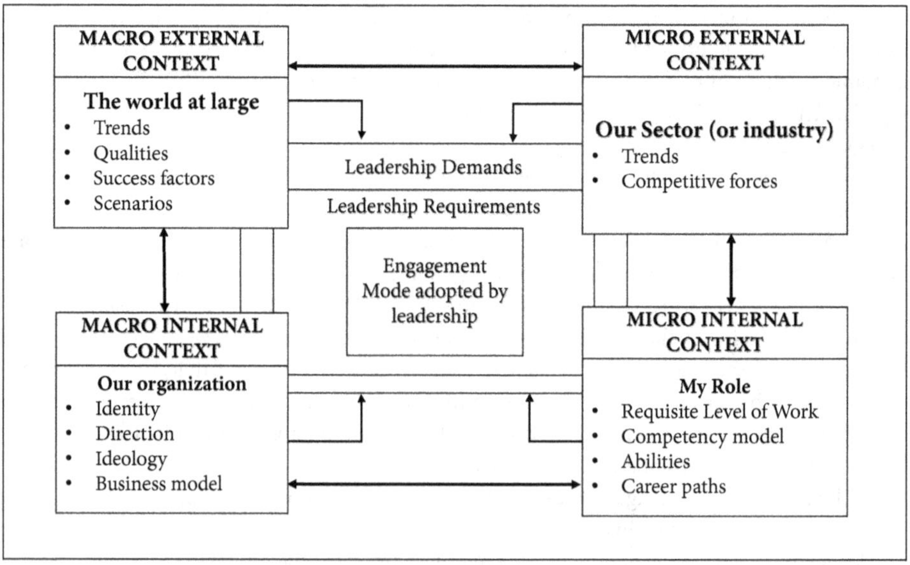

Figure 2.3: The leadership context

The degree of contextual complexity of the Operating Arena discussed above affects the nature and dynamics of the contextual dimensions of the organisation's Operating Arena as depicted in Figure 2.3. Using the sports analogy again, this is the level of the game the organisation needs/

wants to play to make it successful in its chosen league. The emerging world of tomorrow is briefly discussed next with regard to each of the above four contextual dimensions, and the accompanying future-fit leadership challenges, demands and requirements are highlighted.

Macro, External Context: The world at large

Figure 2.4 provides an overview of the most dominant features of the emerging world order.[6]

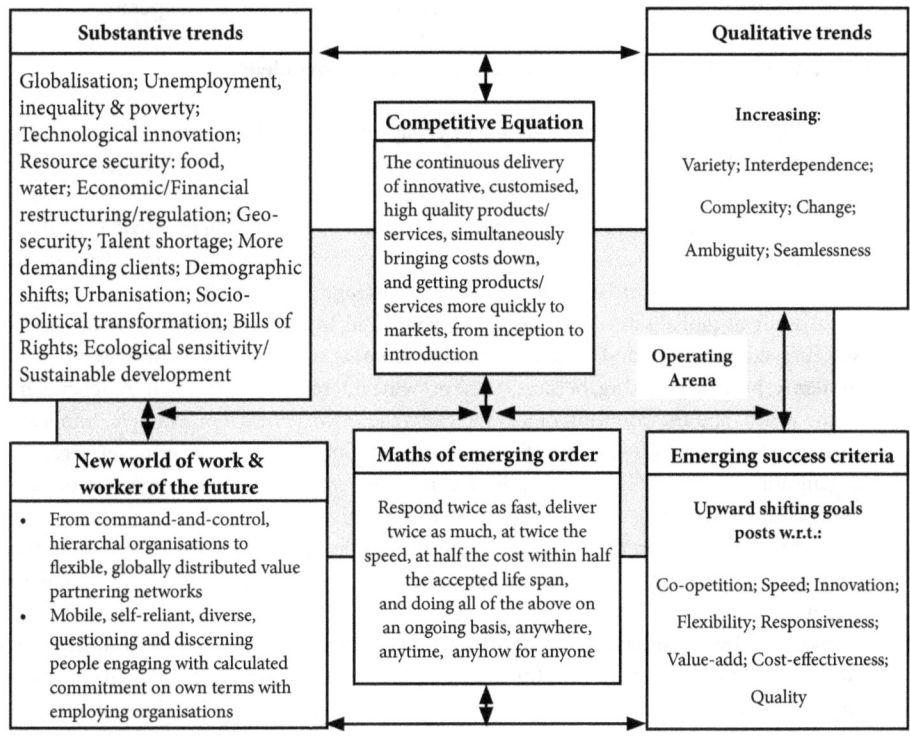

Figure 2.4: The emerging world order

According to Figure 2.4, leadership is facing a vastly different future – the VUCA world:[7] [i] a world dominated by <u>V</u>olatility, <u>U</u>ncertainty, <u>C</u>omplexity and <u>A</u>mbiguity – culminating in a specific competitive equation and associated maths. The emerging new order therefore requires leadership to rethink radically the *Why, What, How, Who, Where,* and *Whereto* of their organisations, not only in the present, but also, in particular, while moving into the significantly different future of the emerging order. Very often this future thinking is formulated in scenarios, which are probable stories about what the future will look like, and how to respond appropriately to these possible futures.

---

i The US Army War College conceptualised VUCA to describe the world which arose after the ending of the Cold War (Kinsinger and Walch, 2012). The acronym, however, only came about in the 1990s. The "V" refers to volatility: the nature, speed, volume, and magnitude of change has an unpredictable pattern. The "U" stands for uncertainty, or the lack of predictability w.r.t. issues and events, making it difficult to use past experiences as predictors of future outcomes (Sullivan, 2012b). The "C" relates to complexity, which in combination with the turbulence of change and the absence of past predictors, adds to the difficulty of decision making. This results in confusion, which in turn causes ambiguity, the last letter in the acronym.

In general, what are the future-fit leadership demands and requirements imposed by the emerging new order? At least eight emerging leadership demands and/or requirements can be discerned:

1. Given the emerging world order – radically different from what has been in place to date – it is required of organisations to reconsider from first principles the organisation's definition of **Leadership** and its **Leadership Landscape** – in particular the choices made regarding its Landscape, especially its current **Leadership Stance and Excellence** – in order to assess whether they fit the world of tomorrow in which the organisation must operate.

The following **emerging leadership requirements will be demanded:**[8]

2. The adoption of a **different worldview** to engage with a 20/20 vision with the emerging world order. At present a complexity/chaos worldview appears to supply the most powerful insight into the true nature and dynamics of reality.
3. **A global mindset**, because the world has become a global village. Most boundaries restricting the movement of information, people, stakeholders, products/services and resources across the world have disappeared/are disappearing rapidly.
4. As a result of globalisation, the need for **cross-** and **intercultural competence** because societies, communities and organisations are becoming more culturally diverse.
5. **Systemic, holistic thinking**, because of the growing interconnectivity and interdependency of the world, and the adoption of a complexity/chaos worldview. For example, implicated in the emerging world order, with the concurrent need for a new mindset regarding organisations befitting this order, is the requirement to view the organisation as a contextually embedded, dynamic, interconnected, and systemic whole.
6. **Authentic relationship formation**, because leadership has to build and maintain lasting, deep relationships with multiple, diverse stakeholders in order to build social capital and goodwill.
7. **Rapid, real time, responsiveness/agility** in combination with a **large-scale organisational navigation ability** flowing from the emerging world of tomorrow's competitive equation together with its associated maths, which implies accelerating speed and ongoing change (see Figure 2.4).
8. **Continuous innovation, creativity and experimentation**, requiring ongoing disruptive innovation. If an organisation is to remain a thriving, sustainable entity going into the future, it will have to be set up as a learning organisation. Central to a learning organisation is action learning, enabled by a learning/teaching culture. Such a culture can be typified by continuous experimentation, risk taking, a tolerance for mistakes, and a high degree of autonomy to act, and to be institutionalised in the organisation as a way of life.[9] More specifically, organisations need to consider strategic innovation in five domains: its markets/customers; products/services; delivery; context; and business model (see the next discussion of the Micro, External Context).[10]

Micro, External Context: The Sector (or Industry) of our organisation

There is hardly a Sector globally that is not being affected by re-invention (for example, online retail, online education); convergence (for example, the emergence of a seamless Information Communication Technology (ICT) Sector/Industry); or a (threatening) extinction (for example, printed mass communication, such as newspapers) being the cause of and a result of the new, emerging world order. Many Sectors have to rethink their business models radically in view of the emergence of the application-enabled, on-demand, peer-to-peer economy.[11]

Macro, Internal Context: Our Organisation

Because of the dynamics and features of the emerging new order (see Figure 2.4), and radical, disruptive innovation, a significant mindset shift is taking place in re-thinking the critical ingredients of future-fit organisations, and consequently their resultant organisational designs. This is in contrast to the ingredients making up the traditional organisations associated with the old world order. Figure 2.5 depicts the general mindset shift taking place regarding the organisation of the future,[12] which may differ somewhat by specific Sectors.

TRADITIONAL ORGANISATION	➡	EMERGING ORGANISATION
Objectives, plans, standards	➡	Mission, vision, philosophy
Static, self-sufficient	➡	Self-designing, distributed value web
Local, physical	➡	Global, virtual
Standardised, formalised	➡	Flexible, ambidextrous (= Work Unit specific designs)
Jobs, Functions, Individual	➡	Roles, Work domains, Teams
Procedures	➡	Culture
Positional power	➡	Expert power
Top/Down decisions/relationships	➡	Multi-directional decisions/relationships
Management: Efficiency	➡	Leadership: Effectiveness
Over-inspection	➡	Self management/governance
Activities	➡	Outcomes
Compliant loyalty	➡	Negotiated contributions
Information-scarce	➡	Information-rich
Products	➡	Markets/Customers
Self interest	➡	Corporate Citizen
Engaging only Body and Head	➡	Engaging total person, including Heart and Spirit

Figure 2.5: The general mindset shifts in thinking about the organisation of the future

The traditional mindset of the organisation (on the left of Figure 2.5) represents the conventional command-and-control organisational design. The emerging mindset of the organisation (on the right of Figure 2.5) represents the high flexibility/high involvement (or network/value web) organisational design. Table 2.3 below gives a comparison of the two designs. Implicated in the emerging mindset of the organisation is a shift in leadership demands and requirements.[13]

Table 2.3: Comparison of different types of organisational design

Conventional command-and-control organisational design	Emerging high flexibility/high involvement (or network/value web) organisational design
One person to one prescribed task (= job) with few skills, little decision-making power, little information, controlled by rules, procedures and rank, linked to others through the hierarchy, focusing on efficient processes, quantity and continuous improvement	Multi-skilled and multi-disciplinary autonomous teams/ mini-business units performing broad chunks of the organisation's overall core work processes (or the total core work process for a product/service/client/market) with a high degree of decision-making power, self-generated information, driven by and linked to others by an internalised vision and philosophy, focusing on customers, quality and relentless innovation

Infusing the emerging high flexibility/high involvement (or network/value web) organisational design are four broad trends affecting future-fit leadership demands and requirements:

- **Trend 1: Globalising organisations.** Being a global organisation, or intending to become a global player, has become common in the emerging world order of an increasingly interconnected world. The major challenge to globalising organisations is to find the right balance simultaneously between an *integration need:* the capability to act globally in concert as a total organisation AND a *responsiveness need:* the capability to address client/customer needs at the local, coalface level of day-to-day delivery. Expressed in leadership language: "Think globally but act locally".
- **Trend 2: Virtualised organisations** (also as a means to globalise). As seen in Figure 2.4, the maths of the emerging new order necessitates delivery by organisations on an ongoing basis, anywhere, anytime, anyhow, for anyone. This implies the imperative of a virtually connected organisation.[14]
- **Trend 3: Digitalised organisations** (being global from the onset). The emergence of organisations designed around a technological, network-based application that brings customer needs and service provision through the internet together virtually; that is, an organisation that is from its inception completely virtual, such as Uber, Lyft, Washio, Handy, Amazon's Mechanical Turk, and Airbnb. These completely (globalised) digitalised, virtual organisations are manifestations of the snowballing rise of the new on-demand, peer-to-peer economy.[15]
- **Trend 4: Automated organisations.** On all fronts the automatisation of organisational processes and decision-making is growing exponentially, the so-called Fourth Industrial Revolution through, for example, automated decision-making algorithms, robotics, and 3D printing.[16]

The globalised, virtualised, digitalised and/or automated organisation imposes additional and different leadership demands and requirements against the backdrop of the high flexibility/high involvement (or network/value web) organisational design as the emerging mindset change regarding the organisation.

As can be deduced from the above discussion, at least five future-fit leadership demands and requirements imposed by the organisation of the future can be identified:

1. **Systemic, holistic thinking and actions** requiring one to view and deal with the organisation as a contextually embedded, dynamic, interconnected, and systemic whole (see Figure 2.5 above).

2. **An outside-in perspective, leveraged from a steward/servant mindset/attitude.** The shift in thinking towards sustainability – adopting the triple bottom line of planet, profit, and people – and the growing requirement by leading securities and stock exchanges worldwide of integrated reporting for listed companies is forcing organisations to reconsider in a fundamental way how to bring the different voices of their diverse, multiple stakeholders into their organisation. The emergence of multiple-purpose organisations, for example, the Benefit Corporation (the B Corp) is a concrete manifestation of this thinking.[17]

    Leaders have to master the art of building and nurturing deep, morally-based relationships with stakeholders, informed by the qualities of legitimacy, fairness, and equity. The above shift requires a steward (or servant) mindset/attitude in which the organisation sees itself as an inherent part of the intricate fibre and DNA of the communities/societies in which it operates. Organisations with a stewardship mindset/attitude strive to create abundant prosperity through the value they unlock and the wealth they create by delivering enriching products/services to customers, simultaneously sharing – fairly and equitably – the wealth created with the people who contribute to creating the wealth.[18]

3. **"And/Both" instead of "Either-Or" thinking and actions.** Given the shift in the playing field of the emerging world order (see Figure 2.4, future-fit organisations will have to move away from "*Either-Or*" organisational design choices, for example, a product/service OR market/customer basic delivery logic. They should preferably consider "*And*" delivery logic-choices, for example, a product/service AND market/customer delivery logic; a functional AND a process logic in architecting a fit-for-purpose future organisational shape.[19] This type of design logic will demand an increase in their requisite contextual complexity, especially with regard to the scope of and variety in the organisation (see Table 2.1).

4. **Partnering.** The emerging world order (refer to Figure 2.4), and the organisation of the future design (refer to Figure 2.5), demand reinvention of the value-generation logic of the organisation to be based on a strategic *partnering* delivery logic in which relationships move centre stage in respect of how the organisation functions. Relationship-centric organisations imply the emergence of a new form of organisation: the value network organisation based on collaborative, partnering relationships. Partnering pertains to two or more individuals, groups, or organisations that are able and willing to engage in a mutually beneficial, two-way value exchange through cross-boundary relationships based on trust in joint pursuit of mutual value-unlocking and wealth creation.[20]

5. **Technological savviness.** The virtualisation, digitalisation and automation of organisations, in combination with the snow balling proliferation of the social media, demand future-fit leaders who have a high degree of technological savviness, able to use technology in putting their organisations ahead of the game in their chosen Operating Arenas, and dominating the communication space of their followers.[21]

Micro, Internal context: My Role as a leader

For the purposes of this chapter, the contextual perspective on the role of a leader in the Micro, Internal Context that will be discussed here is the need for leadership to meet the demands of their work roles at the requisite Level of Work (LOW). Stratified Systems Theory provides a handy way of conceptualising LOWs with their respective requisite complexities.[22] Seven LOWs can be distinguished: from LOW 7: Corporate prescience (that is, global systems) through to LOW 1: Quality (that is, daily operational delivery). Table 2.4 provides an overview of the seven LOWs.[23]

Table 2.4: An overview of the respective Levels of Work

SHIFTS IN WORK CONTEXT CHARACTERISTICS	LEVEL OF WORK	THEME OF WORK	WORK SETTING	WORK ELEMENTS	TYPICAL DECISION-TIME HORIZON *	TYPICAL WORK ROLES
From LOW1 to LOW7 • Predictable, certain to Unpredictable, ambiguous • Tangible, visible to Intangible, invisible variables • Facts to fuzzy probabilities • Simple, ordered to Complex, chaotic • Linear causality to Systemic patterns • Single to multi-variables/ dimensions • Past/ Present-into-Future to Future-into-Present	7: Corporate Prescience	Global influence and presence	World at large	• World/ global mindsets, philosophies, policies, and systems	20 years plus	Global organisation Leader/ Director
	6: Corporate Citizenship	Industry protection and enhancement Business oversight/ longevity	Industry, locally and internationally Organisation	• Context shaping • Corporate Governance	10–20 years	Industry leader Board Director
	5: Strategic Intent	Strategy crafting	Organisation	• Returns/ Yields • Direction, Objectives, Philosophy	5 to 10 years	CEO/ MD
	4: Strategic Translation/ Implementation	Strategy development	Organisational Function/ Work	• Organisational Policies & Standards • Organisational Systems • Work Unit Direction, Objectives, Philosophy, Return/ Yields	3–5 years	Enterprise/ BU Executive Functional Executives
	3: Operational Execution	Practice	End-to-end Work (Unit) Process	• Resourcing • Delivery Work Processes	2 to 3 years	Process Leader
	2: Operational Practices	Work Unit Service	Work Unit	• Delivery Standards	1 year	Front Line Leader (=Supervisor)
	1: Operational Delivery	Quality	Work Station	• Daily Delivery	Up to 3 months	Operator/ Practitioner
CONTEXTUAL COMPLEXITY Low to High: • Location and Time Boundaries • Scope of and Variety within organisation • Degree and Rate of Change						

* These are typical time horizons: The more complex time-/space-wise and unstable the context of an organisation, the longer the time horizon must be.

Chapter 2: The world of tomorrow: leadership challenges, demands and requirements

It is important to note the following with regard to Table 2.4: (1) how the context of a leadership role changes as the LOW changes. For example, LOW 7 and LOW 5 respectively have the world at large and the organisation as contexts; and (2) the requisite complexity of the respective LOWs are mediated by the contextual complexity of the Operating Arena (as discussed above) in which they are embedded. For example, LOW 5, Strategic Intent will look qualitatively different in a low compared to a high contextual complexity context, although it still remains strategic work. Total Work Requisite Complexity is thus equal to:

Requisite LOW x Contextual Complexity

Each LOW comes with its own leadership demands and requirements in terms of expected actions. These cannot be discussed here because of space constraints.[24][25]

The facets of Operating Arena: The depth of the context

Up to now the *"breadth"* of the Context has been discussed: the *contextual dimensions* making up the Context. This section addresses the *"depth"* of the Context, that is, the facets of the Context. These facets can be seen metaphorically like an iceberg, depicted at the centre of Figure 2.6 in the form of a triangle (the topic of fit will be discussed in the next section):

- The **visible part above the water** that represents (1) the **features** of, and hence **dynamics** within, the Regions/Countries where the leadership and their organisation are operating (Facet 1).
- The **invisible part below the water** which represents (2) **deep Global Cultural Orientations** that frame and inform the actions and conduct of persons in those Regions/Countries (Facet 2) as well as (3) (consequential) **Expected Leadership Attributes** related to a Region/Country (Facet 3).[26][ii]

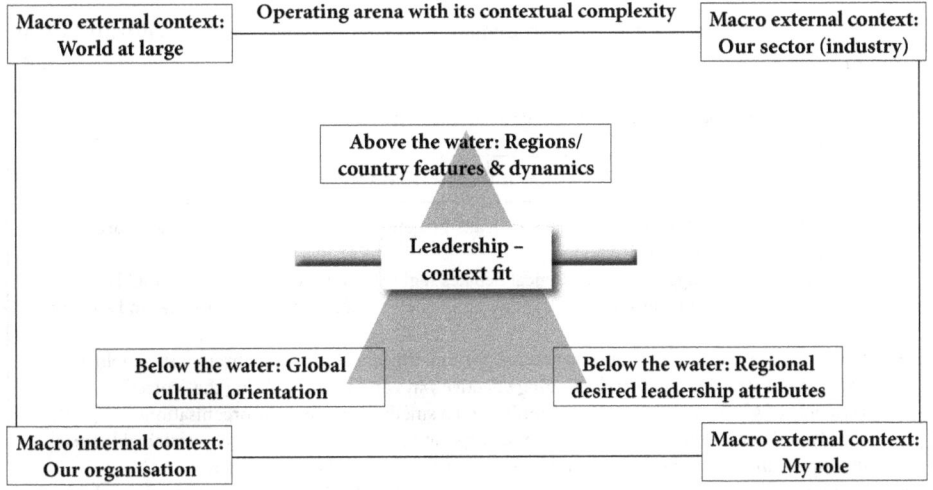

Figure 2.6: The facets making up the Operating Arena

---

ii It is argued that human beings are wired for culture (Pagel, 2012). The part of the iceberg that is under the water embraces the anthropology of business, or organisations.

Leadership in Context

Facet 1 of the Operating Arena: Regions/country features and dynamics

Leadership has to have an in depth understanding of the features and dynamics of the countries included in its Operating Arena as its playing field, the above-the-water Facet 1 of the contextual fit triangle (see Figure 2.6). For example, Emerging Countries (ECs) have become part of the Operating Arena of many organisations, given the growing importance of ECs in the world economy. Figure 2.7 graphically illustrates the generic features, and, by implication, the dynamics of ECs.[27]

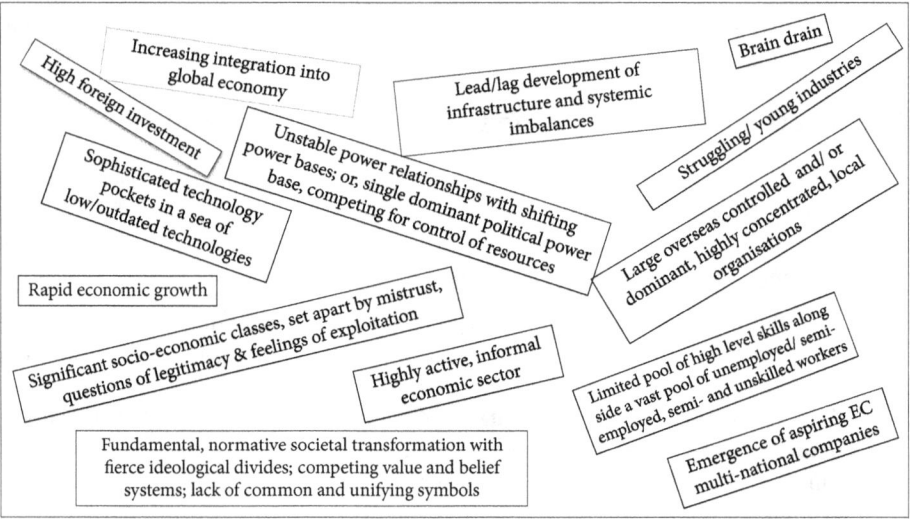

Figure 2.7: Generic unique features of ECs

Some of the more important leadership demands and requirements associated with ECs are listed in Table 2.5.[28]

Table 2.5: Leadership demands and requirements associated with ECs

ECs LEADERSHIP DEMANDS
• Given the fundamental, normative societal transformation, having a high contextual awareness, understanding and responsiveness
• Given the power struggles and ideological debates raging in the society, adopting a highly visible, clearly articulated and communicated values and beliefs stance: "This is who we are, and what we stand for"
• Based on an expanded view of stakeholders, formulating a well-thought-through stakeholder engagement strategy, and thereby finding effective ways and means to bring the "voices" of different segments of society at large and communities on a smaller scale into the organisations
• Visibly and concretely demonstrating good corporate citizenship through real, sustainable social upliftment interventions from an embeddedness perspective: "We belong here"
• Building a global competitive capability in local, emerging (business) organisations through co-value-creation alliances and partnerships
ECs LEADERSHIP REQUIREMENTS
Responsiveness/Agility; Value-based, purpose-driven leadership; Large scale change navigation; Stakeholder engagement; Cross-cultural; Social conscienceless; Corporate citizenship; Partnering and collaboration; a Global mindset; Holistic, systemic thinking

Facet 2 of the Operating Arena: Global cultural orientations

Global Cultural Orientations form the second point of the contextual fit triangle, the invisible portion of the iceberg below the water. Three types of Global Cultural Orientations inform the world – shown in Figure 2.8[29] – and can therefore form part of organisations' Operating Arenas, if any of these countries fall into their Arenas. Globalisation, seamlessness, and the maths of the emerging world order (see Figure 2.4) has made more than one Global Orientation part of many organisations' Operating Arena.

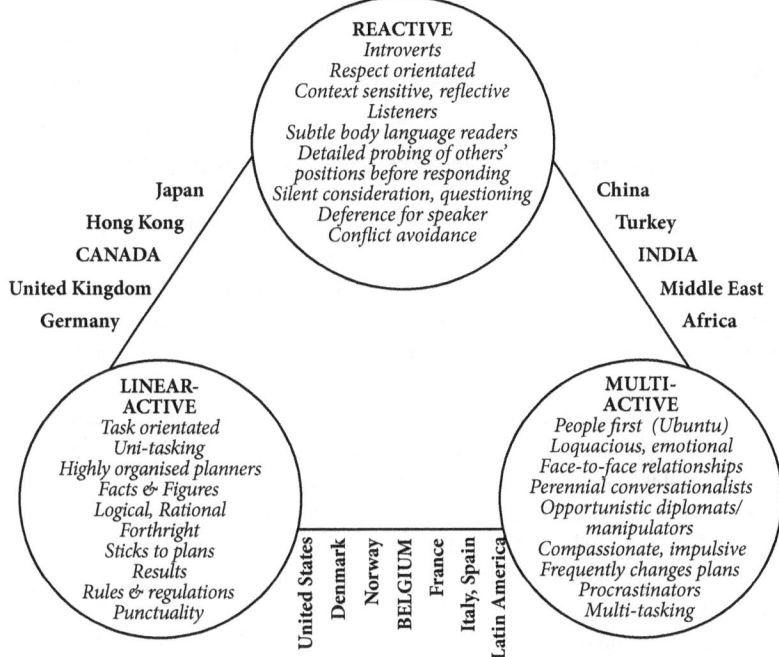

Figure 2.8: Global cultural orientations

Global Cultural Orientations impose the leadership demand and requirement on leadership to have the intercultural (or transcultural) intelligence to understand their own and the Cultural Orientation of others they are interacting with.

Facet 3 of Operating Arena: Expected Leadership Attributes

Expected Leadership (= desired) Attributes form the third point of the contextual-fit triangle, also under the water as part of the iceberg. Whereas Global Cultural Orientations are reflective of broad national cultural differences, Expected Leadership Attributes are specific to national differences regarding societally desired leadership characteristics. Generic desirable leadership attributes exist across nations. Concurrently nation-specific attributes also exist.[30] Leadership effectiveness is strongly influenced by the degree of congruence within these expectations.

Leadership-Context Fit

As a departure point, it must be accepted that the understanding of and the search for fit is an ongoing, dynamic process since the Context, and by implication the reciprocal Context-Leadership relationships, is forever changing and shifting. Based on the above discussion, a comprehensive leadership-contextual-fit model can now be explicated. Figure 2.6, introduced above, simultaneously depicts this model. According to this model, as illustrated by this figure, leadership-contextual fit is a function of the best fit between:

1. On the one hand, the leadership challenges, demands and requirements of the Operating Arena with its contextual complexity as manifested in the contextual dimensions: the outer periphery of the figure, and the contextual facets, the triangle in the centre of the figure. This represents the "demand" side of the leadership-contextual fit; and
2. On the other hand, the desired profile of leadership as manifested in leadership abilities, representing the "supply" side of the leadership-contextual fit.

The better the fit – the dynamic balancing of demand and supply in real time – the higher the likelihood of leadership mastery, outcomes and excellence being demonstrated, all other things being equal.[31] [iii]

Future-fit Leadership Requirements

The focus of the discussion up to now has been predominantly on the demand side of the leadership-contextual fit. In this section the supply side will be addressed: future-fit leadership requirements. What could this future-fit leadership profile look like?

It can be argued that the world of tomorrow will require well-rounded, "intelligent" leaders who at the requisite complexity (= Level of Work x Contextual Complexity) understand who they are as individuals; can deal effectively with daily leadership demands of their roles; can interact with others at interpersonal, team and unit levels in productive, meaningful and mature ways (= achieving with people); can negotiate the organisational landscape successfully in order to realise a sustainable, desirable future for their organisation, in this way through constructive engagement with their context; can fundamentally transform their organisation to be aligned to a different world; and can do this throughout while acting ethically and responsibly.[32] [33] As the outcome of the set of meta-abilities, given in the circle, future-fit leadership needs to manifest the 5 Cs of future-fit leadership excellence: Character, Connected, Caring, Committed and Competent.[34]

Table 2.6 provides an overview of the critically more important abilities expected to make up the profile of future-fit leadership as based on and deduced from the above discussion in this chapter.[iv] [35] [36] [37] Critically more important are the predicted 20% abilities that will make the 80% difference (the Pareto principle) in the world of tomorrow as a consequence of the emerging world order.

Table 2.6: Overview of the more important expected abilities in the profile of future-fit leadership

ABILITY DOMAIN	ABILITIES
Intelligence Modes	• **Personal and Interpersonal Intelligence** (including Emotional Intelligence): having a resilient, well crystalised, authentic Identity as a leader – who and what am I; what do I stand for; how I relate to and impact on others, and build genuine relationships with them • **Systemic Intelligence** (including Cognitive Intelligence): able to craft and use a dynamic, integrated, systemic map of a chosen Operating Arena and world, used to navigate the Arena with insight

---

iii Three distinct types of person-environment, or Context fit can be distinguished: Demands-Abilities, D-A; Individual Needs-Supplies, ability of environment to fulfil needs, N-S; and Values as personal attributes-Environment congruence, OVC, Yu, 2014. See also Hoffman & Woehr, 2006.

iv The abilities could be categorised into Personal Attributes, Attitudes and Values, Knowledge, Skills and Expertise and Conduct/Behaviour, which will not be done in this case.

Chapter 2: The world of tomorrow: leadership challenges, demands and requirements

ABILITY DOMAIN	ABILITIES
Intelligence Modes (continued)	• **Ideation Intelligence** (including Spiritual Intelligence): able to conceive increasingly, more daring and inspiring dreams (= ideas) about different/new futures, along the way triggering creative construction that will lead to lasting, worthy legacies • **Action Intelligence**: able to bring about lasting, meaningful change because leadership think and act in terms of a knowledge-guided, reflective action research-and-learning process • **Contextual Intelligence** (including (Trans)Cultural Intelligence): able to engage constructively, at the requisite level of complexity, with their Operating Arena through a carefully chosen, appropriate, Interpretative Framework – worldview, decision making framework, value orientation – which make them exceedingly fit for, and matched to their context
Understand who they are as individuals	Self-awareness; Self-driven; Integrity; Resilience; Responsiveness; Agility (or Flexibility); Internal locus of control; High tolerance for ambiguity; High risk-taking; Creative/ Innovative/Experimental; Curiosity; Psychosocial maturity; Courage; Perseverance
Can deal effectively with daily leadership demands of their roles	Integrated global/local, systemic ("big picture") thinking: Convergent (i.e. synthetic) and Divergent (i.e. analytical); An understanding of and ability to effect changes in mindsets and worldviews; Strong technical/professional base with the ability to localise/customise; Resourcefulness; Multi-lingual; E-technologically savvy; Large-scale, systemic change ability; Continuous learning and teaching attitude; Multiple learning approaches, e.g. learning to learn, learning by reframing
Interact with others at interpersonal, team and unit levels in productive, meaningful and mature ways (= achieving with people)	Persuasiveness; Personal presence and stature; Empathy/Caring; Active listening; Accessibility; Diversity sensitivity (i.e., inter-race, inter-gender, inter-values, inter-generational and intercultural); Deep insight into organisational culture and dynamics; A deep understanding of interpersonal and teaming dynamics within a multi-cultural setting; Internal partnering/networking
Negotiate the organisational landscape successfully	Cross-functional insight and collaboration; Social networking; Deep understanding of organisational dynamics and culture within a multi-cultural setting; Partnering; Network and coalition building; Organisational branding; Intrapreneurial attitude
In order to realise sustainable future for organisation	Strong transformation (= Vision/ Values)/Transcendental (= Purpose/ Meaning) leadership; Pursuit of a purpose bigger than merely seeking profits; Proactive futuring; "Can do-"/Resourceful attitude
In this way, through constructive engagement with the context, fundamentally transforming their organisation to be aligned to different world	Global mindset; External partnering/Networking; Stakeholder engagement; Cross-cultural ability
Throughout acting ethically and responsibly	Value-centric; Corporate citizenship; Social consciousness; Integrity

Conclusion

The Context in which leadership is embedded is changing in fundamental ways. Without doubt the future is going to look radically different, and so consequently will the leadership challenges, demands and requirements associated with the changing Context. The need is for better *and* different leadership in order to establish a best Context-Leadership fit. The bias of this chapter has been towards a *different* type of leadership as required by the emerging world of tomorrow, using a contextual vantage point of a predominantly futuristic Transform/Recreate Frame, leveraged from the Strategic Posture of being a Proactive, instigator of change. This is not to deny that some leadership challenges, demands and requirements will remain the same going into the future.

Attaining a best fit is an ongoing process demanding constant attention as the Context changes, and an organisation interrogates its Strategic Intent in response, in the present and going into the future. As was discussed in this chapter, this necessitates giving constant, in depth attention to any changes and shifts in one's contextual vantage point; one's chosen Operating Arena with its corresponding contextual complexity and stakeholders; and the contextual dimensions and facets informing the Operating Arena.

Endnotes

1. Cf. for example: Beugré, Acar & Braun, 2006; Clawson, 2009, 45ff; Dihn, Lord, Gardener, Meuser, Liden, & Hu, 2014; Fairhurst, 2009; Kanter, 2010; Linden & Antonakis, 2009; Obolensky, 2010; Osborn, Hunt & Jauch, 2002; Porter & McLaughlin, 2006. For a conceptual exposition of the term 'Context', see Johns, 2006.
2. Yu, 2014.
3. For example, Kanter, 2010.
4. Schneider, 2002.
5. Acquaah, Amoako-Gyampah & Nyathi, 2014; Kanter, 2010; Schneider, 2002.
6. Clawson, 2009, 45ff; Kanter, 2010; Schneider, 2002; Veldsman, 2015a, 2015c.
7. See also Rodriguez & Rodriguez, 2015.
8. Cf. Glover & Friedman, 2015; Kanter, 2010; Midddleton, 2014.
9. Veldsman, 2015a.
10. Veldsman, 2015a.
11. Colvin, 2015; Murray, 2015.
12. Kanter, 2010; Osborn, Hunt & Jauch, 2002; Schneider, 2002; Veldsman, 2015a.
13. Cf. Galbraith, 2000, 2014; Kanter, 2010; Marquardt, Berger & Loan, 2004, quoted in Kim & McLean, 2015; Veldsman, 2015a; Visser, 2011.
14. Veldsman, 2015a.
15. Colvin, 2015; Murray, 2015; Steinmetz, 2016; Stein, 2015; *The Economist*, 2015.
16. Brynjolfsson, E. & McAfee, A., 2014; Ford, 2015; Schwab, 2016; Susskind & Susskind, 2015.
17. Kelly, 2012; Mackey & Sisodia, 2013; Saporito, 2015.
18. Aßländer, 2011; Bennis, Parikh & Lessem, 1994; Broomes, 2013; Delios, 2010; Fisher & Grant, 2012; Kanter, 2010; Kelly, 2012; Pless, Maak, & Waldman, 2012; Mackey & Sisodia, 2013; Rajak, 2011; Veldsman, 2015b; Visser, 2011.
19. Cf. Galbraith, 2014.
20. Veldsman, 2015a.
21. Brynjolfsson & McAfee, 2014; Colvin, 2015; Ford, 2015; Murray, 2015; Schwab, 2016; Steinmetz, 2016; Susskind & Susskind, 2015; *The Economist*, 2015.
22. Jaques, 2006; Jaques & Clement, 1994; Osborn, Hunt & Jauch, 2002; Shephard, Gray, Hunt & McArthur, 2007.
23. Veldsman, nd.
24. Ibid.
25. Kanter, 2010. See also Luthans, Luthans & Luthans, 2015, p. 404.
26. See, for example, Denny & Sunderland, 2014; Northouse, 2007.
27. Dalglish, 2014a; Veldsman, 2015b, 2015c.
28. Dalglish, 2014a; Veldsman, 2015b, 2015c.
29. Sourced and expanded from Lewis, 2003.
30. Dalglish, 20149b; House, Dorfman, Javidan, Hanges & Sully de Luque, 2014; Trompenaars & Hamden-Turner, 2002.
31. Yu, 2014. See also Hoffman & Woehr, 2006.
32. See also Hoffman & Woehr, 2006.
33. Veldsman, 2015c.
34. Wort, 2004.
35. Bücker & Poutsma, 2010; Gentry & Sparks, 2012; Kanter, 2010; Kim & McLean, 2015; Luthans, Luthans & Luthans, 2015; Molinsky, 2012; Osborn, Hunt & Jauch, 2002; Rodriguez & Rodriguez, 2015; Taylor & Vorster, 2016; Veldsman, 2015c.
36. Kim & McLean, 2015; Veldsman, 2015c.
37. See, for example, Kim & McLean, 2015; Veldsman, 2015c.

References

Aßländer, MS. 2011. 'Corporate social responsibility as subsidiary co-responsibility: A macroeconomic perspective'. *Journal of Business Ethics*, 99(1):115–128.
Acquaah, M, Amoako-Gyampah, K & Nyathi, NQ. 2014. *Measuring and valuing social capital: A systematic review*. GIBS, Cape Town & Pretoria, ZA: Network for Business Sustainability South Africa. [Online]. Available: http://nbs.net/knowledge. [Accessed 1 July 2016].
Bennis, W, Parikh, J & Lessem, R. 1994. *Beyond leadership. Balancing economics, ethics and ecology*, Cambridge, Blackwell.
Beugré, CD, Acar, W & Braun, W. 2006. 'Transformational leadership in organisations: an environment-induced model'. *International Journal of Manpower*, 27(1):52–62.
Broomes, V. 2013. 'Enhancing impact of CSR on economic development and livelihoods in developing countries'. In K Haynes, A Murray & J Dillard. (eds.). *Corporate social responsibility. A research handbook*. New York, NY: Routledge.
Brynjolfsson, E & McAfee, A. 2014. *The second machine age: Work, progress and prosperity in a time of brilliant technologies*. New York, W.W. Norton.
Bücker, J & Poutsma, E. 2010. 'Global management competencies: a theoretical foundation'. *Journal of Managerial Psychology*, 25(8):829–844
Clawson, JG. 2009. *Level three leadership*. Upper Saddle River, Pearson/Prentice-Hall.
Colvin, G. 2015. 'The 21st century corporation'. *Fortune*, 38–47, 1 November.
Dalglish, C. 2014a. 'The African context'. In E van Zyl (ed) with C Dalglish, M du Plessis, L Lues & E Pietersen. *Leadership in the African context*. Cape Town, Juta, 40–60.
Dalglish, C. 2014b. 'Leadership in a multicultural context'. In E. van Zyl (Ed.) with C. Dalglish, M. du Plessis, L. Lues & E. Pietersen. *Leadership in the African context*. Cape Town, Juta, 61–80.
Delios, A. 2010. 'How can organisations be competitive but dare to care?' *Academy of Management Perspectives*, 24(3):25–36.
Dihn, JE, Lord, RG, Gardener, WL, Meuser, JD, Liden, RC & Hu, J. 2014. 'Leadership theory and research in the new millennium: current theoretical trends and changing perspectives'. *The Leadership Quarterly*, 25:36–62.
Denny, R & Sunderland, P (eds). *Handbook of anthropology in business*. Walnut Creek, CA: Left Coast Press Inc.
Fairhurst, GT. 2009. 'Considering context in discursive leadership research'. *Human Relations*, 62:1607–1633.
Fisher, J & Grant, B. 2012. Beyond corporate social responsibility: Public value and the business of politics'. *International Journal of Business and Management*, 7(7):2–14.
Ford. M. 2015. *Rise of the robots*. New York, NY: Basic Books.
Galbraith, JR. 2000. *Designing the global organisation*. San Francisco, CA: Jossey-Bass.
Galbraith, JR. 2014. *Designing organisations*. San Francisco, CA: Jossey-Bass.
Gentry, WA & Sparks, TE. 2012. 'A convergence/divergence perspective of leadership competencies managers believe are most important for success in organisations: A cross-cultural multilevel analysis of 40 countries'. *Journal of Business Psychology*, 27:15–30.
Glover, J & Friedman, HL. 2015. *Transcultural competence. Navigating cultural differences in the global community*. Washington, DC: American Psychological Association.
Hoffman, BJ & Woehr, DJ. 2006. 'A quantitative review of the relationship between person-organisation fit and behavioural outcomes'. *Journal of Vocational Behaviour*, 68:389–399.
House, RJ, Dorfman, PW, Javidan, M, Hanges, PJ & Sully de Luque, MF. 2014. *Strategic leadership across cultures*. Los Angeles, CA: Sage.
Jaques, E. 2006. *Requisite organisation: A total system for effective managerial organisation and managerial leadership for the 21st century*. Baltimore, MD: Cason Hall & Co. Publishers.
Jaques, E & Clement, SD. 1994. *Executive leadership: A practical guide to managing complexity*. Cambridge, MA, Cason Hall & Co. Publishers.
Johns, G. 2006. 'The essential impact of context on organisational behaviour'. *Academy of Management Review*, 31(2):386–408.
Kanter, RM. 2010. 'Leadership in a globalising world'. In N Nohria & R Khurana (eds). *Handbook of leadership theory and practice*. Boston, MA: Harvard University Press. 569–609.
Kelly, M. 2012. *Owning our future. Journeys to a generative economy*. San Francisco, CA: Berrett-Koehler.
Kim, J & McLean, GN. 2015. 'An integrative framework for global leadership competency: Levels and dimensions'. *Human Resource Development International*. [Online]. Available: http://dx.doi.org/10/\.1080/13678868.2014.1003721. [Accessed 1 July 2016].
Lewis, RD. 2003. *The cultural imperative*. Yarmouth, ME: The Intercultural Press.

Linden, RC & Antonakis, J. 2009. 'Considering context in psychological leadership research'. *Human Relations*, 62(11):1587–1605.

Luthans, F, Luthans, BC & Luthans, KW. 2015. *Organisational behaviour. An evidence-based approach*. 13th ed. Charlotte, NC: Information Age Publishing.

Mackey, J & Sisodia, R. 2013. *Conscious capitalism*. Boston, MA: Harvard University Press.

Middleton, J. 2014. *Cultural intelligence. CQ: The competitive edge for leaders crossing borders*. London, UK: Bloomsbury.

Molinsky, AL. 2012. 'Skills every 21st century manager needs'. *Harvard Business Review*, 139–143, January–February.

Murray, A. 2015. 'Uber-nomics'. *Fortune Editor's Desk*, 1 January.

Northouse, PG. 2007. *Leadership. Theory and practice*. 4th ed. Thousand Oaks, CA, Sage.

Obolensky, N. 2010. *Complex adaptive leadership*. Farnham, UK: Gower.

Osborn, RN, Hunt, JG & Jauch, LR. 2002. 'Toward a contextual theory of leadership'. *The Leadership Quarterly*, 13:797–837.

Pagel, M. 2012. *Wired for culture. Origins of the human social mind*, New York, NY: WW Norton & Company.

Pless, NM, Maak, T & Waldman, DA. 2012. 'Different approaches toward doing the right thing: Mapping the responsibility orientations of leaders'. *Academy of Management Perspectives*, 26(4):51–65.

Porter, LW & McLaughlin, GB. 2006. 'Leadership and the context: Like the weather?' *The Leadership Quarterly*, 17:559–576.

Rajak, D. 2011. *In good company. An anatomy of corporate social responsibility*. Stanford, CA: Stanford University Press.

Rodriguez, A & Rodriguez, Y. 2015. 'Metaphors for today's leadership: VUCA world, millennial and "Cloud Leaders" '. *Journal of Management Development*, 34(7):854–866.

Saporito, B. 2015. 'Making good, plus a profit'. *Time*, 23 March.

Schneider, M. 2002. 'A stakeholder model of organisational leadership'. *Organisation Science*, 13(2):209–220.

Schwab, K. 2016. *The fourth industrial revolution*. Cologny, CH (CHE): World Economic Forum.

Shephard, K, Gray, JL, Hunt, JG & McArthur, S. 2007. *Organisation design, levels of work and human capability*. Ontario, CAN: Global Design Society.

Steinmetz, K. 2016. 'The way we work. A new poll reveals the size of the peer-to-peer revolution'. *Time*, 34–37, 18 January.

Stein, J. 2015. 'Baby, you can drive my car. And stay in my guest room. And do my errands. And rent my stuff. My wild ride through the new on-demand economy'. *Time*, 9 February.

Susskind, R & Susskind, D. 2015. *The future of the professions*. Oxford, UK: Oxford University Press.

Taylor, N & Vorster, P. 2016. Chapter 42 of this book.

Trompenaars, F & Hamden-Turner, C. 2002. *21 Leaders for the 21st century. How innovative leaders manage in the digital age*. New York, NY: McGraw-Hill.

The Economist. 2015. 'The future of work. There's an app for that'. 15–18, 3 January.

Veldsman, TH. 2015a. *Whereto organisational design? In search of design criteria for future-fit organisations?* 11th European Conference on Management Leadership and Governance (ECMLG), Military Academy, 12–13 November.

Veldsman, TH. 2015b. 'The power of the fish is in the water'. *African Journal of Business Ethics*, 9(1):63–83.

Veldsman, TH. 2015c. *Leadership in emerging economies: Challenges, requirements and profile*. 2015 JvR Africa Conference of Psychology: People Development in Africa, 18-1–19 May. Kruger National Park, Mpumalanga.

Veldsman, TH. nd. 'Organisational design as a critical organisational discipline'. *Architecting organisational operating models for fit-for-purpose delivery logics (tentative title)*. Book manuscript in preparation. To be published in Johannesburg, ZA by Knowledge Resources.

Visser, W. 2011. *The age of responsibility. CSR 2.0 and the new DNA of business*. Chichester, UK: John Wiley.

Wort, A. 2013. Evaluating a leadership authenticity programme. Unpublished doctoral thesis. Johannesburg, ZA: University of Johannesburg.

Yu, KYT. 2014. Inter-relationship among different types of person-environment fit and job satisfaction. *Applied Psychology*, 65(1), January. doi:10.1111/apps.12035.

SECTION 3
SECTORIAL CONTEXTS

Chapter 3

SCHOOL LEADERSHIP

Louise van Rhyn, Gail McMillan and James Ndlebe,
in association with business leaders and principals
in the Partners for Possibility community

What we contribute through our taxes, we get back through the high quality of our public services.
That is why we have:
- *Good schools with well-educated, trained and caring teachers; ...*

Each community has:
- *A school;*
- *Teachers who love teaching and learning; ...*

South Africa's Vision 2030, (Preamble to the National Development Plan)

The above excerpt from South Africa's Vision 2030 statement presents an ideal future, both for the many South African children who currently do not have access to adequate education, and for the country as a whole. The Vision 2030 document has been described as an ambitious document for its highly positive description of a possible future for South Africa. In the practice of Appreciative Inquiry, as pioneered by David Cooperrider, this type of description would be called a provocative proposition, which is a statement that "bridges the best of 'what is' with your own speculation or intuition of 'what might be.'"[1]

A provocative proposition stretches the status quo while suggesting real possibilities. In our view, the Vision 2030 description of South Africa is a provocative proposition for the country – a description of the possibilities that lie within the country, just waiting to be tapped. South Africa's Vision 2030 is a description of a flourishing South Africa, a country that works for all.

The ideals espoused by Vision 2030 are provocative, precisely because of the disparity between what is and what could be. In the realm of education, certainly, the disparity is huge. South Africa does not currently have the education system described in the Vision 2030 statement. In fact, it falls far short. In spite of high spending on education and the implementation of some good policies, there are many clear indicators that the public education system in South Africa is in crisis.[2][3]

Estimates vary, but around 80% of South Africa's schools are considered to be dysfunctional.[4][5] This means that the majority of the 12 million children currently attending South African schools are at under-performing schools, which could have a very negative effect on their future prospects. More than half of the children who start school never finish, and only 35% of those starting school receive a Grade 12 certificate. To achieve the education goals set by Vision 2030, one needs highly effective leadership in all schools. Leadership is the key to achieving a high-performing education system. The purpose of our chapter is to address the challenges, demands and requirements of school leadership. To this end the following topics are addressed: the South African school landscape; unique school leadership challenges; a school leadership competency standard: Principalship; the need for innovative solutions; and a case study.

The South African School Landscape

To best understand the challenges faced by South African schools, it is important to consider the composition of the school sector. Professor Ruksana Osman describes the South African school landscape as follows: "The South African schooling sector is large, complex and unevenly distributed in terms of the communities it serves. There are public schools, faith-based schools, secular, corporate and low-fee private schools."[5] Figure 3.1 reflects the situation graphically.

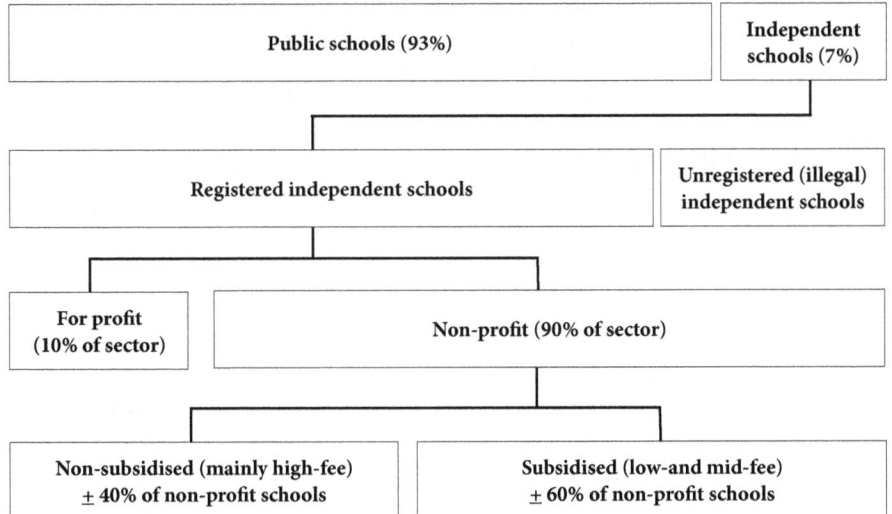

Figure 3.1: South African school sectors in 2015
Source: *ISASA (Independent Schools Association for South Africa)*

Broadly speaking, however, there are two main categories of school, recognised by the South African Schools Act (SASA) 84 of 1996: public and independent. Public schools are state controlled, and independent schools are privately governed.

In 2015, there were 25 691 registered schools in the South African education system. Of these, 93% were public schools and 7% were independent. Public schools accommodate approximately 12 250 million pupils, while 566 000 learners attend independent schools.[6]

The independent school sector is growing as a result of a high demand for quality education coupled with the perception that this level of education is not currently readily available in the public education system in South Africa.[7]

As indicated in Figure 3.1, there are several types of independent schools, and each of these experiences unique leadership challenges. Principals in high-fee, well-resourced, independent or semi-private schools are expected to run their schools like a business. They typically have large teams to manage, relatively easy access to resources, and very demanding stakeholders to deal with. The role of principals in a high-fee, well-functioning school is very similar to that of a CEO in a medium-sized business.

In stark contrast, many of the stakeholders of low-fee independent schools and under-resourced public schools are absent or disengaged, and principals routinely lack the resources they need. This leaves almost all of the management and support responsibilities in the hands of the school's principal, and many of these principals do not receive the necessary training to enable them to address the challenges they face. Considering that 93% of learners in South Africa attend public schools, the challenge described above is significant and hence the focus of this chapter will be on challenges in the public school sector.

South Africa's government schools: 'A tale of two systems'

Dr Nic Spaull, a researcher at the University of Stellenbosch, has described South Africa's education system as "A Tale of Two Systems"[8] because when the outcomes of the 20%–25% of well-resourced schools – both public and private – are compared with those in the 75%–80% of predominantly public under-resourced schools, the differences are radical. His research shows a strong correlation between language, socio-economic status and current school choices.

In January 2016, the Minister of Basic Education, Angie Motshekga, addressed delegates at the Basic Education Sector Lekgotla – a meeting convened by government to discuss policy issues. She called for a paradigm shift in addressing the reality of "two education systems in one country", one being a high-performance system with pockets of excellence; while the other she called the "Cinderella" system, deprived of resources and characterised by "pockets of disaster."[9]

Spaull[10] created a theoretical framework that explains these results:

> "A minority of students (about 25%) who come from wealthy backgrounds of all races attend high-quality primary and secondary schools and go on to study at university or other institutions of higher learning. Consequently, these students gain access to the top end of the labour market where they earn high incomes in high-productivity jobs.
>
> The second schooling system consists of the majority of students (75%) who come from poorer backgrounds, attend low-quality primary and secondary schools, and have very little chance of accessing higher education opportunities due to the low quality of their education. Most of these students move directly into the labour market, with either no matric qualification or a low-quality matric pass. These students will either fill the ranks of the unemployed or the informal sector, or become part of the second-tier labour-market, which offers low-productivity jobs and low incomes. These jobs are often manual labour or low-skill jobs, which pay the minimum wage."

Spaull concludes that this cycle will continue, with wealthier parents continuing to send their children to good schools, while parents on the lower rungs of the labour market and their children will remain stuck in the dysfunctional part of the education system. It is this part of the system where the parents received their training as well. With this in mind, without intervention, the "current style of poverty and privilege" will continue.

Resources and education outcomes

Education continues to receive the lion's share of South Africa's national budget. In 2014/2015, 20% of government expenditure, amounting to R254 billion, was allocated to education,[11] and in the 2015/2016 budget, it was further increased to R297.5 billion[12].

With regard to spending and academic outcomes, Spaull notes:

> "Looking at the Grade 6-aged population in South Africa, 25% were deemed to be functionally illiterate, while 39% were classified as functionally innumerate. This is in stark contrast to Kenya where the rates are only 8% (functional illiteracy) and 11% (functional innumeracy). What is more striking, is that South Africa spends almost five times as much per pupil ($1 225) compared to Kenya ($258). On functional literacy rates, South Africa also performs worse than Namibia ($668 per child), and Swaziland ($459 per child).

South Africa has the same percentage of Grade 6-aged children that are literate as Uganda (71%), yet spends more than 18 times as much per child! Clearly, more resources are not the silver bullet – we are not using existing resources anywhere nearly as effectively as other African countries."[13]

The cost of poor education outcomes for South Africa

The social impact of this education inequality does not affect only South Africa's social fabric. According to the OECD (Organisation for Economic Co-operation and Development), Global School Ranking report (2015), South Africa's GDP would grow by 2,624% over their lifetimes if all students achieved a basic level of education to just the age of 15.[14]

Unique School Leadership Challenges

Why we need to focus on school leadership

Research has shown that the leadership of school principals has a direct and substantial effect on pupil achievement,[15] and that this effect occurs across the spectrum of schools.[16] Moreover, the evidence shows that the influence of school principals on educational achievement is considerably greater in schools where the needs of learners are acute and the circumstances of the school are difficult, as in the 75% of public schools described above.

A growing volume of literature recognises school leadership as the critical factor in turning around an education system in crisis.[17] Education systems are characterised by high levels of complexity.[18] The need to satisfy the demands of a large and diverse group of stakeholders, which includes teachers, learners, parents and politicians, contributes to this high level of complexity. Another generator of complexity in the South African Education system is the impact of socio-economic ills such as hunger, poverty, HIV/AIDS and violence.

A significant volume of research, rooted in complexity science, has revealed that a useful approach in attempting to bring about change in large complex systems is to identify the largest units of change and then to work with those individual units, rather than attempting to change the entire system.

Within an education system, the largest unit of change is the school.[19] Intervening at school level and building the leadership capacity of principals therefore have the potential for significant leverage in facilitating change in the SA education system.

The approach of focusing on schools as the largest unit of change and using school leadership as the primary lever is supported by University of Stellenbosch researcher Gabrielle Wills. Wills conducted research, published in December 2015, on "[i]mproving the calibre of school leadership in South Africa." In her report, Wills stresses her concern that policy makers in South Africa are not giving "sufficient attention to the way good school leadership can improve the quality of education."[20]

The leadership challenge in under-resourced schools in South Africa

It is clear that being a school principal in an under-resourced school in South Africa is a difficult task. Professor Brian O'Connell, former Rector of the University of the Western Cape, describes the role as "the most difficult leadership job in South Africa."

There is increasing recognition that the role of school principals is not only critical, but highly specialised.[21] In South Africa, however, the majority of school principals are not being sufficiently equipped with the knowledge, skills and expertise required for their specialist role,[22] let alone with the ability to lead the major turnaround that is required in the education system.

The challenges faced by principals at the head of under-resourced schools in South Africa

In June 2015, a group of school principals were asked what their key challenges were. This is what they said as depicted in Figure 3.2:

Figure 3.2: Challenges faced by principals

According to Figure 3.2 principles said the following:

- They are under-equipped and ill-prepared for the financial, administrative and managerial demands that are placed on them as managers and leaders of their schools.
- Teachers are not being sufficiently trained for their task. Many teachers give instruction in subjects such as maths and science, which they have not been fully equipped to teach.
- Teachers are disengaged and often absent from their classrooms. In a speech by Minister Motshekga in January 2016, she calls teacher absenteeism the "elephant in the room", and notes that "teachers are hardly found in class" and that many "only teach 40% of scheduled lessons." She continues by referring to a 2010 Human Sciences Research Council study, which found that "almost 20% of teachers in South Africa are absent on Mondays and Fridays and that teachers in former-African schools teach an average of 3.5 hours a day compared with about 6.5 hours a day in former model C schools. This amounts to a difference of three years of schooling";[23]
- There is a severe lack of human resources. Many principals reported having no one to whom they can delegate tasks. Deputy principals often have full teaching loads and are unable to take on any of their administrative or governance responsibilities. Many principals in under-resourced schools have to teach classes because of a shortage of teachers at the school.

- The lack of human resources at under-resourced schools is also clear in the absence of leadership and administrative support. In well-resourced schools, principals typically have a team of people that they can ask for help, or they have the financial resources to pay relief teachers to stand in for teachers who are sick or on special leave. Principals are also expected to be IT literate and able to manage a wide range of administrative responsibilities.
- Overcrowding in classrooms is a further challenge. Although the teacher–pupil ratio is officially not expected to exceed 35 : 1, principals report that many classrooms accommodate up to 90 learners. There is wide-spread agreement among education experts that it is impossible for one teacher, no matter how competent he or she may be, to facilitate learning with such a large number of learners in a class. The use of technology is often cited as the solution to this problem. However, teachers first need to learn how to use the technology within the teaching process, and many teachers currently don't have a strong enough foundation in teaching methodologies to build on.
- Significant challenges exist with regard to infrastructure. Many schools still do not have essential services and facilities such as water, electricity and adequate sanitation, let alone libraries, science laboratories, and sports fields. According to Minister Motshekga: "Some schools have no desks for learners, neither do they have sanitation facilities. We must consider the lack of sanitation in schools as an affront to our children's inherent right to dignity."[24]
- Parents are absent and disengaged, and expect schools to take full responsibility for all aspects of their children's education, while they take no part in the process. This is often not done intentionally, but many parents do not know how to support their children because their own education was poor and they experienced very little parental support themselves.
- Working with large numbers of children whose ability to learn is negatively impacted on by social and economic problems, which include hunger, drug- and gang-related issues, trauma resulting from neglect and/or abuse, poor living conditions, and other problems that are prevalent in poor households. Many children are hungry and tired when they reach school in the morning. Some schools are able to provide food, but the nutritional value of the meals that learners receive is often low, and it is common knowledge that children who are inadequately nourished are unable to concentrate, and that this sometimes triggers behavioural problems which exacerbate their difficulties in the classroom.[25]

Another challenge faced by most principals in under-resourced schools is the limited support they receive from their School Governing Bodies (SGBs). This is because members of these SGBs seldom have the necessary knowledge and skills to enable them to provide the kind of support that principals require.

In theory, principals should receive support from district education officials. Many principals, however, report that they receive little or no support from these officials. In Minister Motshekga's address, she calls this the other "elephant in the room" – the Provincial Education Departments (PEDs) which are not managing education appropriately in their respective spheres of authority. In the Minister's view: "We allow mediocrity to spread like cancer to the highest echelons of the basic education system, thereby threatening the very foundation of the system."[26] Just as principals have often not been prepared for their role, most district officials are also not well equipped for their responsibilities, and are sometimes seen by principals as a hindrance rather than a help.

A School Leadership Competency Standard: Principalship

In August 2014, Minister Motshekga published a proposed 'South African Standard for Principals' in the *Government Gazette*.[27] This was a big step forward in a system that has traditionally not given this very important role the attention it deserves'. It acknowledged the importance of leadership in the role of a school principal, and the many areas where good school leadership could make a significant difference to the school, its pupils, and the surrounding community.

The purpose of the new standard is to define the role of the school principal and the competencies required to fulfil it:

> "The South African Standard for Principalship provides a clear role description for school leaders and sets out what is required of the principal. He or she, working with others in the school and wider communities, must effectively promote, record, manage and support the best quality teaching and learning; the purpose of which is to enable learners to attain the highest levels of achievement for their own good, the good of their community and the country as a whole."[28]

The Department of Basic Education (DBE) acknowledges that there are "differentiated development needs for the professionalisation and development of the role of principal and other school leaders. These are:
- The improvement of the recruitment and selection procedures for principalship
- The induction and mentoring of newly appointed principals
- The enhancement of the skills and competencies of principals in posts
- The professional preparation for principals and the enhancement of the skills, attributes and competencies of deputies and middle managers; and
- The twinning of new appointees with experienced principals."[29]

This is a massive task for the DBE, as it applies to both incumbent principals and the large number of principals who need to be appointed. In research done during 2015, Gabrielle Wills found that 33% of school principals are aged 55 or older. This means that every year a large number of principals retire. Consequently, around 1 000 new principals must be appointed each year for the next decade. Wills also found that the demand for principal replacements is highest in the poorest schools,[30] where the need for good leadership is greatest.

It therefore becomes clear that the biggest challenge for South Africa today lies with almost 20 000 principals who have been equipped for their task as educators, but who have not been prepared for the task of managing and leading a highly complex organisation with many different stakeholders and significant challenges that need to be addressed at most of these schools.

The South African Standard for Principalship acknowledges the multi-faceted nature of the role, as reflected in Figure 3.3.

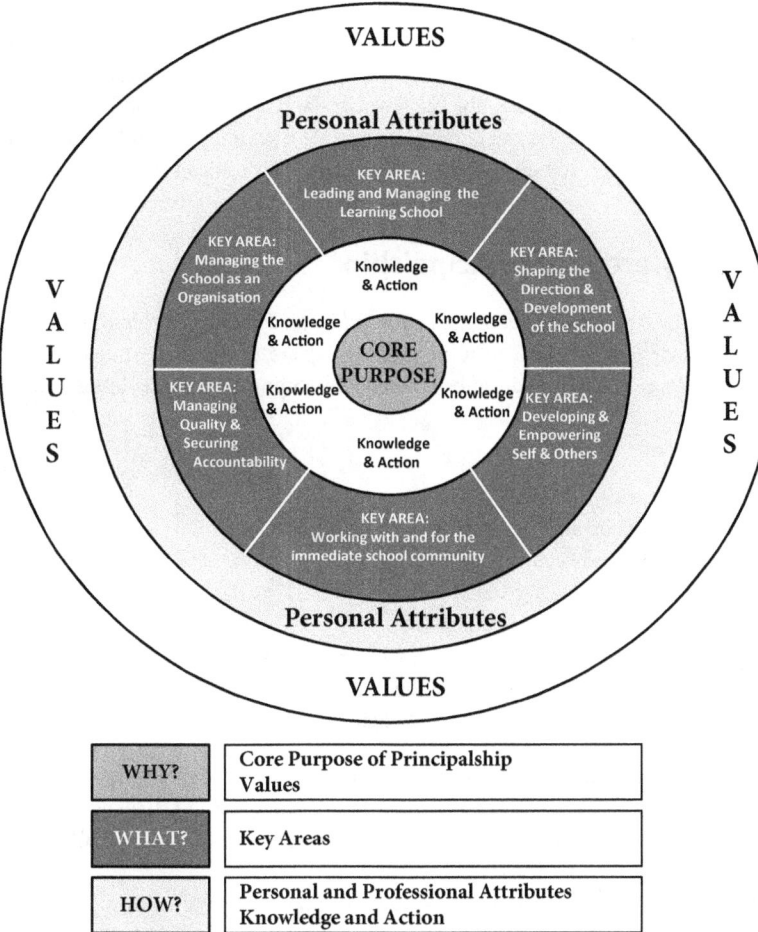

Figure 3.3: South African standard for principalship

From this graphic depiction give in Figure 3.3, it is clear that school principals are expected to both manage the school and lead through vision, support and direction. It is also clear that a principal's role extends beyond the learners and teachers to the community surrounding the school.

The core purpose of principalship

In the *Government Gazette* in which the Standard was tabled, the core purpose of the role is described as "the creation of an environment in which the highest possible level of teaching and learning can take place." The Standard also refers to the Principal's role in providing clear direction and having a strategic plan for the school, which is implemented in conjunction with the School Governing Body (SGB).

Once goals and strategies are set, principals, like business leaders, are required to translate the schools' vision and mission statements into "action plans and achievable outcomes."[31] During this process, they must liaise with and be accountable to various supervisory bodies, including the SGB, the DBE, and the local community.

The Standard articulates another dimension of the important role of a principal, namely responsibility for creating a safe and nurturing environment within which teaching and learning can take place. Such an environment enables teachers to do their best work and encourages continual improvements in teachers' subject knowledge and teaching methods.

Last, the Standard reiterates the important role that a school plays within the community, and it requires the principal to build strong community relationships for the benefit of both the school and community[32].

The eight key areas of principalship

With the purpose established, the *South African Standard for Principalship* identifies eight distinct roles[33] that a principal is expected to fulfil. These roles are described as interdependent, and include primary roles related to education and equally important roles as leader and manager of a school.

The eight key roles are:

1. "Leading the Learning School
2. Shaping the Direction and Development of the School
3. Managing Quality and Securing Accountability
4. Developing and Empowering Self and Others
5. Managing the School as an Organisation
6. Working with and for the immediate school Community as well as the broader community
7. Managing Human Resources (staff) in the school
8. Management and advocacy of extra-curricular activities."[34]

The above list gives an indication of the size and scope of the task that school principals face. Principals are expected to lead and manage all aspects of a complex and challenging organisation in the same way as a general manager in a manufacturing plant, who has overall responsibility for all aspects of the operations at the plant.

However, a general manager is almost always supported by a team of people who are responsible for specialist support functions, such as Information Technology (IT), Human Resources (HR), and Financial Management. Similarly, in well-resourced government or independent schools, principals are typically supported by SGB members who assume responsibility for such specialist support functions. Unfortunately, in under-resourced schools, particularly those where most parents are poorly educated, the principal has to assume responsibility for all the management functions that enable teaching and learning to take place. There can be no doubt that school principals face a massive task. While assuming the role of general manager of their schools, they are expected to inspire and lead a major turnaround in the quality of education. This is the provocative proposition of Vision 2030.

In addition to the above, principals of under-resourced schools in South Africa need high levels of resilience and tenacity. How best to develop the required skills set and to support principals in South African schools demands a radical rethink.

An important question that arises from the requirements outlined in the Standard for Principalship is whether it is possible for prospective principals to accumulate all the required knowledge and skills by the time they are appointed to the role, especially if they have not benefited from attending well-functioning and successful schools. Once they are appointed, very few principals in under-resourced schools benefit from high-quality management and leadership skills development. Fewer still participate in mentorship programmes in which an experienced principal or business leader supports the principal to acquire the knowledge and skills that their role demands.

There are almost 20 000 principals across South Africa who urgently need to acquire the knowledge and develop the skills and competencies in all eight key areas of leadership specified in the Standard for Principalship. This, however, cannot be easily achieved. It is not feasible for principals simply to put their jobs on hold while they undertake comprehensive Masters-level development programmes lasting several years.

To use an analogy, South African citizens from across the spectrum of government, business and civil society must fix the plane while it is flying, and support principals as they acquire the knowledge and skills they require. As a nation, we need to engage our collective intelligence and creativity to find ways to support principals so that they can lead the change that is so desperately needed in our schools.

The Need for Innovative Solutions

In the South African corporate world, the best leaders are usually developed over a number of years. Many receive several days of training every year from top institutions, focused on leadership development. By contrast, most who are appointed as school principals do not benefit from management or leadership development. Typically, they are teachers one day and principals the next, and have to assume a role that is incredibly complex and very different from their previous one as teacher or Deputy Principal. Since they have not been adequately prepared for their role, most principals are generally ill-equipped to fulfil it.

Simply 'throwing money at the problem' is not the solution. Vast sums of money have been channelled into education without any real impact, and this calls for a new course of action of how we are to expect real and lasting change.

Formally sanctioned training for school principals

One way of addressing this need for leadership training in schools is through formal tertiary education. In 2007 the Department of Education recognised this need and introduced an Advanced Certificate in Education: School Leadership (ACE:SL).

The ACE:SL programme acknowledged that school management is very different from classroom teaching and that traditional teacher training does not prepare teachers for the leadership and management roles they have to play when elected to the position of school principal. The ACE:SL courses were taught with a standard curriculum across several institutes of higher learning across South Africa, and offered current or prospective principals a fair balance between theory and practice in equipping them for their roles as the leaders of their schools.

This training programme was superseded in 2011 when the Minister of Higher Education and Training issued the national policy on the minimum requirements for teacher qualifications in terms of section 8(2)(c) of the National Qualifications Framework Act 67 of 2008. This policy was designed to align qualifications for teacher education with the Higher Education Framework of 2007. This new policy direction meant that the Advanced Certificate would be phased out and be replaced by an Advanced Diploma in School Leadership and Management, which changes the status of the qualification from a National Qualification Framework (NQF) exit-level 6 to an NQF exit-level 7 status.

The new Advanced Diploma in School Leadership and Management is to be built on the same principles as those of the ACE:SL, and will include modules on leading and managing the school, managing the school as an organisation, developing and empowering self and others, and working with and for the community. It is envisaged that this programme will be applicable to both the principal and the school management team (SMT). At the time of writing, this programme was still under development.[35]

Addressing the urgent need for better leadership in schools

The advances in formal training for principals and future programme development do not address some of the most pressing problems faced by principals and under-resourced schools, and it is clear that there is a need for a more innovative approach. This approach would have to consider the time, resources, and capital constraints faced by many principals, and should in some way bridge the gap between the school and the outside world.

A small group of leadership development practitioners[36] has been working since 2010 to develop an innovative solution to principal development – informed by cutting-edge thinking about leadership development. They are informed by the ideas behind Asset-Based Community Development (ABCD) and Positive Deviance. Instead of studying what's wrong in the 20 000 struggling schools, they asked: "Why do 5 000 schools work so well?"

They have found the following two commonalities – without exception – in schools that work well:

- The *principals have been equipped for their task* through being part of a well-functioning school community for many years. Most of these principals grew up in privileged communities, taught in well-functioning schools, and were members of School Management Teams before becoming principals in well-functioning schools.
- Many of these principals have also had *access to support and guidance from parents and other members of the community* around the school – typically professionals who have the capacity to get involved in their children's school as members of the School Governing Body (SGB).

Most principals in under-resourced communities had a challenging childhood, often in a poor black township or community. Many of these principals have not had the opportunity to experience a well-functioning and well-resourced school system since they themselves attended under-resourced schools. Furthermore, in under-resourced communities, because of historic inequities, the SGB usually consists of unemployed and often illiterate parents, who are unable to provide the same levels of support to principals and School Management Teams (SMTs) that are accessible to principals in well-resourced schools.

Asset-Based Community Development (ABCD) challenges practitioners to look at the assets that are widely available in the community, but possibly being under-utilised. In South Africa, there are thousands of business leaders who have had the opportunity of receiving formal business education, such as an MBA, or who have benefited from a variety of management and leadership development opportunities. These executives have many of the skills that principals need and which are identified in the South African Standards for Principalship.

Equipping the pilot while the plane is flying

The preceding overview of the challenges faced by the majority of public schools has identified the urgent need for leadership training in schools and the large resource of competent leaders and leadership training available in the private sector. The question remains as to how one can address this challenge by combining the available resources and the challenge of training school leaders, with cognisance of the constraints of time – faced by both the private sector and school principals – and money that most often plague these under-resourced schools.

Any solution, be it a tertiary training programme or any other intervention, should also consider the practical application of any proposed training. One successful model is the 70:20:10 model of learning,[37] which emphasises the importance of learning and developing leadership skills through experience. According to the 70:20:10 model, 70% of a programme's training should be experiential in the workplace, addressing challenges that are faced and solutions would be suggested and applied as the problems appear. This allows the person being trained to internalise the solution while problems are being solved. The model further says that the second most important area of learning is to learn and develop through interaction with others, which should constitute 20% of the training. The last 10% is assigned to learning and developing through structured courses and training programmes.

The 70:20:10 model allows for a flexible training model that can fit in the time constraints faced by all leaders, while ensuring a high level of success and retention by the participants.

A case study: Symphonia for South Africa's Partners for Possibility initiative

Partners for Possibility, which places the school at the centre of a community, is a cutting-edge social change innovation that partners business leaders with school principals in a reciprocal co-learning and co-action partnership where both leaders learn from each other and apply their learning to improve the school where the principal is the leader.

The programme offers a formal structure in which principals learn from business leaders who have been equipped with general management and change leadership skills; and business leaders learn from principals about leading in under-resourced environments, getting work done with few resources and collaborating across boundaries.

Often, business leaders also bring their network and resources to bear, resolving in a short while many of the infrastructure or administrative burdens that have been hampering progress at the school for years. In doing this, business leaders utilise their networks and demonstrate their networking skills to lobby for support from within their own organisations and industry contacts and, most importantly, from the businesses surrounding the school. This is of vital importance as the businesses in the vicinity of the school can get involved in a more sustainable way.

These business leader and principal partnerships join in groups of similar partnerships, where they regularly share ideas, insights and challenges, while each individual partnership receives professional coaching throughout the year of formal training. Through this process, business leaders and members of their teams and communities are able to provide practical hands-on support where it is most needed – at the school.

A Future Perspective

Education is foundational to the economy. Trends in this sector should be on the radar of every business leader. This is especially true in South Africa, where the education sector finds itself buffeted by global changes – including changes in teaching methods and the rise of technology – and a myriad of local structural, philosophical and political challenges. Many of these challenges facing the education sector will resonate in corporate corridors soon, which warrants careful consideration and intentional support from corporate South Africa.

With this in mind, there are a number of major considerations that should be on every leader's agenda, both leaders in the education sector and those planning for the future of their enterprises.

Skills versus competencies

In contrast to the era in which our current pedagogical methods were created, the world is now awash with free and easily accessible information and knowledge. Information has changed from something that should be sought, memorised and catalogued to something that is freely available and should be critically analysed, evaluated and applied. In a recent study by the World Economic Forum and Boston Consulting,[38] this new reality has created a vacuum in the teaching of higher order skills or competencies. These competencies are required to be an active and efficient member of the economy and one that can survive in this new knowledge economy.

Some of the competencies listed by both the WEF-Boston Consulting study and recent research by Harvard[39], includes critical thinking, problem solving, persistence, collaboration, personal communication skills and curiosity. It should be clear that many of these traits and competencies cannot be taught in the traditional teacher-centred classroom where information is taught through rote learning and where standard proficiency tests dictate what is memorised and recalled.

There is surely a need for these higher order skills, even as most schools and even universities do not consciously teach it. Businesses often also report a need for suitably competent employees. This emphasises the need for leaders in education to address this glaring gap and leaders in the corporate sector to consider their response to an influx of inadequately skilled workers.

Facilitating learning and growth

In keeping with the disparity between the current teaching environment and the skills and competencies needed from future job applicants, one should consider the urgent need for teachers to change their mind-set and approach. Gone are the days in which the teacher was the first and final authority on knowledge and skills. In a connected context teachers should forget about being the centre of all attention and all learning and move to a more collaborative method of teaching.

In much the same way, the new generation of employees will not learn or be challenged by a strict hierarchical and authoritarian leadership style. Rather, leaders will be required to facilitate and challenge employees as part of their learning process, thereby helping employees to build many of these modern day competencies that are seen as critical for future business survival.

Participatory leadership

The new methods that are required in education will resonate in corporate South Africa. Studies, such as those quoted here, call for a more participatory teaching style, which engage learners and makes them responsible for finding answers and solutions. Through this process of actively engaging learners, teachers can instil a culture of initiative and responsibility in the learners. And in much the same way a more participatory form of leadership will find good application in the business environment, where leaders will find an increase in next generation employees that are often ill prepared for the challenges that they are about to face. This method of leadership also calls for leaders who are comfortable with disruption. Education remains at its very core a disruptive force and it will require teachers, and leaders, who are comfortable with disruption.

Breaking down the barriers

This point speaks to the broader challenges facing education in South Africa. With over 20 000 schools listed as being under-resourced or in crisis, there is a never ending requirement for support of these schools and for finding new ways of solving their problems. Many of these schools address their unique challenges and make progress through sheer determination and courage, often finding a solution despite their very limited management experience and resources.

Sadly, many of the solutions needed in the South African education sector are available in great supply in the corporate sector, but that remains out of reach of most under-resourced schools. Corporate South Africa is a shining example of the leadership talent available in South Africa, and most leaders in this sector are the product of many hours or even years of leadership training and mentorship.

At the same time, schools exist within a community and the opportunities exist for it to become the centre of that community and for it to draw on the skills, enthusiasm and manpower available. This is where a great opportunity for dramatic leverage exists. If leaders could cross boundaries and share insights, resources and contacts they would be able to make a significant impact. They will also find themselves inspired by the hearts of the leaders at under-resourced schools and by their ability to make a difference, without necessarily opening a cheque book.

By some measurements, South Africa will need to appoint over 1 000 new school principals per year to fill vacant or soon to be vacant positions.[40] Most of these principals have not been exposed to any form of leadership training or development. Yet they will soon find themselves at the helm of a highly complex organisation with limited resources and a myriad of social and administrative challenges. Breaking down the barriers between corporate leaders and school leaders holds great potential. Not least because it offers the opportunity for the systemic change that is called for and it allows for problem solving at a school level, which is the largest unit of sustainable change.

Business has a vested interest in the success of the education sector. It also has much to learn from the changes in training and education in the way in which it interacts with employees and adapts to the modern competitive environment. Business can positively impact the business environment by applying many of the skills and solutions that it has access to, while it stands to learn immeasurably from the brave men and women that work tirelessly in the South African education sector.

Conclusion

There is a real opportunity here for corporate citizenship. The task of school principal is massive. In well-functioning schools, principals are supported by staff members with the capacity to help as well as members of the community who are able to provide practical support with regard to support functions such as IT, HR and Finance.

There are approximately 20 000 under-resourced schools in South Africa. Principals in these schools do not have enough staff and they typically don't have skilled and experienced people on their SGBs who can share the load. Yet they urgently need assistance and support.

Imagine if all business leaders with these kinds of skills in South Africa made themselves available to support under-resourced schools? Imagine if one could involve professional organisations such as the South African Institute of Chartered Accountants (SAICA) or the South African Board of People Practitioners (SABPP), and they expected their members to offer help and support in their respective field of expertise at just one school in their area?

South Africa needs innovative solutions to deal with its education crisis. The level of unequal distribution of resources and support is largely due to former apartheid policies. Business can play a huge role in addressing this by sharing knowledge and skills where they are most needed rather than just expecting more from people who are already under huge pressure.

Through highly effective leadership in schools where all learners receive quality education, the provocative proposition of what might be – a high-performing education system, the foundation of a flourishing South Africa – is possible.

Endnotes

1. Cooperrider, D. 2002. Appreciative inquiry.
2. Spaull, 2013.
3. Wilkinson, 2015.
4. Spaull, 2012.
5. Osman, 2015.
6. DBE, 2015 (October).
7. CDE, 2013 (August).
8. See endnote 4.
9. Motshekga, A (Minister of Basic Education). 2016.
10. See endnote 4.
11. National Treasury, RSA. 2015.
12. National Treasury, RSA. 2016.
13. See endnote 4.
14. OECD, 2015.
15. Marzano et al., 2005.
16. Leithwood et al, 2004.
17. Jensen, 2013.
18. Morrison, 2006.
19. Goodlad, 1975.
20. Wills, 2015.
21. Bush, 2008.
22. Bush, Kiggundu & Moorosi, 2011.
23. See endnote 9.
24. Ibid.
25. Ross, 2010.
26. See endnote 9.
27. DBE, 2014 (August), pp. 6–29.
28. Ibid, p.1.
29. Ibid, p.7.
30. Wills, 2015.
31. DBE, 2014 (August), p. 12.
32. DBE, 2014 (August), p. 12.
33. Note further that the Standard identifies 72 knowledge and skills domains across the 8 areas.
34. DBE, 2014 (August), p. 9.
35. Parliament of the RSA, 2015.
36. Collins, 2014.
37. Kajewski & Madsen, 2013.
38. New Vision for Education – Unlocking the Potential of Technology. www3.weforum.org
39. Education for the 21st Century – Executive Summary. April 24 – 26, Harvard University.
40. Wills, 2015.

References

Bush, T. 2008. *Leadership and management development in education*. London, UK: Sage.

Bush, T, Kiggundu, E & Moorosi, P. 2011. 'Preparing new principals in South Africa: The ACE: School Leadership Program'. *South African Journal of Education*, 31:31–43.

Centre for Development and Enterprise (CDE). 2013 (August). *Affordable private schools in South Africa*. Johannesburg, ZA: Centre for Development and Enterprise.

Collins, M. 2014. *Partners for possibility*. Johannesburg, ZA: Knowledge Resources.

Cooperrider, D. 2002. 'Tips for crafting provocative propositions'. *Appreciative inquiry*. [Online]. Available: https://appreciativeinquiry.case.edu/practice/toolsPropositionsDetail.cfm?coid=1170. [Accessed 1 July 2016].

Department of Basic Education (DBE). 2014 (August). 'South African standard for principalship'. *Government Gazette* 37897. Pretoria, ZA: Government Printer. 1–29.

Department of Basic Education (DBE). 2015 (October). *School realities*. Pretoria, ZA: Department of Basic Education. [Online]. Available: http://www.education.gov.za/reports/2015 school realities. [Accessed 1 July 2016].

Goodlad, J. 1975. Schools can make a difference. *Educational Leadership*, 33(2):108–117.

Jensen, B. 2013. *The five critical steps for turnaround schools*. Carlton, AUS: Grattan Institute. [Online]. Available: http://www.alliance21.org.au/.../Jensen_Alliance-21-Education-Innovation.pdf. [Accessed 1 July 2016].

Kajewski, K & Madsen, V. 2013. *White Paper: Demystifying 70:20:10*. Melbourne, AUS: DeakinPrime Corporate Education, Deakin University. [Online]. Available: http://deakinprime.com/media/47821/002978_dpw_70-20-10wp_v01_fa.pdf. [Accessed 1 July 2016].

Leithwood, K, Louis, KS, Anderson, S & Wahlstrom, K. 2004. *Review of research: How leadership influences student learning*. Minneapolis, MN: Center for Applied Research and Educational Improvement, University of Minnesota.

Marzano, RJ, Waters, T & McNulty, BA. 2005. *School leadership that works: From research to results*. Alexandria, VA: Association for Supervision and Curriculum Development (ASCD).

Morrison, K. 2006. 'Complexity theory and education'. Paper presented at the APERA Conference, Hong Kong, Macau Inter-University Institute, Macau. 28–30 November. [Online]. Available: http://edisdat.ied.edu.hk/pubarch/b15907314/full_paper/SYMPO-000004_Keith%20Morrison.pdf. [Accessed 1 July 2016].

Motshekga, A (Minister of Basic Education). 2016. 'Keynote address'. Basic Education Sector Lekgotla. Saint George Hotel, Pretoria, 20 January. [Online]. Available: http://www.education.gov.za/newsroom/speeches/ . [Accessed 1 July 2016].

National Treasury, RSA. 2015. *Estimates of national expenditure 2015*. Abridged version. Pretoria, ZA: Communications Department, National Treasury. [Online]. Available: http://www.treasury.gov.za/documents/national%20budget/2015/ene/FullENE.pdf. [Accessed 1 July 2016].

National Treasury, RSA. 2016. *2016 budget highlights*. Pretoria, ZA: National Treasury. [Online]. Available: http://www.treasury.gov.za/documents/national%20budget/2016/guides/2016%20Budget%20Highlights%20Card.pdf. [Accessed 1 July 2016].

OECD Home Directorate for Education and Skills. 2015. *Universal basic skills*. Organisation for Economic Co-operation and Development (OECD), 13 May [Online]. Available: http://www.oecd.org/edu/universal-basic-skills-9789264234833-en.htm. [Accessed 1 July 2016].

Osman, R. 2015. *Private vs public schools in South Africa: It's not a simple numbers game*. The Conversation Media Group. 1 June.[Online]. Available: https://theconversation.com/private-vs-public-schools-its-not-a-simple-numbers-game-41899. [Accessed 30 July 2015].

Parliament of the RSA. 2015. Overview and analysis of basic education report on the introduction of the advanced diploma in school leadership and management. 12 May. [Online]. Available: https://pmg.org.za/files/150512overview.pdf. [Accessed 1 July 2016].

Ross, A. 2010. *Nutrition and its effects on academic performance. How can our schools improve?* MA (Education) thesis. Marquette, MI. Northern Michigan University. [Online]. Available: https://www.nmu.edu/sites/DrupalEducation/files/UserFiles/Files/Pre-Drupal/SiteSections/Students/GradPapers/Projects/Ross_Amy_MP.pdf. [Accessed 1 July 2016].

Spaull, N. 2012. 'Education in SA: A tale of two systems'. *Politics Web*. [Online]. Available: http://www.politicsweb.co.za/politicsweb/view/politicsweb/en/. [Accessed 1 July 2016].

Spaull, N. 2013. *South Africa's education crisis: The quality of education in South Africa 1994–2011*. Johannesburg, ZA: Centre for Development and Enterprise.

Wilkinson, K. 2015. 'Checked: 80% of South African schools indeed "dysfunctional"'. *Mail & Guardian*, 25 March. [Online]. Available: http://mg.co.za/article/2015-03-25-are-80-of-south-african-schools-dysfunctional. [Accessed 1 July 2016].

Wills, G. 2015. *Improving the calibre of school leadership in South Africa*. ReSEP Policy Brief.

Chapter 4

LEADING IN SOUTH AFRICAN HIGHER EDUCATION

Crain Soudien

Many South African publications issued around about 18 October 2015 carried the extraordinary image of the Vice-Chancellor of the University of the Witwatersrand, Adam Habib, sitting on the floor in the atrium of Senate House. Surrounded by students, most of whom are standing, there he is, in classic Habib mode, holding forth, chin upright, leaning on his left arm, his right arm extended in an emphatic flourish. What is going on? This very public figure in the higher education and political community is attempting to engage with his students at the height of the student uprising. On the floor though he may be, this is clearly not the posture of a hostage.

In this chapter, I argue that we see in this image of Habib the full amplitude of the complexity of, and in some ways an experimental response to, the leadership question of higher education. The chapter is an attempt to describe and analyse the new approaches which are emerging in the higher education sector in terms of its management and leadership. It begins with the basic argument that the sector is going through an intense transition This demands on the part of leadership, as is the case in other leadership contexts involving transitions, the capacity to cope with unpredictability; to be able to map out the variety of scenarios that are possible within the context; and to be able to develop what in the leadership literature is described as transformational leadership.[1]

The contribution begins with a brief review of the major leadership theories in the discussion. It then moves on to an analysis of the nature and structure of the higher education system, and introduces the work of higher education sociologist Martin Trow, who describes the features of higher education systems. The discussion pivots on Trow's descriptions of systems and their transitions from one stage to another. The question of transition is focused upon in order to describe the current crisis in higher education in the country. The chapter makes the argument that this crisis is the product of the transition. It describes the features of this transition and, on the basis of this discussion, looks at the experience of higher education leadership in 2015. The chapter closes with a consideration of the qualities and competencies that are necessary for leadership in the current period.

Leadership Theories and their Relevance for Higher Education

Interestingly, the leadership literature is characterised by two forms of writing. At its popular end, one can find any number of texts crafted in clichéd 'principles'. Much of this kind of work is superficial, dependent on anecdote, and structured around the identity of a de-contextualised universal manager with a knapsack of ready-made solutions. At its serious end, it works with psychology and sociology in deep ways. While both have their uses, it is the latter which is of interest for this work.

The discussion of higher education leadership took a serious turn in the 1970s with the work of Clark.[2] Clark's work constituted the first attempt to describe the sociology of the university. The most critical element of this work was its description of universities as 'loosely coupled' systems. Later scholars[3] would elaborate on this analysis to describe universities as sites of 'organised anarchy'. The sociological feature which, in this genre of writing, distinguished the public university from other kinds of organisational settings was essentially the individual – the individual to be formed, the individual to be protected, and the individual to be celebrated.

It was the duty of the university, in the midst of all the other things that it would do – producing knowledge and knowledge-producing subjects, disputing knowledge, recreating knowledge, acting in the public good – to ensure that the basic conditions for the survival and flourishing of the free-thinking and creative individual would never be undermined. This individual had the benefit of both resources which he/she could expect from his/her institution and the freedom to determine a developmental path for him-/herself. He/she was not subjected to the kinds of accountability typical of corporate or government structures. Having to manage this put the role of the university leader, the president (in the United States), the vice-chancellor (in the English-speaking colonial community), the rector (in the Germanic tradition), or the dean in a very different light. He/she did not sit at the apex of an institution in the same kind of way as a corporate leader. Instead, in a much more collegial mode, he/she was required to facilitate the development of the many individually-minded people around him/her and mediate in and between them rather than pronounce and dictate what they should do. This is now what is accepted as the ideal of the modern public university.

Of course, it is the case, that higher educational systems develop cultures and traditions. And so it is, for example, that academic freedom is a much stronger feature of the Anglo-American tradition in higher education than it might be in systems that have grown up with other histories. It is also the case that institutions within systems, depending as they do on the role players inside them and the dynamics between them, evolve quite distinctive ways of managing and leading, even if the dominant characteristic of their system is quite pervasive.

In the South African setting, two traditions have evolved: the British and the Germanic tradition. But academic freedom and institutional autonomy have persevered as strong features of what the systems looks like. These have, moreover, been enshrined in the South African Higher Education Act 101 of 1997 and in the founding statutes of institutions. As we shall see below, it is the founding traditions that have emerged as major areas of contestation in the protests that have erupted in the country, with many role-players seeking the placing of limits on academic freedom and its complementary value of institutional autonomy.

In this context of higher education, standard leadership approaches and theories have not been without value and relevance. Those that have found resonance include the transformational, charismatic, situational and moral leadership approaches.[4][5] Common to all these approaches are issues relating to inclusion, respect, and the distribution of responsibility and accountability. Growing out of this work, largely informed by scholars working against the backdrop of the north American academy, has been a line of thinking focused on the capacity of leaders in the 'loosely coupled' context of the university to provide strong diagnostic and evaluative leadership underpinned by principles of distributed responsibility and inclusion.

As Geering[6] points out, a number of generalisations relating to the principles and the methods of leadership in higher education have taken root and come to be accepted as standard points of departure in the sector over the course of the development of this discussion. These include the following:

> "Leadership is a shared process and a group function, being the product of interaction; leadership does not result from position or status, but rather how a person behaves in an organisation; leadership positively changes organisational effectiveness and group activity; leadership implies change; leadership cannot be structured in advance; and most groups have more than one person occupying the leadership role."[7]

While this discussion has been developed in the more wealthy systems of higher education in the world, they have come to be seen as useful for leaders elsewhere too. Critically, however, as the situation in which an important leader such as Habib finds himself makes clear, they do not constitute a tool-kit. While sharing and awareness of behaviour are undoubtedly deeply critical for leaders anywhere, it is still the very particular set of dynamics which arise in particular settings which higher education leaders need to have a deep understanding of. It is this particularity, I would like to argue, which gives the South African university its very distinctive identity. What are these dynamics?

The Nature of the South African Higher Education Sector

The dynamics which give the contemporary South African university its character take their substance directly from the history of colonialism and apartheid. The questions of 'race', class, and, it needs to be said, gender, are core to the story of the development of the South African university. Many of South Africa's leading universities have their origins in educational initiatives which begin in the formative days of the Union of South Africa.

I would like to argue that the South African academy is constituted in ambivalence. This ambivalence is the direct result of the encounter, and even contest, between the *idea of the university*, especially in its deeply liberal Newmanian intonations – the university as a place of strangers with students and professors from all quarters bringing knowledge from all quarters – and *the idea of South Africa* – South Africa as a place of destiny for the realisation of white privilege.

The higher education system that emerges out of this contestation is in the end essentially the triumphal product of white supremacy. Constitutive closedness eclipses and overwhelms the constitutive urge to make the university an open place. The knowledge project is yoked behind the social and comes to be used through the admissions practices of the emerging universities and the content of their teaching as the means by which a white elite is produced and reproduced. This process is brought to a climax with the passing of the Extension of University Education Act 45 of 1959, which formally bars people of colour from the white universities and forces them into a new generation of ethnic and tribal universities. The critical point to take away from this discussion is that the system that emerges from this experience is a racially defined white elite one.

In the current era, we are now, more than fifty years after the passage of the Extension of University Education Act, in a fundamentally different place. What makes the situation so different? The South African higher education system has been significantly remodelled through a process of mergers and realignments. It is made up of 26 institutions, and the old divide between technikons and universities has been removed. Most critical, however, is that the system has tipped over from being an elite system to becoming a mass-based system. At this point I draw on the work of Trow[8] to help us understand the leadership implications of this shift in the fundamental dynamics of the South African university.

Trow, using Weber's definition of the *ideal* (a typification which may not exist in an empirical sense), classified higher education systems into three ideal types: elite, mass and universal.[9] By definition, a system ceased to be elite when its enrolment exceeded 15% of the people, the youth in the main, eligible to attend. Beyond 15% enrolment, they become mass higher education systems. When they attained the benchmark of 50% enrolment, they became universal systems. Trow revised that figure to 30% in 2006. Why he did this is unclear. Table 4.1 below captures the characteristics typical of the three systems.

Table 4.1: Trow's definitions of Elite, Mass and Universal Higher Education

	Elite (0–15%)	**Mass (16–50%)**	**Universal (over 50%)**
Attitudes to access	A *privilege* of birth or talent or both	A *right* for those with certain qualifications	An *obligation* for the upper and middle classes
Functions of higher education	Shaping mind and character of ruling class; preparation for elite roles	Transmission of skills; preparation for broader range of technical and economic elite roles	Adaptation of 'whole population' to rapid social and technological change
Curriculum	Highly structured in terms of academic or professional conceptions of knowledge	Modular, flexible and semi-structured sequence of courses	Boundaries and sequences break down; distinctions between learning and life break down
Institutional characteristics	Homogeneous, with high and common standards	Comprehensive with more diverse standards	Great diversity, with no common standards
	Small residential communities	'Cities of intellect' – mixed residential/ commuting	Aggregates of people enrolled, some of whom are rarely or never on campus
	Clear and impermeable boundaries	Boundaries 'fuzzy' and permeable	Boundaries weak or non-existent
Locus of power and decision-making	'The Athenaeum' – small elite group, shared values and assumptions	Ordinary political processes of interest groups and party programmes	'Mass publics' question special privileges and immunities of academe
Academic standards	Broadly shared and relatively high	Variable; system/ institution: 'become holding companies for quite different kinds of academic enterprises'	Criterion shifts from 'standards' to 'value-added'
Access and selection	Meritocratic achievement based on school performance	Meritocratic plus 'compensatory programmes' in order to achieve equality of opportunity	'Open', emphasis on 'equality of group achievement' (class, ethnic)

	Elite (0–15%)	Mass (16–50%)	Universal (over 50%)
Internal governance	Senior professors	Professors and junior staff, with increasing influence from students	Breakdown of consensus-making institutional governance insoluble. Decision-making flows into hands of political authority

Source: *Based on Trow*[10]

There are two important observations to make about Trow's work. The first is the value to be derived from his ideal types. In each are to be seen important attributes. Relevant for the purposes of this discussion are the different attributes relating to access and their significance for learning, administration and governance. Access in elite systems is based on *privilege;* in mass systems on *right;* and in universal systems on *obligation* for the privileged.

With regard to governance, his comments have great relevance for the South African situation. The elite system is managed in 'The Athenaeum', a small elite group with shared values and assumptions. He saw, and perhaps even supported, elite systems as virtuous structures which were able to nurture "(r)elatively close and prolonged relationships between student and teacher ... this form of higher education conveys ... to students that they can accomplish large and important things in the world, that they can make important discoveries, lead great institutions, influence their country's laws and government".[11]

The mass-based system, and this is crucial for the South African system, is subjected to the ordinary political process of interest groups and party programmes. The administration in this mass-based system is now no longer in the hands of amateur administrators, but is managed by a large and fulltime bureaucracy. The system concentrates on the transmission of skills and knowledge between teachers and their students. Exchanges between professors and students are briefer, less personal, and aimed at preparing students for more modest roles in society.[12]

Trow's second point of significance for this discussion relates to the transition from one type to another:

> "These problems can be understood better as different manifestations of a related cluster of problems, and ... they arise out of the transition from one phase to another in a broad pattern of development of higher education, a transition underway in every advanced society – from elite to mass higher education and subsequently universal access. Underlying this pattern of development lies growth and expansion."[13]

This expansion had serious consequences for the management of the system. Trow[14] remarked that "when a very large proportion of all the members of an institution are new recruits, they threaten to overwhelm the processes whereby recruits to a more slowly growing system are inducted into its value system and learn its norms and forms."

Trow's analysis is important for understanding the leadership challenge in South Africa. The system has moved from being an elite system to becoming, distinctly, a mass-based system. This is evident in the dramatic shifts in the composition of the student community. In 1993 African enrolment was 191 000 students.[15] While growth was to be seen in all the colour groups of our population, it was most dramatic amongst the African group, where between 1993 and

2013, a period of 20 years, enrolment increased by almost 261% (see Table 4.2 below). In the period from 2000 to 2007, the participation rates of black students grew from 10% in 2001 to 12% in 2006; for coloureds from 8,5% to 13%; and Asians from 42% to 51%. From 2000 to 2010 the average annual increase for black students was 6.5%. In terms of absolute numbers, black African enrolments in the period from 2008 to 2013 went up from 515 058 to 689 503. Over the periods from 2000 to 2013, the increase in total enrolments was 76.7%, from 556 700 to 983 698 students.[16][17] For the entire period, it was also 116.8%. Interestingly, the white participation rate remained stable at 59%. Female participation increased from 15% to 18%, while the male rate went up from 13% to 14%.

Table 4.2: Headcount enrolment and growth by race, 2000-2013

Actual enrolment	African	Coloured	Indian	White
2000	317 998	30 106	39 558	163 004
2001	353 327	32 900	43 436	173 397
2002	370 072	37 906	47 567	178 871
2003	403 325	42 390	51 611	184 964
2004	453 621	46 091	54 326	188 714
2005	446 945	46 302	54 611	185 847
2006	451 107	48 538	54 859	184 667
2007	476 680	49 001	52 579	180 435
2008	515 058	51 647	52 401	178 140
2009	547 686	55 101	53 562	179 232
2010	595 963	58 219	54 537	178 346
2011	640 442	59 312	54 698	177 365
2012	663 123	58 692	52 296	172 654
2013	689 503	61 034	53 787	171 927
% increases for the whole period	116.8	102.7	36.0	5.5

Source: *Compiled from CHE*[18]

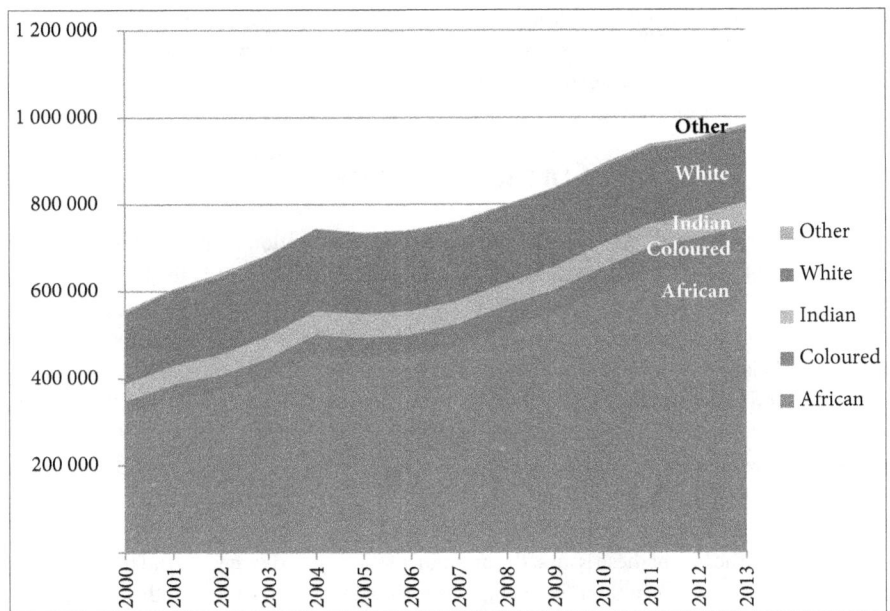

Figure 4.1: Headcount student enrolments in public higher education by race, 2000 to 2013
Note: Other includes students from race groups not classified here, for example Asian students.

In 2005 the participation rate for the whole 20–24 age cohort was 12%.[19] By 2013, the rate for the African segment of the population, not focusing on the 20–24 age group, had increased to 16,3% (own calculation). In Trow's terms, the system had tipped over. It was no longer elite but now mass-based.

In putting Trow's analysis into larger perspective, also important for this discussion, is the composition of the teaching force in the university. In Trow's, we see how the pedagogical and governance elements of the elite university depend on homogeneity: shared values and impermeable boundaries. In mass-based systems a schematisation of instruction develops, using more remote, impersonal forms. What has happened, critically, giving this instructional aspect of the situation in the country a particular dynamic, is that the profile of the professoriate has remained largely white and male. While improvements have taken place in the period between 2003 and 2009, with the percentage of white members of staff declining by almost 10%, they still constituted 57,6% (25,067 out of 43,446) of the number of academic members of staff in the system total.[20] Higher Education South Africa (HESA) (now Universities South Africa) commented on this, saying that "there is a great deal more progress to be made".[21]

Against this backdrop, Trow's insights about what happens to systems when they grow are directly relevant for the South African discussion. He observes that:

> "...systems of mass higher education differed from elite systems not just quantitatively but also qualitatively. They differed obviously in the proportions of the relevant age group they enrolled, but also in the way in which students and teachers viewed attendance...; in the functions of gaining entry for the student; in the functions of the system for their society; in their curricula; in the typical student's career; in the degree of student homogeneity; in the character of academic standards; in the forms of instruction; in the relationships between students and faculty... In other words, the differences between these phases are quite fundamental and relate to every aspect of higher education."[22]

What is the significance of this for leadership in the South African system? Trow's observations about the ease with which countries manage the transitions of their systems are crucial. He says: "If the transition is made successfully, the system is then able to develop institutions that can grow without being transformed, until they start to admit over 30% of the relevant age group."[23]

Current Challenges

Using Trow, I argue that what we are seeing in the higher education landscape are the complex consequences of the system tipping over from one state to another. It is in the throes of that transition. The university system is currently experiencing a student uprising. The uprising emanated out of a protest against the imposing presence of a statue of Cecil John Rhodes, a major imperialist figure in South Africa's colonial history, on the campus of the University of Cape Town. It quickly expanded to other issues, the most pertinent of which was that of access: the right to learn; and a question, less clearly articulated, but a question, nonetheless, about the modes of government in the university. The curriculum has been a focus of student criticism. This criticism is essentially that the curriculum is Euro-centric and does not sufficiently engage and use African scholarship.

In terms of the first of these issues, the question of the right to learn was fundamentally about the proposed increases in student fees being put forward by universities and their exclusionary impact on poor and largely black students. With regard to the second issue, the question arose of the legitimacy of university councils and their defence of the argument of institutional autonomy. As central as the right to learn was to the question of access, so was the legitimacy of the councils to determine by themselves questions such as the employment conditions of staff members, particularly administrative staff, within the university.

The protest was led by the #FeesMustFall (#FMF) movement, a national initiative found on most campuses without a discernible leadership or accountability structure. The #FMF provided the 2015 protest with its symbolic and organisational resources. Through a series of important symbolic marches, first on Parliament in Cape Town, then on the Union Buildings, and finally on Luthuli House, the headquarters of the African National Congress, #FMF succeeded in first stopping and later securing the reversal of decisions that had already been made by many universities in the country to increase their fees. Critically, it also managed to bring most of the major universities in the country to a standstill. Epitomising this shut-down was the image of Habib, surrounded by Trow's new recruits to the higher education system, who actually succeeded in overwhelming the contemporary university. The protests did not throw open the gates of learning, but they brought to the fore the question of the new South African university. They brought a new poignancy to the question of what the new mass-based South African university is to become. Central to this poignancy, and here I seek to recast Trow and to render his analysis in the grounded realities of South Africa, is its sociological complexity.

Central to the South African complexity is the real matter of how Trow's new entrants to the system: people with complex traditional, patriarchal, gendered, racialised and class histories – many of which would have been in the apartheid era marginalised and delegitimised – enter into the space of the learning commons of the university with its own complexities. These complexities are its tangle of oppressions and exclusions, on the one hand, and freedoms and affordances, on the other.[24]

The reality is that the post-apartheid university is still a place of the elite. This elite is now no longer white, but it is still a powerful new social force. But the university is for many a place of intense self-discovery and, significantly, even self-liberation. Keeping some out as it does, it offers for others critical new opportunities in their lives. This is an important point with which to think through and analyse the complexity of a university. Even as it becomes mass-based, it is still a place for particular kinds of elites in terms of how society is differentiated and ranked. In elite systems one has an alignment between the social groups and the content and character of the university. In mass-based systems, the elite nature of the enterprise remains, but the reproductive loop between the distribution of power outside the university and inside it is broken. The university is no longer a vehicle and instrument for the socially privileged.

What does one take away from this discussion? Most critical, it seems, is the need to recognise that the South African university in moving from an elite to a mass-based university is undergoing difficult changes. Particularly in its student composition, the system is made up of a constituency which is new to higher education. Its professoriate remains largely white. How does one lead in this complexity?

Critical Competencies

It is important to acknowledge the value of the general literature on leadership in higher education for South Africa. The general qualities to which Geering drew attention for loosely coupled systems have direct relevance for South African universities. It is important to emphasise this point to remind ourselves that the South African university as a university is a member of a structure which is, *sui generis*, different from other kinds of institutions. Its distinctiveness, as the North American leadership literature is helping us to understand, and we must agree that this distinctiveness is important to protect, requires South African universities to be managed and led in ways that remain recognisable and in conformity to what is happening in the leading institutions in the world.

These ways are:

1. Making leadership *a shared responsibility and a group function* and so distributing power in terms of decision making and the determination of the direction of an organisation. In the case of students, this entails ensuring that they are able to participate at all the levels of the organisation where their participation is appropriate and proper.
2. Ensuring that leadership is *a process and the product of interaction*. Protocols and guidelines must be cultivated which make it possible for the most vulnerable members of the organisation serving in committees to participate with confidence and without fear of victimisation. In these terms, critical for the university is a sense of collegiality. The demonstration of collegiality is crucial for the shared distribution of power.
3. Ensuring that leadership does not result from social position or status, but rather from *capacity*. Only people who are able to demonstrate competence with regard to the responsibilities attached to them should be considered and eligible for appointments.
4. Making leadership *accountable* for organisational effectiveness and being able to demonstrate *the capacity to both diagnose and act* in relation to the decisions it has made.

What these now widely-accepted approaches to leadership suggest is that it is possible for good leaders in the system to come from anywhere. However, they have to understand the nature and character of the university. They have to manifest the maturity to operate at both macro- and micro-levels of the organisation. This means being able to read into and engage with the large structural complexities of the system in which they find themselves. They must have the acumen for or the ability to recognise the need for training to be able to identify, work with and resolve problems which arise out of the structural realities in which they find themselves – the funding and governance prescripts which determine their base-line operations, both internally and in relation to the larger system. This requires basic levels of financial and governance literacy.

Critically, this is in the space of public higher education, the capacity to be able to manage the tension between, on the one hand, compliance with the financial and governance performative requirements of the system, and, on the other, the courage to take risks which ensure that their institutions can respond, quickly and agilely, to opportunities which might arise. Their capacity to diagnose, against this, must be more than simply adequate. They need to analyse quickly and deconstruct a situation in order to be able to understand what is not working, who the accountable people are, and to respond effectively.

This means having a good sense of the structures at their disposal and their effectiveness, a sense of the individuals holding down positions of responsibility, and their strategic and task-orientated abilities. Their organisational sense needs to be highly developed. Within the dynamics of their institution's loosely coupled structure, they also need to manage the flows and surges of power and the paralysis that circulate within the complex structure of the institution. This requires an awareness of how ideas, attitudes and conceits circulate in the environments and the effective maturity to deal with disappointment, resentment, jealousy, elation, joy and hubris. In these the leader in South Africa is no different in the basic suite of capabilities to his/her counterpart anywhere in the world.

If the job that is to be done is to be carried out with any sense of understanding, he/she has to have a deep grasp of the psychology and sociology of the exclusions and inclusions that characterise a society such as South Africa. The leader has to have some of the panache of a Habib, but also the wisdom of vice-chancellors and rectors who have come to recognise the immediate reality of working in a space of transition. The leader needs to recognise that he/she stands at the head of a structure that has historically struggled with inclusion: the inclusion of particular groups of people, and the inclusion of particular kinds of knowledge.

At the same time, he/she needs to have a fine appreciation of the accumulated knowledge resources inside the disciplines practised in the university and to work with these in critically respectful ways. At the core of the capacity required with this psychology and sociology is acknowledging the strengths and weaknesses of the inherited university – with its centuries' old legacy – and the university that is to be built, and then, on top of all that, a self-awareness honed to a fine edge.

What this psychosocial literacy talks to is a multi-dimensionality which includes the following competencies:

1. *A self-awareness of one's strengths and weaknesses* and the demonstrative capacity which shows, repeatedly, an understanding of how to stop doing some things and when to start others. Essential in this self-awareness is also an understanding of one's own positionality, 'race' in the current conjuncture, but always also gender, class, sexuality, language, and many of the other forms of power that matter in relationships between individuals and groups.
2. The capacity to smell *the inclination to exclude and to privilege* – to see racism or sexism, or indeed any other exclusionary power – and to act in relation to it in ways that produce better social outcomes for everybody. This requires the understanding of and the capacity to know how to manage affirmation, criticism, rewards and sanctions.
3. *The capacity to build trust.* This is in some ways, in the space of the transition, the most critical issue which the leader has to deal with. He/she has to work out how the re-norming of the university is to work. He/she has to be clear and decisive about which practices and norms must be preserved and which must be discarded. He/she then must have the ability, once a reasonable degree of consensus around these questions has been achieved, to have a fairly good idea of how a re-norming process inside an organisation can be undertaken.

4. *The capacity to plan into the future.* Once an organisation has come to a reasonable consensus of what its normative order should be, it has to develop the capacity to move forward in the tension between risk and opportunity. It needs to be able to set goals for itself and to develop the structures to facilitate and support the achievement of its goals, such as attending to the psychological well-being of members of the organisation, resourcing them appropriately, and setting in place the accountability structures which will ensure that the system is able to operate on its own logic. In this, the leader needs to be a project manager, task-orientated, and a visionary.
5. *The ability to communicate.* The ability to communicate in transitional spaces is central. It is central to the degree in which transitional spaces are marked by discursive ambiguity. Confusion is easily sown and spread socially in order to produce mistrust. The purpose of good communication is to reveal and make transparent the source of a message and to create the conditions for how it is received and how it may be responded to. This is the kernel of the process for re-norming a context. Leadership needs to communicate timeously and judiciously. It needs to acknowledge fault and take blame, but it also needs to explain, make clear, and point the way forward. In a context such as South Africa, where complexities in social networks easily lead to breakdown of trust and the precipitation of lines of action that multiply risk needlessly, this is deeply important.
6. The last quality which the leader needs to be aware of is that he/she is playing *a central role in the process through which the new university becomes a South African university*. He/she needs to have a sense of what the university needs to hold on to and what it needs to do to make it distinctly South African.

A Future Perspective

The leadership discussion in South Africa is no different in its major elements to that which one would find anywhere else in the world. It depends here, as it does elsewhere, fundamentally on an analysis of where the country is and where it is likely to go. Diagnosis and a prognosis are important features of such an analysis.

Diagnosis

What might a diagnosis of South Africa look like? It would depend on who is doing it. The following are important segments of opinion-making in the country: The dominant political grouping inside the African National Congress (ANC); disaffected supporters of the ANC; the core of the established business community; liberal and largely white political opposition; populist political opposition; conservative white political opposition; black nationalist political opposition; radical trade union movement; radical political opposition; disaffected and alienated young people outside of organised political structures and formation; and disaffected and alienated people in general.

Outside of this list is the general public. The opinion-makers are drawn largely from the country's elite – the new and old elite. The general public do not have the same material means and access to the media that the elite would have. Their ability to change and shape opinion is constrained. But they are drawn behind the elites often, and in different forms.

Each of these groupings has a view of what is both right and wrong about the country. There is no consensus among them about the diagnosis at all. Optimism and pessimism circulate among them in varying degrees of intensity and duration. It can be suggested that there is agreement that the country is in something of a crisis. However, what this crisis is would elicit very different responses. For many it would be a crisis of the enduring effects of colonial whiteness. For others it would be a crisis of capitalism and neo-liberalism. For yet others it would be a crisis of the greed of the new elite. A version of this diagnosis would have it that what is going on is a problem of black nationalism. A frequent diagnosis would look to the global economy and talk of the recession and the collapse of the world's financial system. For others, it is a crisis of how the old and the new in South Africa, with all their inherited and conjoined problems, manifest themselves in the present.

Prognosis

As this diagnosis can shift and change, so too would the prognosis. Among certain sectors of the white community, whether they are in business or politics or the academe, there is acute uncertainty about their futures. How nationalists, populists and radicals see the future is unclear. Present in their assessments are the whole range of short-term and long-range views of what is going to happen to the country.

Different as these views are among the elite opinion-makers, one can venture an opinion to say that there is widespread unhappiness in South Africa at the moment. There is not the generalised optimism of the country that produced the reconciliation discourse that itself led to the rainbow metaphor. Where the country is at the moment is in a state of considerable confusion about the future.

This confusion is compounded by some objective realities, such as the crisis of the economy and the challenge that this crisis poses to many of the medium- and long-term plans that the country has relatively wide agreement about, such as the National Development Plan (NDP). While initiatives such as the NDP project create quite optimistic targets to which the country should be looking in the long-term, the financial crisis in particular is casting serious doubt over the major assumptions that are embedded in the NDP. All of this is making it really difficult for all the major stakeholder groups to predict confidently and clearly where the country will be in even five years.

Diagnosis and prognosis in higher education

How different is the higher education sector from the rest of the economy and the political situation in which the country finds itself? Very interestingly, higher education in South Africa was able until very recently to develop and move on a very different trajectory to what was unfolding in the country, particularly in the economy. It was able to grow and to sustain itself even as the rest of the economy was feeling the impact of the global recession. Growth rates in higher education in terms of their enrolments and budgets were consistently larger than those in the general economy. The sector was able to carry on building its personnel and to continue on infrastructural developments.

In 2016 the crisis in which the rest of the country found itself: shrinking growth rates; downsizing of the labour market; and reduced infrastructural development, came to make itself felt in the higher education sector. The sector came then to experience that which its counterparts in Europe had gone through almost ten years earlier. There, though, the financial crash impacted quickly on the universities. Almost immediately after the implications of the crash became apparent, universities, especially in the United Kingdom, were required to downsize. One saw the massive stripping out of the universities of what university managements deemed to be not core business. Catastrophically, this assessment of what constituted core interests excluded the so-called soft disciplines. The arts and humanities came under heavy attack. Now, in 2016, South

African higher education has come to the point where its European counterparts were in the late years of the first decade of the new millennium. Synchronisation of developments with the rest of the economy has arrived.

Leading in uncertain times

The major characteristic facing the higher education sector in South Africa is that of uncertainty. Uncertainty, it needs to be said, formed a major part of what their counterparts in the United Kingdom went through fewer than ten years ago. Uncertainty in South Africa takes a more complex route here, though. It has many more dimensions to it than such countries in Europe would be experiencing.

The first and most crucial issue facing the leadership of higher education right now is that of its ***income.*** There is immense uncertainty in the sector currently around its two major sources of income. The first is in relation to the income the sector receives from the state through its subsidy. The second is in relation to its ability to control the income it receives through student fees.

With regard to the first, it has long been a mainstay of financial planning in higher education that the state would meet the bulk of each university's costs. In the historically white segment of the sector, the expectation was that the state would meet about 62% of those costs. The size of the subsidy has, however, been reducing each year. Even though these reductions have been marginal, they have had major consequences for individual institutions in the higher education economy, which has had to deal with its own internal inflation.

The way in which the wealthier universities have coped with this – in order to retain an essential internal economic equilibrium – has been to increase student fees above the national rate of inflation. This leads directly to an assessment of the universities' reliance on student fees. Most of the country's more established and former white universities have been able, historically, to increase their fees each year. For these institutions, annual increases in the range of 10% per annum have not been unusual. Critically, the student uprising in 2015 put an end to the institutions' ability to meet its budgetary shortfalls through fee increases.

In 2015, through pressure from the students and then as a result of an agreement brokered by the state president and the student movement, universities were not allowed to raise their fees. Following this development, the greatest uncertainty facing the universities in 2016 is whether they will be able to make any adjustments whatsoever to their fee structures. The issue that this raises, in a climate of rising costs inside and outside the university, is whether the universities will be able to continue providing the services that they have been accustomed to offer. If Treasury pronouncements are to be taken seriously, there is little likelihood, as has been the case in the past, that the state is going to step in to make good the universities' shortfalls in their budgets.

The second uncertainty relates to the ***student protest*** itself. While the universities have been able to return to something of a normal programme – not entirely, as weekly occurrences around the country demonstrate – there is uncertainty about how the students will deal with the issues of fees, and, in relation to what the fees that they do pay make possible, the provision of services they expect of the university, such as improved curricula, improved housing, and improved extra-curricular support, such as the provision of healthcare, transport, and other services on the campuses. A feature of the student protests over the last few months has been the consistent presentation of new and different demands. University leadership has found itself embroiled in sequence after sequence of new issues which students have put in front of them which they have had difficulty in addressing.

A third uncertainty which university leaders are having to face relates to their *staff*, both academic and support. In the historically privileged universities, members of staff have put forward a range of disparate demands, ranging from supporting or not supporting the student protests to insisting on salary increases and in-sourcing of outsourced workers, and, in general, agitating for improved conditions of service. Dissatisfaction is opening up the institutions to vulnerabilities they did not have before, chief among which is the loss of their most accomplished staff. Institutions that would have been able to build layers of highly rated, globally recognised academics confront the danger of their best staff moving out of the universities.

What all these uncertainties demonstrate is that South African higher education is in exactly the same position in which its counterparts would have been ten years earlier in the economically developed world. However, its problems, as suggested above, are more acute. These problems relate to the fact that the transition through which the system is going from being an elite to becoming a mass-based system makes the South African case more complicated. In becoming mass-based, the leadership is having to confront the reality that it cannot govern as it did in the past.

It also cannot, in its core business of teaching and learning, carry on working in classrooms and in interactions with students as it did before. It is going to have to come up with new strategies and tactics. These considerations make South Africa a different case from that of its counterparts. Its counterparts underwent their transition to a mass-based system in much less stringent financial times. South Africa is having to reinvent itself in deeply difficult financial times. This is the challenge that it will have to confront.

The dilemma facing the university leadership then is how it can do the incredibly difficult work of increasing its student numbers and at the same time continue to provide services of the same or even higher standards than before. In assessing this challenge, it is clear that the next five to ten years in the sector are going to be increasingly difficult. Many institutions that would have built up reputations for global excellence will find themselves in danger of internal collapse. Weaker and poorer institutions will largely remain much as they are but without the presence of stronger institutions to provide them with benchmarks, even if these benchmarks are problematic.

Leadership in times such as these has to be endowed with creativity. This creativity begins with new and innovative strategies of bringing along the disaffected and disgruntled with them, to enable them to see the larger picture of financial and intellectual stability which a system requires as its *sine qua non*. Without this, there is no prospect of a system that upholds and promotes excellence. It will be inclusive, but it will be mediocre.

If the base requirement of stability has been achieved, creativity demands the capacity to determine what excellence means, what it stands for, and how it can be attained. This is asking a great deal of intellectual leaders who need to be outstanding stewards of their estates but also deeply sensitive nurturers. They have to marshal their rands and cents with a diligence which will lose for them important friends and supporters.

Having done that, they must then bring into play the insight which finds new learning opportunities and possibilities where there were none before. In working within a new mass-based system, they have to overhaul fundamentally the ways in which their institutions induct young people into the essentially arcane and deliberate world of thinking. This will require imagination such as has not been in great evidence before. What will they do with their talents, future generations will ask? But it is not just their responsibility to carve a path forward in a world of uncertainty. It is that of the whole nation. But they must have the nation alongside them. For this they will have to secure the trust and confidence of the South African people.

Conclusion

The challenge of leading in this new context is almost too great for a single individual. It has to be a shared task. That shared task, however, demands the very qualities of individualism that I have argued define the public university. This individualism has to distinguish itself from the individualistic. It is about the courage of sharing ideas, about the individual willing to put his/her thinking into the density and maelstrom of debate and to help the individuals in the space of the university who so easily succumb to self-centredness to begin the great task of imagining how free-thinking individuals commit themselves in solidarity to building a new society and a new world.

Endnotes

1   Clawson, 2006.
2   Clark, 1973.
3   Baldridge, Curtus, Ecker & Riley, 1982.
4   Avalio & Yammarino, 2002.
5   Wren, 1995.
6   Geering, 1980.
7   Ibid.
8   Trow, 2007.
9   Trow, 2007, p. 243.
10 Trow, 2007, p. 244; emphasis in the original.
11 Trow, 2007, p. 250.
12 Ibid.
13 Oromaner, 2012.
14 Trow, 2007, p. 245.
15 CHE, 2004.
16 CHE, 2008.
17 CHE, 2015.
18 CHE, 2008, 2015.
19 Scott, Yeld & Hendry, 2007.
20 HESA, 2011.
21 Ibid.
22 Trow, 2007, p. 248.
23 Trow, 2007, p. 253.
24 Maluleke, 2016.

References

Avalio, B &, Yammarino, F. 2002. *Transformational and charismatic leadership: The road ahead*. San Diego, CA: Emerald.
Baldridge, JV, Curtus, DV, Ecker, GP & Riley, GL. 1982. 'Alternative models of governance in higher education'. In GL Riley & V Baldridge (eds). *Governing academic organizations*. Berkeley, CA: McCutchan Publishing Corporation. 2–25.
CHE, 2004. *South African higher education in the first decade of democracy*. Pretoria, ZA: CHE.
CHE, 2008. *South African higher education statistics*. Pretoria, ZA: CHE.
CHE, 2015. *South African higher education statistics*. Pretoria, ZA: CHE.
Clark, B. 1973. 'Development of the sociology of higher education'. *Sociology of Education*, 46(1):2–14. W73.
Clawson, J. 2006. *Level three leadership: Getting below the surface*. New York, NY: Pearson.
Geering, A. 1980. 'An analysis of leadership theory and its application to higher education'. *ERIC*. [Online]. Available: http://eric.ed.gov/?id=ED196394. [Accessed 29 January 2016].
Higher Education South Africa (HESA). 2011. *A generation of growth. A proposal for a national programme to develop the next generation of academics for South African higher education*. Pretoria, ZA: HESA.
Maluleke, T. 2016. 'Current heat is forging a new university'. *Mail and Guardian*, 29 January to 4 February. 29.
Oromaner, M. 2012. 'A sociologist looks at higher education. A review'. *H-Education*, May. [Online]. Available: http://www.h-net.org/reviews/showrev.php?id=35332. [Accessed 12 January 2016].
Scott, I, Yeld, N & Hendry, J. 2007. 'A case for improving teaching and learning in South Africa'. *Higher Education Monitor*, 6. Pretoria, ZA: CHE.
Trow, M. 2007. 'Reflections on the transition from elite to mass to universal access: Forms and phases of higher education in modern societies since WWII'. In J Forest & P Altbach (eds). *International handbook of higher education*. Dordrecht, NL: Springer.
Wren, J. 1995. *The leader's companion: Insights on leadership through the ages*. New York, NY: Free Press.

Chapter 5

PUBLIC SECTOR LEADERSHIP
Vain Jarbandhan

Leadership and leadership development, or the lack thereof in public sector institutions, are central to everyday conversations. Modern society has questioned the role of public sector leaders in upholding the values of society and promoting the public interest, given the plethora of challenges faced by the young South African democracy. It is commonly argued that in order to provide for the basic needs of society, there is a requirement of public leadership to promote good governance.

The concept of governance is understood to be the "way in which the underlying values of a nation (usually articulated in some way in its Constitution) are institutionalised".[1] In order to uphold a country's values, as enshrined in its Constitution, there is a need for a leader who understands the reality of the society that he/she serves. It is important that countries identify good administrative leaders and nurture them through training and development initiatives in order to achieve "a better life for all" ultimately. Political leadership must strive to accelerate the transformation of society by ethical and principled leadership, based on the tenets of democracy and not solely by narrow political agendas.

Among the key challenges facing public sector leadership are the following:

- An appreciation of the impact of globalisation (including the financial crisis and austerity measures) on effective service delivery,
- The complexity of modern day problems, with no simple solutions,
- Growing gap between the "haves" and "have-nots" and finding ways to solve them,
- The growing emphasis on market-based solutions to address public policy issues (more so the role of economic solutions to social problems),
- Effective leadership for transformation,
- An ethical requirement and greater transparency among government leaders, and
- The service delivery challenge.

Given the nature of the challenges, it is important to foster a leader who is alert, principled, and adaptive to these realities. This chapter will commence with setting the scene in South Africa post-1994 by examining the political landscape under the leadership of Presidency of Nelson Mandela, Thabo Mbeki and Jacob Zuma. It will be followed by examining the service delivery challenges that bedevil South Africa, in relation to its administrative leadership challenge.

State-owned enterprises (SOEs) have been identified as key engines of economic growth globally. However, in South Africa, that has not been the case. The numerous attempts by government to bail out financially stricken state-owned enterprises puts a strain on the fiscus, and hampers economic growth, as was recently pointed out by President Zuma. It is incumbent on the state as shareholder and the management and board members of state-owned enterprises to show leadership in turning state-owned enterprises around in order to develop into the drivers of economic recovery.

This chapter also highlights the need for a competent cohort of administrative leadership, hence a competency approach to promoting leadership among the most senior of public servants. Finally, the understanding of leadership is ever-evolving: traditionally, leaders were understood to be those who found solutions to the wicked problems of the world. However, today, leaders are understood to set the vision and strategic direction for complex organisations, as it is these that are closest to the point of delivering services seen as being equally important, those at the coalface.

From Mandela to Zuma

The release of Nelson Mandela from prison in 1990 ushered in an era of hope for most South Africans. Prior to Mandela's release, the South African apartheid sociopolitical landscape, its economy and its image around the world lay in tatters. Internationally the apartheid legacy had placed South Africa among the pariah states of the world, and domestically the loss of numerous lives as a result of political unrest had rendered the country rudderless from a leadership perspective.

The De Klerk government had no option but to announce the release of Mandela from prison, after twenty-seven long years of incarceration, on 2 February 1990. The release of Mandela was greeted either with great joy, or with a sense of disappointment, depending on the side of the political diaspora to which one felt allegiance. The pessimists believed that a government led by the ANC would result in widespread bloodshed, and the optimists believed in the promised "better life for all".[2]

The widespread bloodshed never materialised, but just over two decades into democracy the "better life for all" is a far-cry from reality. So what, then, actually went wrong, and is the dream of a "better life for all" now deferred? This chapter will commence by briefly looking at the post-apartheid political leadership transition, under the post-democratic political leadership.

The Mandela era

The first democratic parliament consisted of members of the Tripartite Alliance being in the majority, that is, members from the ANC, the SACP, and COSATU. The macro-economic policy that was favoured during this period was the Reconstruction and Development Programme (RDP); after all, the ANC-led alliance had fought the election on this ticket. The idea behind the RDP was to lift the masses up from the levels of poverty by building houses, schools, and clinics, by creating employment, and by improving water and sanitation.

The leadership shown by Mandela as President portrayed the country in a very positive light. International investment improved dramatically over his Presidency, and the outlook for the country remained positive. However, all on the domestic political landscape did not seem rosy. The value of the RDP, which was aligned to the left, was questioned by Thabo Mbeki (who was Deputy President), and the role of trade unions was brought under the microscope. In essence, Mbeki questioned the leftist element within the alliance and the influence that they were having on the country's foreign policy.

In the words of Plaut and Holden,[3] "with foreign currency leaving the country and the rand on the slide, the authorities had to rein in the left". The tensions between members of the Tripartite Alliance became palpable, and somewhat dysfunctional, with the introduction of the Growth Employment and Redistribution (GEAR) macro-economic policy framework that was favoured by Mbeki.

The Mbeki era

Thabo Mbeki ascended to the Presidency of the ANC in 1997. He favoured the GEAR macro-economic policy which focused on the re-establishment of liberal market economies; primarily, his focus remained heavily on transitioning the economy. The move towards the GEAR policy raised many eyebrows among the leftist element within the Tripartite Alliance, who believed that this policy favoured the elitist classes and not the workers.

The SACP/COSATU alliance members believed that the GEAR policy under Mbeki's leadership had moved the ANC to the right of the political spectrum. The SACP/COSATU alliance members were unhappy under Mbeki's leadership and often accused him of marginalising them, and even using state agencies to silence his opponents. An example of this was when he accused Cyril Ramaphosa, Tokyo Sexwale and Matthews Phosa of being part of a Jacob Zuma plot against him. This incident heightened tensions between Mbeki and Zuma.[4]

In 2000 a case of corruption, using state institutions, was hatched against Zuma. It began with the 'arms deal' probe and the gathering of evidence against the person who was at the time Zuma's financial advisor, Schabir Shaik. Evidence was gathered against Zuma, fingering him as the beneficiary of kickbacks and bribes in securing the French armaments producer, Thales. After a lengthy trial, Schabir Shaik was found to have benefited from the arms deal. Zuma was found to be complicit in the deal, but not much could be done to him because his popularity among the tripartite membership was solid.

The rift between Mbeki and Zuma came to a head in June 2005, when Zuma was sacked from his position as Deputy President. Both men could now barely tolerate each other. In December 2007, at the ANC Conference in Polokwane, Zuma emerged as the most popular leader of the ANC by garnering 2 329 votes to Mbeki's 1 505 votes. In 2008 Mbeki was accused of political interference in Zuma's case and was asked to step down as President of the ANC. He was succeeded by President Kgalema Mothlanthe, who served a mere six months as President of the Republic, and was often referred to as a 'caretaker president'.[5]

However, Zuma could not be sidelined, and he remained president-in-waiting. On 9 May 2009, Zuma became the President of South Africa. It must also be noted that Mbeki's Presidency was clouded by his views on HIV/Aids, where he was labelled an Aids 'denialist'. It was argued that his lack of understanding on the pandemic influenced the government's policy decisions on the pandemic.

The Zuma era

During the initial stages of the Zuma era, the ANC Youth League under Julius Malema showed undying support for Zuma. Furthermore, the role of the policies such as black economic empowerment (BEE) became entrenched in society, where the black elite found themselves beneficiaries of lucrative business deals. The redistribution of land and the nationalisation of mines debates gathered momentum during Zuma's tenure as President. The support from the left of the Tripartite Alliance had found favour with him.

It became evident that the state of corruption and escalating levels of corruption became entrenched during Zuma's Presidency. The levels of corruption were especially questioned by COSATU, when the movement noted that: "Because of the frighteningly rapid emergence of a powerful predator elite, abusing access to the state to accumulate wealth, the question of tackling corruption has become a growing national priority".[6] To add to the challenge facing Zuma's ANC and its alliance partners, there was a thrust of powerful figures jockeying for positions closer to him.

One of those wanting to get closer to him was the leader of the ANC Youth League, Julius Malema. Malema was an ardent supporter of Zuma, and on occasion threatened to "kill for Zuma". Malema's outspoken nature on issues of nationalisation of mines and land placed the Zuma-led government at risk of losing allegiance with international investors. Malema went further with regard to the internal mechanisations of the ANC and its alliance partners by questioning the position of the Secretary-General of the ANC. This annoyed many senior figures within the alliance. Malema was now becoming a liability to Zuma, so much so that in 2010, Zuma informed the ANC's National General Council that juniors in the party ought to respect seniority – a long-held custom of the organisation.

This strained relationship led to the formation of the Economic Freedom Fighters (EFF) on 17 August 2013, under the leadership of Julius Malema. Implicit in the party's ideology were anti-capitalism, left-wing populism, Marxism-Leninism and Pan-Africanist principles, to name but a few. In the 2014 national elections, the EFF managed to secure 25 seats in the National Assembly and seven seats in the National Council of Provinces. The EFF, together with other opposition parties, has been vociferous on issues such as the Nkandla issue, where on many occasions Parliament was disrupted by members calling for Zuma to "pay back the money", as had been requested by the Public Protector, Advocate Thuli Madonsela.

Furthermore, the globally publicised Marikana massacre was a great blot on his Presidency. The rift in the alliance partners led to a once-close Zuma ally, Zwelinzima Vavi, being ousted as Secretary-General of COSATU, because of gross misconduct and ill-discipline. It became clear that those who opposed Zuma and his policies were quickly placed on the periphery of politics.

Political commentators are quick to point out that during the Zuma era, the levels of service delivery protests increased, crime escalated, unemployment became rampant, and the general economic prospects of the country looked bleak. Whether this could be ascribed to his leadership style, the global economic crisis, the alleged corrupt behaviour with regard to politically connected families, or a combination of any of these issues, remains unanswered. During the Zuma era, the support for opposition parties increased, especially in metropolitan areas, as attested to in the 2014 national elections, where the support for the ANC in large budget metros had decreased, with the Nelson Mandela Metro losing most ground.

With the looming local government elections scheduled for 2016, there is a sense of unease among the upper echelons with the Tripartite Alliance. A final challenge for the Zuma-led alliance is the National Development Plan (NDP), which was released in 2011. The NDP was not well received by the left, especially the trade union partners. Among the criticisms levelled against the NDP were the complexity of the document, the definitions of key concepts such as unemployment, and the youth wage subsidy.[7]

What is evident from the discussion above is that leadership is complex and individualised. It is complex in the sense that many actors and actions influence the leader–follower relationship; and individualised in the sense that an individual can use his or her innate capacities to direct action towards his or her own goal attainment. The Mandela era was dominated by a process of healing and reconciliation. Mandela was a charismatic figure, an icon and global brand. Mbeki was a leader who was distanced from his followers, sometimes he was criticised as being aloof (for example, on the AIDS issue), and sometimes he was hailed as being a leader who was driven by ultimate goal attainment, which possibly led to his downfall. Zuma, on the other hand, is regarded as a pragmatist who would protect his party at all costs. He is regarded at times as a leader whose competence, honesty and judgement are often questioned, but a very strong ideologist and party supporter.

The ushering in of democracy in South Africa brought in winds of change, a feeling of renewal in South Africa when Nelson Mandela in 1994 envisioned, "For we must first, together and without delay, begin to build a better life for all; this means creating jobs, building houses, providing education, bringing peace and security for all".[8] It is now 2015, and South Africa needs a reality check. South Africans need to ask the pertinent question: "How are we doing [when measured] against this vision?" The intention of this chapter is not to answer this question, but to get South Africans to think around the issue of future fitness for public sector leadership.

Contextual Complexities Related to Service Delivery

Among the challenges faced by the post-apartheid government is the challenge around service delivery. The onset of democracy in 1994, and the expectation of the "better life for all" created an unrealistic expectation among the citizenry, especially those who lived in abject poverty. Opposition political parties are quick to point out the ANC-led government's shortcomings when delivering services. The country has seen a spike in service delivery protests over the years. Municipal IQ, a web-based data and intelligence service, provided the following graphic representation in Figure 5.1 in 2014 to support the fact that service delivery protests are on the increase.

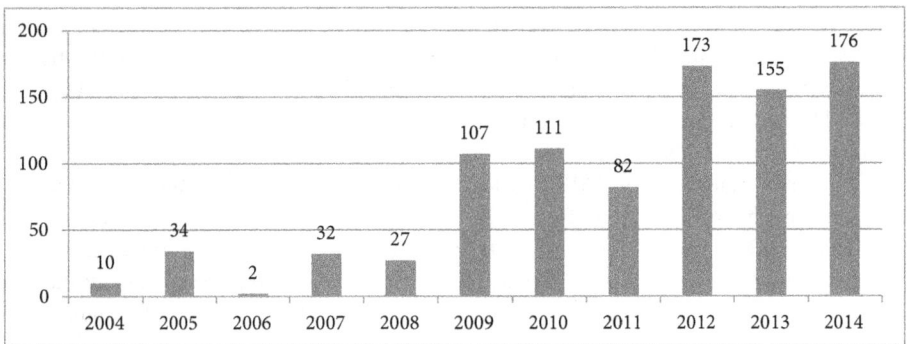

Figure 5.1: Major service delivery protests, by year: 2004 – October 2014
Source: Municipal IQ, 2014 [9]

The reason for this increase is not clearly understood. Based on the information presented in Figure 5.1, the Mandela era was met with the lowest levels of service delivery, followed by the Mbeki era, and currently the Zuma era. Did the Mandela magic keep communities satisfied, or is the government under President Zuma a poor role model? A simplistic answer to this conundrum would be dangerous.

It can be argued that the reason for the spike in service delivery protests could be attributed to the lack of leadership acumen at the local level of government, because that is where most of the protests take place. Rapid urbanisation has led to the country's metropolitan structures not being able to provide for the citizens' needs. Furthermore, the maintenance and development of infrastructure, for example, municipal waste treatment plants, has been neglected and inadequately monitored. Nationally, inadequate maintenance of the country's power-generating capacity led to 'load-shedding', which did not help the country's economy. President Zuma has recently mentioned that the economic downturn in the country is largely to be blamed on the Eskom debacle.

General distrust among communities around the leaders who serve them also escalates service delivery protests. Over the past years, the homes of councillors have been set alight when citizens could get no answers to their grievances. Communication around community projects has been very limited, with only a handful of closely connected citizens getting access to these projects. This has led to the further distrust and alienation of councillors at the local level of government.

To compound the above issues, the lack of skills across all spheres of government has led to poor service delivery and, ultimately, protests by communities with regard to the services that they receive. The lack of skills must be placed in its context. The Bantu education system did not adequately prepare South African school leavers for the place of work. The general degrees that senior managers in the public service possessed post-democracy did not equip them to hold management positions. Many degrees were awarded in theology and in the fine arts, with a small percentage of the degrees awarded being in management and/or finance. The skills that were lacking included, *inter alia*, financial, communication, knowledge management and change management skills.

Having realised the need for these skills, the Department of Public Service and Administration (DPSA) introduced a Senior Management service (SMS) competency framework in 2003 and the Leadership Development Strategic Management Framework (LDSMF)[10] in 2005 in order to upskill management and leadership capability. The competency framework for senior management leadership competency development will be discussed in later sections of this chapter.

From the discussion above it is clear that service delivery is a challenge for the public sector. However, the government has made steady progress in rolling out services to all South Africans, especially those that have been previously disadvantaged. On 11 September 2012 President Zuma addressed the South African Local Government Association, where he indicated that: "No country could have produced the delivery we have produced over the last 18 years".[11]

In a press statement, the SAIRR backed up Zuma's statement when they produced data to indicate that he was correct in his analysis. Frans Cronje, the CEO of the SA Institute of Race Relations (SAIRR), indicated: "A myth has taken hold in South Africa that service delivery was a failure. However, research that we have published over the past several years suggests that that is not the case".[12] He produced the following evidence (data gathered between 1996 and 2010) to back up his pronouncement:

- The number of South Africans living in formal households increased from 5.8 million to 11 million (an increase of 89%),
- The number of households with access to electricity increased from 5.2 million to 11.9 million (increased by 127, 9%),
- The number of households with access to piped water increased from 7.2 million to 12.7 million (an increase of 76,6%),
- Social welfare reached over 15 million South Africans, and
- The population of South Africans living on less than $2 a day declined form 12% to 5% in 2010.[13]

It is often said that leadership lies in the eye of the beholder: some see it as viewing artwork, and that what appeals to one may not appeal to another. The same applies to public leadership in South Africa, in the sense that some view their political leaders as being messiahs, while others view them as failures. The complexity of leadership leads to the view that there is no "one-size-fits-all" when it comes to leadership.

From Executive Leadership to Administrative Leadership: Implications for the Public Sector

One of the complexities of public sector leadership rests in the demarcation or separation of executive and political leadership; and administrative and managerial/supervisory leadership. The perennial debate in public administration, and the separation of politics from administration, was popularised by Woodrow Wilson's essay of 1887 entitled *The Study of Administration*. In this essay, Wilson expanded on the normative relationship between those who were elected (politicians) and those who were appointed (officials). He postulated that politics is inherently different from administration, where politicians should focus primarily on policy formulation and administrators should carry out the policy directives.

His notion was squarely focused on competent administrators who were politically neutral. This notion is regarded as being outdated in the current political-administrative interface because senior managers within government (senior management services) play a crucial role as policy advisors to politicians who may not have the technical know-how on policy issues. One needs to remember that the period of office of politicians generally spans a five- or ten-year term of office, while that of a public servant can span that of his or her career.

The challenge with administrative leadership is the interface that it has with executive leadership. Van Wart[14] is quick to point out that the dearth of research on administrative leadership within the public sector does not add to the challenge of understanding the phenomena around the concept of administrative leadership. One of the issues with which authors grapple is the role of administrative leadership in modern, democratic organisations. The central debate around the issue is the role played by administrative leaders in promoting the public good in public institutions: are they simple implementers of policy as managers, or do they add value to the supply chain of service delivery in an ever-changing environment? In addition, the role of administrative leaders in transforming the societies that they serve needs to be investigated. After all, they can be seen as change agents, as those individuals who buy into a vision of the organisation's strategic goal in order to change the societies which they serve.

Leadership and Governance Challenges in State-Owned Enterprises

State-owned enterprises (SOEs) have a crucial role to play in the transformation of South African society and the economy. SOEs in South Africa have been criticised for being bloated and inefficient, and lacking good leadership skills to promote good governance. A survey of SOEs in South Africa indicates that almost all of them are in a state of disarray. Among the worst-performing SOEs are PetroSA, South African Airways, the South African Broadcasting Corporation and Eskom.[15]

The South African government has had, on numerous occasions, to pump in billions of rands to keep these SOEs financially solvent. A great challenge for these SOEs is a lack of clear leadership and direction in the areas of good corporate governance, financial management, and leadership. The current electricity debacle is a case in point, where the state is investing billions of rands, but the outcome is not encouraging. In addition, international ratings agents have commented on the negative outlook of these SOEs, and this has a direct impact on the economic future of these SOEs and the country as a whole. The leadership of these enterprises has constantly come under the spotlight because many of its leaders have either falsified qualifications, or are incompetent, or are given leadership positions based on nepotism and corruption, in, for example, the SABC, Transnet and the Post Office.

Khoza and Adams[16] point out that good corporate governance, the role of government (as shareholder) and having a savvy board of directors are critical to the success of SOEs, and they focus specifically on ESKOM by adding that "… good corporate governance is ultimately about effective leadership. An organisation depends on its board to provide it with direction, and the directors need to understand what their leadership role entails".

What is of importance to the success of SOEs is a clear understanding of the leadership roles of the board and the shareholder. Very often these lines are blurred where the board have a vision that is not in synch with that of the shareholder or even the management of the SOE. This has been evident in the case of the SABC over the recent years, where board members would resign, or were forced to resign, owing to the challenge of understanding their respective roles.

It is also apparent that many of the board members of SOEs are not passionate about upholding the key principles of corporate governance as listed in the King Reports. The King III Report[17] Chapter 1, which is entitled *Ethical Leadership and corporate citizenship*, makes it clear that the board "… should ensure that the company is and is seen to be a responsible corporate citizen by:

- Considering not only financial performance but also the implications of the company's operations on society and the environment,
- Protect, enhance and invest in the well-being of the economy, society at large and the environment,
- Ensure that the company's performance with all stakeholders is based on sound principles that are embedded in Chapter 2 (Bill of Rights) of the Constitution,
- The promotion of ethical conduct and good corporate citizenship is encouraged, and,
- Ensure that management ensures corporate citizenship policies".[18]

The King III Report makes it incumbent on the leadership of boards to ensure that the economic, social and environmental aspects of societies need to be upheld. However, within the South African context, the King III principles are relegated to secondary importance because of the highly politicised nature of appointing board members. Furthermore, the leadership values of board members need to be beyond reproach. Over the recent past, the *bona fides* of SOE board members have been publicly questioned, with some of the public applicants even having a criminal record. Some, on the other hand, do not even have a grasp of the business of the SOE of which they intend to serve as board member.

Government's role in promoting the business of SOEs has come under sharp criticism. Government policies, the nationalisation debate, and the global financial meltdown have also jeopardised the outlook for SOEs. The nationalisation debate has muddied the waters somewhat with foreign investors feeling unsafe to invest in the country. Political interference in SOEs in South Africa, and the frequent changing of political public enterprise ministers, do not help the situation.

The model that South Africa has to investigate is the model that is used globally, where SOEs are created as a distinct legal entity which is entirely run by the government or companies in which the state may be a major shareholder. The role of government is to set public policies so that the SOEs can prosper and generate income for the state. Colin Coleman of Goldman Sachs pointed out in *Business Day* in 2014 that the Chinese have raised over $120bn over the last 30 years by listing SOEs, while retaining control over them.[19] South Africa can benefit from this model in that the floating of these entities would result in major flows of revenue which could be used to upgrade infrastructure that the country so badly needs and deserves.

It is evident that the political will to resolve the problems in SOEs is missing. As long as leaders of SOEs are appointed solely based on political affiliation, SOEs will remain a blot on the South African public landscape. A solution to the SOE challenge from a leadership perspective is to appoint management and board members based on principles of merit. The performance of management and board members should be closely monitored and reported on by an independent forensic unit, for example, an independent auditing and advisory company. Furthermore, any member of management or boards, if found guilty of misconduct, should face the rule of law, rather than being offered a "golden handshake".

Currently, the South African government has not managed the issue of SOEs well. The bailouts offered to SOEs could go a long way to stimulating economic growth. To the contrary, SOEs, if well-governed, can be drivers of economic growth and infrastructure development.

A Competency-Based Approach to Leadership: A Public Sector Approach

The post-1994 South African public sector realised that the challenges of globalisation and rapid change required leaders who could shape the direction and influence the outcomes of public sector organisations. However, the May 2000 Baskin Report[20] indicated that all was not well in the senior echelons of government. Among the challenges highlighted was poor performance of senior managers who acted as leaders, which resulted in poor service delivery. A key recommendation of the report was for a competency-based development model for senior managers who fulfilled leadership roles. Internationally, countries such as the United States, New Zealand, Australia, the Netherlands, France, South Korea and Tanzania have adopted a competency framework for senior managers, or what they refer to as senior executives.

In South Africa, competency models were used primarily in the private sector. Research published by Charlton[21] indicates that leaders need to possess the following generic competencies in order to be effective:

- Leaders need to capture people's attention through inspiring a future vision,
- Leaders need to be effective communicators, and
- Leaders need to manage 'the self'.

The post-1994 South African public sector faced many challenges. Among them was the challenge to transform the public sector as a whole to deliver on the developmental goals of the state and, among others, to create a "more competent public administration". The need to transform the public sector into one that was responsive to the needs of the citizens was paramount for government. The words of the former Minister of Public Service and Administration, Geraldine Fraser-Moleketi, summed-up the leadership challenge faced by the South African Public Service: "The talent search for contributing leaders who are able to distribute their primal leadership throughout the Public Service demands a steady supply of experienced knowledge workers with competencies".[22]

With the development of the Leadership Development Strategic Management Framework of 2005, the following competencies given in Table 5.1 were developed for the Senior Management Services (SMS). Core competencies were meant to be a representation of the content of what needs to be done (or demonstrated) by the SMS members in their roles and functions. The process competency was the manner in which the function is to be performed, in essence the process competencies 'the how?' as represented in Table 5.1.

Table 5.1: Senior Management Services competencies[23]

Core competencies	Process competencies
1. Strategic capability and leadership 2. People management and empowerment 3. Project and programme management 4. Financial management 5. Change management	1. Service delivery innovation 2. Knowledge and information management 3. Problem solving and analysis 4. Communication 5. Client orientation and customer focus

Core competency 1: Strategic capability and leadership, as listed in Table 5.1, will be elaborated on. This competency makes it incumbent upon senior managers in the public service to "drive the vision, strategy and lead" subordinates to execute government's mandate, which is to deliver quality services, as their core function. This core competency is supported by five core 'dimensions' to support the attainment of the competency.

These dimensions are as follows:

- Showing innovation in service delivery,
- Leadership with clear communication guidelines,
- Lead with accurate problem solving skills,
- Lead in political and cultural contexts in keeping with the *Batho Pele* principles, and
- Lead through knowledge and learning.[24]

The strategic capability and leadership competency is crucial to service delivery. Any 21st-century public organisation has to set strategic goals and show leadership on how the goals are to be attained. Innovation is key to achieving service delivery goals, an innovative leader will find clear solutions to the challenges of service delivery. Effective leadership communication also supports effective service delivery, where a senior manager needs to communicate in a clear and concise manner the vision of the organisation, and the expected outcomes from subordinates.

Problem-solving skills are a basic requirement of any senior leader. The challenges posed by globalisation, both domestically and internationally, require a senior leader to think of creative solutions in order to solve the problems of society which the leader serves. The politicisation of the public sector and the cultural context of leadership cannot be overlooked. The diversity and complexity of the South African society must be understood if one is to be an effective public sector leader.

The *Batho Pele* principles support citizens as 'customers' of government and require services to be delivered based on eight service delivery principles, namely: consultation, service standards, access, courtesy, information, openness and transparency, redress, and value for money. In order to implement the *Batho Pele* principles, the leader needs to act as a servant, one who wishes to serve his customer, rather than a bureaucrat.

A shocking finding by the Public Service Commission (PSC) in August 2000 was that the *Batho Pele* principles were not being practised as they ought to be. The PSC surveyed 130 government departments (national and provincial) and found that compliance across the departments was lacking. Furthermore, the lack of practical skills to deliver services within the *Batho Pele* framework was inadequate among the departments surveyed. It therefore becomes a leadership requirement for public sector managers to understand clearly the eight principles when interacting with communities and delivering public services.

The key issue that needs to be raised with a competency model for the public sector is the relevance of the set competencies given the current situation, both domestically and globally. It is of crucial importance that senior managers within the public sector identify the environment of the future, predict future public sector challenges and develop a competency framework for future-fit public sector leadership. In addition, the role of training institutions, for example, the National School of Government (NSG), has to align its training and development initiatives for future leaders with curricula that are relevant for the environment in which leaders operate, with a vision of future fitness.

A Future Perspective

The public sector leadership dilemma

Public sector leadership has come under sharp criticism over the recent past. Leadership crises at a political level, for example the 'Nkandla' scandal, and at the administrative level, for example, the hiring of incompetent cadres; and the challenge at the level of state-owned enterprises do not bode well for the country's future. To add to this, the falling rand, the lack of adequate infrastructure development, and political uncertainty place a greater emphasis on developing leaders who are ethical, professional and competent.

The clarion call for a professional public sector leader has to be clearly articulated, and the relevant government training institutions (National School of Government (NSG), the South African Local Government Agency (SALGA), and higher education institutions (HEIs)) have to make a concerted effort to attract the best candidates based on merit. The idea of a merit-based public sector has been at the forefront of many debates across the South African landscape. However, the debate has its own challenge in that the country has to deal with the imbalances of the apartheid legacy.

Affirmative Action (AA) and Broad-Based Black Economic Empowerment (BEE)

The challenge of balancing the inequalities of the past; the role of South Africa in the global economy; and the need for socio-economic transformation at home is an onerous challenge. With the onset of democracy, it had become constitutionally imperative for those who were previously disadvantaged to be included in the mainstream economy. However, involving the previously disadvantaged into the mainstream economy had become a further constraint because many of the disadvantaged did not have the skills to participate in the economy.

Currently, a poor basic education system does not bode well for the cohort of students who seek access either into higher education or into the job market. An assessment of the country's maths and science results do not make palatable reading, despite the massive budget investment in basic education. The recent student protest at universities has underscored the challenge faced by university students despite 21 years of democracy. To further complicate the country's transition, political analysts and commentators have argued that the country's BEE endeavours have favoured the political elite at the expense of the majority of the previously disadvantaged. Moreover, the implementation of AA has been questioned. Despite the good intentions of AA, the process to a large extent has been questioned. The deployment of politically connected cadres who lack the relevant competencies has rendered the ideals of AA vulnerable.

The South African Institute of Race Relations[25] argued that "entrepreneurial activity in South Africa was 13% below the global average for comparable countries, such as Argentina, Brazil and Malaysia". In addition, it was noted that the socio-economic environment was "skewed against them" as a result of the poor skills level of black entrepreneurs; the lack of access to capital; uncertain energy costs; a very rigid labour regulatory framework; and slow economic growth.

This has an impact for the country's future, given the targets set by the National Development Plan (NDP). The NDP has its own set of challenges with organised labour, COSATU, rejecting the plan. Furthermore, the targets set by the NDP are under threat if the leadership dilemma is not resolved. Interestingly, the NDP itself does not focus directly on leadership. In order to roll out the NDP, it is important for the public sector and its stakeholders to set a national leadership agenda to bring the plan to fruition. Besides AA, BEE has also posed a challenge for the country's development as the majority of BEE beneficiaries have been a small group of politically-connected individuals.

A merit-based public sector leadership

A merit-based public sector would go a long way towards addressing the challenges that face South Africa. Candidates chosen on merit (rather than on political affiliation), seniority, and competence would be a significant step forward in improving service delivery. This is the model that is used in Korea, with promotions based on the outcomes of formal written examinations. In addition, the performance of public servants is closely monitored, with those performing well above the levels of competence receiving special bonuses and allowances. French public servants are appointed after successfully completing an entry examination. Promotions are based on merit, and poor performance is cautioned, with the pay structure being based on egalitarian principles.[26]

The lessons that the South African public sector can learn from the Korean and French models are to appoint staff, especially the senior management service, based on merit. Furthermore, promotions must be linked to a performance management system. A career-orientated public service, with public servants showing an ethos to transform society, must be promoted. All of these proposals must be counter-balanced against the transformation agenda of the country.[27]

Turning public sector leadership into stewards of social needs

Despite the leadership challenges faced in the South African public sector, progress has been made post-democracy. To be globally competitive, a cadre of public sector leaders has to be developed, leaders who understand the challenges of delivering services in an ever-changing environment. The politicisation of the public sector is unavoidable. However, changing the mindsets of public officials and getting them to separate narrow party-political allegiances at the expense of service delivery has to be paramount in the debate to transform the public service.

Public sector leaders have to be aware of societal needs; they have to be geared to be stewards. The curricula of training institutions that deal with public sector training (NSG, SALGA and HEIs) must include stewardship as part of the curricula so that service can be placed above self-interest. Training in stewardship will enforce ethical values in public servants, and will see them earning the trust of communities that they serve. In addition, the development of the skills of public servants cannot be over-emphasised, given the changing environment in which they operate.

Available public sector leadership

Finally, the success of the public sector depends on the type of leadership available to deliver on government's mandate. A leader who understands the challenges facing the country's future, a leader who understands where we come from, and a leader who views the world through different lenses is required; after all, as Albert Einstein once said "We can't solve problems by using the same kind of thinking we used when we created them".

Conclusion

The discourse around public sector leadership has gained momentum, given the service delivery challenges, the rapid pace of globalisation, and the current sociopolitical tensions that South Africa faces. Furthermore, the politicised nature of the 'predatory state', the contestation for senior management positions within the public sector, and the lack of a well-skilled and competent senior management service magnifies the challenge faced by the young South African democracy. This chapter highlighted the key public sector leadership challenges by focusing on the contextual complexities, which included, *inter alia*, the service delivery challenges, the role of state-owned enterprises, and the key skills that are required to propel South Africa onto the global stage as a key player.

The ANC-led government had introduced a swathe of measures to build capacity among the most senior managers in government by adopting training and development programmes to fast-track skills development. The National School of Government was seen as a champion in spearheading capacity building, with higher education institutions playing a pivotal role in addressing this challenge. However, the challenge of skills development within the public sector stills looms large.

Unfortunately, a quick-fix response to a complex issue of public sector leadership will result in a perpetuation of the current climate. A move to embrace a career-orientated, professional ethos in public sector leadership would help to develop future-fit managers and leaders to make it possible for the state to deliver on its mandate of a "better life for all".

Endnotes

1. OECD, 2001.
2. SAHO, 1994.
3. Plaut & Holden, 2012.
4. Ibid.
5. Mail & Guardian – Zapiro, 2008.
6. COSATU, 2010.
7. COSATU, 2013.
8. ANC, 1994.
9. Municipal IQ, 2014.
10. DPSA, 2005.
11. Ibid.
12. Ibid.
13. Ibid.
14. Van Wart, 2003.
15. *Business Day (BDlive)*, 2014.
16. Khoza and Adams, 2005.
17. IOD, 2009 (King III Report)
18. Ibid.
19. *Business Day (BDlive)*, 2014.
20. Department of Public Service and Administration (DPSA), 2005.
21. Charlton, 1993.
22. See endnote 7.
23. Ibid.
24. Ibid.
25. SAIRR, 2013.
26. Van Wart, 2003.
27. Khoza & Adams, 2005.

References

African National Congress (ANC) – Speech by Nelson Mandela announcing ANC Election victory. 2 May 1994. [Online] Available: http://www.anc.org.za/show.php?id=3658 [Accessed 9 June 2016].

Business Day (BDlive). 2014. 'SA's state-owned enterprises situation of serious concern'. 4 December 2014. [Online] Available: http://www.bdlive.co.za/business/2014/12/04/sas-state-owned-enterprises-situation-of-serious-concern [Accessed] 9 June 2016).

Business Day Live. 2014. 'SA's state-owned enterprise "situation of serious concern"'. *Business Day Live*. [Online]. Available: http:// www.dblive/ business/goldmansachs. [Accessed 22 July 2015].

Charlton, G. 1993. *Leadership. The human race: A guide to developing leadership potential in Southern Africa*. 2nd ed. Kenwyn: Juta & Co.

COSATU. 2010. Central executive committee discussion paper: *The alliance at a crossroads*. [Online]. Available: http://www.cosatu.org.za/discussion paper. [Accessed 27 July 2015].

COSATU. 2013. *Summary of the critique of the national development plan.* [Online]. Available: http://www.cosatu.org.za/docs/misc. [Accessed 1 August 2015.]

Daily Maverick – Khadija Patel. 9 October 2012. 'Look how far we've come: The OTT discourse of government achievements. [Online] Available: http://www.dailymaverick.co.za/article/2012-10-09-look-how-far-weve-come-the-ott-discourse-of-government-achievements/#.V1lvrPl96Uk [Accessed 9 June 2016].

Department of Public Service and Administration (DPSA). 2005. *Senior management service. The Leadership development management strategic framework for the senior management service [LDSMF].* Resource Pack. Part 2. Pretoria: Government Printer.

Institute of Directors in Southern Africa (IOD). 2009. *The King III report on ethical leadership and corporate citizenship.* Johannesburg: Institute of Directors in Southern Africa.

Institute of Directors in Southern Africa (IODSA). 2009. *King Code III.* [Online]. Available: http://www.iodsa.co.za/?kingIII. [Accessed 5 August 2015.]

Khoza, RJ & Adam, M. 2005. *The power of governance – enhancing the performance of state-owned enterprises.* Gauteng: Pan Macmillan & Business in Africa.

Mail & Guardian – Zapiro. 2008. 'Kgalema Motlanthe shown as caretaker president'. 25 September 2008. [Online] Available: https://www.zapiro.com/cartoons/080925mg [Accessed 9 June 2016].

Municipal IQ. 2014. *Press Release: 2014 protests surpass 2012 peak.* 7 November 2014. [Online]. Available: http://www.municipaliq/index. [Accessed 5 August 2015].

OECD. 2001. *Public sector leadership for the 21st century: Executive summary.* [Online]. Available: http://www.oecd.org/docs. [Accessed 1 August 2015].

Plaut, M & Holden, P. 2012. *Who rules South Africa? Pulling the strings in the battle for power.* Johannesburg: Jonathan Ball Publishers.

South African History Online (SAHO). 2 May 1994. 'Speech by Nelson Mandela announcing the ANC election Vitory. [Online] Available: http://www.sahistory.org.za/article/speech-nelson-mandela-announcing-anc-election-victory [Accessed 9 June 2016].

South African Institute of Race Relations (SAIRR). 2013. 'Fast facts'. *Hobbling entrepreneurship and stifling the NDP,* 5.

Van Wart, M. 2003. 'Public-sector leadership theory: An assessment'. *Public Administration Review,* 63(2):214–228.

Chapter 6

COMMUNITY LEADERSHIP
Richard Bricks Mokolo and Mokesh K Morar

South Africa featured prominently in the international media from the late 1980s, especially after the apartheid government of PW Botha declared the second State of Emergency.[1] This intensified the call for sanctions against the South African government by the oppressed people, a call led by liberation movements and others, including the World Council of Churches and the Anti-apartheid Movement,[2] in order to end apartheid and bring about a more democratic society.

The hopes and dreams of people inside and outside South Africa were heightened with the relatively peaceful transition to a democratic government led by Nelson Mandela in 1994. However, in the back of people's minds was the fear that South Africa might become another 'banana republic'.

More than twenty years later, South Africa is still known as the country with one of the biggest Gini-coefficients, which is growing and threatening the future of the country. This legacy of apartheid is characterised by the huge wealth that remains in the hands of a small sector of the white population.[3] Attempts to "share the wealth of the country" through the Black Economic Empowerment programme has resulted in the creation of the *nouveau riche* – "instant millionaires and billionaires" of the new South Africa,[4] and resentment among the poor and the middle class. The BEE programme was therefore expanded to 'broad-based BEE' in order to grow the black middle class. However, many black people, despite the BBBEE shares, ended up indebted to banks and defaulting on their bonds and loans, slipping back into poverty.

On the other side of this widening gap is the painful increase of poverty among the bottom levels of society: visible in the mushrooming of informal settlements around cities and big towns; the alarming unemployment rates; and daily protests against poor services by government and corruption in society.

The neglect of the black townships is hardly noticed by the media, except for major disasters such as the perennial shack fires and floods in Cape Town and Johannesburg. It is clear that the government is unable to cope with the ever-increasing demands for housing; quality education and health facilities; proper roads; electricity or water/sanitation services; or decent jobs for the poor and the working class.

The South African government seems to lack clear and strong leadership and good policies, which in turn seems to have created a 'vacuum' of leadership in the marginalised communities. In reality, there is a layer of leadership that struggled against apartheid and still sees the need to continue under the new democratic government. For them, the material conditions have not improved as expected and promised.

A lot is also happening in terms of leadership 'on the ground', even in the 'forgotten' rural areas, including the former homelands. Black people have realised that the 'freedom and democracy' promised in 1994 will not come to them on a silver platter (as it came to the black elite). They will have to fight for it, over and over again, under dedicated and selfless leadership, in their attempts to deal with inequality and poverty.

This poverty is characterised by high unemployment rates, especially among the black youth (many of whom are poorly educated); the spread of Multiple Drug-Resistant Tuberculosis, which appears to be getting out of hand; the spread of prosperous religions/cults (promising instant salvation and riches, while depriving poor people of their hard-earned money in the name of God); increased tensions among social groups because of the competition for resources;

dispelling the myth of the rainbow nation as an illusion; and neglect of the environment, mostly around mining and industrial areas. Poor communities and their leaders are facing these and other legacies of apartheid and colonialism daily, and they sit with almost no material resources to bring about real change in their lives in the rural areas and townships where they live.

Therefore, the chapter will explore the following themes: the black township context of community leaders, including the origins of townships, and its historical and present challenges. This excursion will include the specific legacies of colonialism and apartheid, and the present-day impact of neo-liberalism. This chapter further endeavours to highlight the unique leadership challenges of the community leader. The competencies which will make for effective community leadership are therefore discussed, and manifest in the story of a community leader of Orange Farm township, Richard Bricks Mokolo.

The Origins of Townships

Tuning in to the radio, especially the English and Afrikaans stations, it appears that many rich and middle class citizens find it hard to understand why township blacks are protesting after 1994. These protests do not seem to fit into the 'new South Africa' when you have a 'black' democratic government. Protests occur almost daily in the black townships[5] and are reported in the traffic reports as an inconvenience. The forebears of these blacks were initially 'imported' as cheap labour and forced to live in compounds/hostels near the mines by mining magnates such as Cecil John Rhodes, who instituted the poll tax for the indigenous people.[6]

Many others moved to farms near towns such as Johannesburg as a result of the dispossession of their land and in order to get the cash to pay the poll tax; it was these farms that developed into 'locations'[7] and later black townships. Alexandra, Kliptown and Soweto are examples, and officially these were deemed by the British and later by the apartheid regime as temporary settlements. At the end of each year blacks had to return to their homelands: all in all there were about ten of these homelands for the indigenous people. According to the homeland policy and based on ethnicity they were set aside for and allocated to: Zulus, Xhosas, Pedis, Tswanas, Ndebeles, Shangaans, Vendas and Swazis.

The expansion of mining and industries led to an increase in the number of townships around South Africa including Orange Farm, Khayelitsha and Umlazi, with no proper housing or decent social services such as health and education facilities. All of the above led to overcrowding and tensions between different communities, including the struggle to bring an end to apartheid. Then came 1994! The hopes and dreams (built on the promises of politicians) of the people were high, but the question was whether such adverse conditions would disappear, and how long would it take?

A 'New' South Africa

The ANC used the Reconstruction and Development Programme[8] to campaign in the first non-racial elections of 1993, promising to right the wrongs of the past and to build a non-racial and non-sexist South Africa, based on the will of the people,[9] under the slogan: 'A better life for all'.

To a limited extent this was achieved, with the emphasis on reconciliation between the racial groups implying that the poor had to be patient. The poor saw the promise of a 'better life' remaining with the rich whites, and this has trickled down to only the black elite. They were told that the government had to maintain the 'good economy' and to let it grow even faster so that the benefits would 'trickle down' to them eventually. When the ANC adopted the Growth, Employment and Redistribution (GEAR) Policy in 1996, some in South Africa, including the labour federation COSATU (an alliance partner of the ANC), saw it as a disguised form of Structural Adjustment Program, usually imposed on countries by the IMF and World Bank. Bond[10] warns: "Virtually all structural adjustment programmes in Africa generated instability".[11] Even the Southern African Catholic Bishops went to the government to raise their concerns about GEAR,[12] which Bishop Hurley called "unbridled capitalism being unleashed on an unsuspecting population".[13] The Bishops were told to "leave economics to the experts", in the same way as they were told by PW Botha to "stay out of politics".[14]

When people were required in 1996 to pay for water, electricity and other basic services as part of GEAR, some community leaders reminded the ANC about their promises of the Freedom Charter that the people would share in the wealth of the country. Why did they have to pay for water, education and other basic services, they asked, when they had been promised in 1993 that these would be free?

They remembered that it was the same ANC that had asked the people to boycott the payment of rent, services and white businesses in order to get rid of apartheid. Now poor people could not make sense of how the ANC had suddenly changed their tune. "How can we pay for services that we cannot afford? Rather scrap GEAR!" they told the ANC government.

When the government refused to scrap their GEAR policy,[15] communities, led by their leaders, took to the streets to protest lack of service delivery. Many attempts were made to recruit and co-opt such leaders into the ANC structures; some acquiesced, while others decided to remain outside the political system in order to fight for 'real and meaningful changes' for the poor and marginalised. One such leader was Richard Bricks Mokolo from Orange Farm, a township south of Johannesburg.

Unique Leadership Challenges in this Context

We will now explore the unique leadership challenges of a community leader against the aforementioned backdrop.

Key challenges in the past

During the colonial period and apartheid, the biggest threats to community leaders in their opposition to colonialism and apartheid were those of harassment, detention and torture by the state.

Religion and the Bible, especially Christianity, were used as part of dispossessing the indigenous people of their land and way of life. They were told that the land had been given as a promise by God to white European Christians. When blacks fought for their land they were met with brutal force, imprisonment, and exile of their leaders. A few exceptional missionaries and whites tried to oppose the 'wrongs' of colonialism and apartheid, but they were not effective owing to their small number and limited strategies. There was hardly any significant opposition to apartheid from the international community, except from a few countries such as Nigeria, the Netherlands, Sweden and India, which would raise objections to apartheid in the United Nations from 1948 onward.

Many black leaders, including Mandela in South Africa, felt ignored and deserted by the International community to such an extent that they sought to take up arms to fight the apartheid government. They received support mostly from China, Cuba, and the former Soviet Union. The armed struggle was often seen as evil by whites and unnecessary, as the government was always willing to talk and negotiate for change.

On the other hand, the West, led by Britain and the USA, supported the South African government with their constructive engagement policy to 'change' the apartheid policy. And so there was not much hope of international pressure for real change for blacks.

Inside South Africa, ordinary black people were fearful of the threats made by the state, so very few would attend public meetings in order to oppose the policies of the government. The 'divide and rule' policy of the British and the apartheid regime worked well, and resulted in a great deal of mistrust in families, and even hatred between language and cultural groupings in South Africa.

Challenges in the past for the community leader in the struggle against apartheid therefore included, *inter alia*: threats of torture, detention by the apartheid state apparatus; opposition by the Dutch Reformed Church, as well as many other main-line churches; minimal international support; limited support for the armed struggle; opposition by major superpowers such as the USA and Britain, with their 'constructive engagement' with the South African regime; little support from the majority of the people in the township, partly because of their fear of the apartheid government; and divisions between cultural and linguistic communities, as well as competition for resources by the different communities.

Present challenges

Some of the past threats and repression are still there for community leaders, although not to the same scale and degree, of course, and only a few will be mentioned here. These leaders are now opposing the neo-liberal policies of the new government today.

When the ANC government campaigned in 1993 they used the Reconstruction and Development Programme and it received widespread acceptance as it 'spoke' to the dreams and wishes of the majority; but when they introduced GEAR, there was opposition to it from many corners of our society, including the religious sector. Many community leaders, who could foresee that these policies would have a negative impact on the poor and the working class, found it difficult to explain their objections and consequences, as they did not have the necessary analytical tools to inform and educate the people.

People listened to leaders like Mandela, who focused on peace and reconciliation, instead of fighting for their rights, as promised in the new South African Constitution. The new government used the media and other state resources very successfully to convince the poor and the working class that 'things will get better – just be patient'. This was a huge challenge to community leaders who read the situation differently, but did not want to criticise Mandela.

Many of the black middle class took out loans and bonds to buy cars and build big, beautiful houses; or they moved to the suburbs (previously reserved for Indians and whites); these were the ones not interested in talking about the 'new' struggle. Many faced foreclosure on their bonds and loans when the economic crisis came, and they realised that the picture was not as rosy as they had hoped for. Most of them were still reluctant to join the new struggle, but many community leaders still try to draw them into the struggle.

Another challenge that community leaders faced was the lure by political parties to join the government in order 'to bring about change for the people'. Promises of positions in high offices, as well as financial advancement via government tenders or contracts, appeared to be very tempting, and some community leaders did and still do fall for such traps. Then there were the challenges from the masses, who appeared not to have learnt enough from the struggle against apartheid, especially to be vigilant and critical at all times. Now, since 1994, it is difficult to call for community meetings, except when there are electricity and water cut-offs.

The very same people will go in their droves to vote for the same government, hoping that things will change. After the elections, all they saw was political leaders driving bigger cars and moving to bigger houses.

Many of the community leaders are unemployed or semi-employed; a few will have pensions to support their families, and rarely can you find a small business person working also as a community leader.

Other leaders would depend on donor funding to operate in community projects – funding that is never guaranteed or sustainable. Jumping through the hoops of funding proposals and requirements is not easy, and many times they take you away from the 'real' work of community organisation and mobilisation. Many community leaders do not have the necessary skills and education to complete and comply with the proposals and requirements. At times the funding suddenly dries up or is diverted to a different sector or sphere of society.

Many times community leaders and their families would end up going to bed hungry and angry as the struggle appeared to be in vain, with little hope of real, meaningful change to their homes and the lives of the poor and the marginalised. Some would try to get a 'real job' or start a small business, and leave the 'struggle' to others.

Present challenges for the community leader therefore include threats and repression by the state; the difficulty of explaining the new policies and implications of them to the communities; the strength of the state and big business propaganda, especially when people are asked to be patient in anticipation of the promise of being rich one day; the lure by political parties and other forms of corruption; as well as being hamstrung in building solidarity among the working class and poor. Then, of course, there are the personal challenges of being unemployed; having poor academic education; and working for NGOs – with precarious funding for community work.

To work as a community leader in the new South Africa is therefore not easy; it is much the same as it was during apartheid, and calls for diligence, foresight, perseverance and sacrifice as never before. Some leaders have managed to persevere despite the challenges and hardships.

Competencies of a Community Leader

Given the challenges facing community leaders outlined above, we argue that for community leaders to lead effectively in such contexts, he/she needs to manifest the following competencies.

Self-regulation

On a very personal level, the community leaders have to build upon the little support that was there during the struggle against apartheid within their own family and immediate community. Many community leaders find it difficult to sustain this support and rather go on this journey alone, becoming 'the voice in the wilderness' for social justice.

Teaching

The leader has to help the community members to understand that despite the promises usually made during election campaigns, the government has limitations, set by the World Bank and the IMF, not to overspend on social services, but rather to allow the market forces (for example, private companies) to take over. When these private companies take over basic services, be it water delivery, electricity, education or health, their first priority is to make profits at all costs. Those who read the newspapers critically and have a political and economic grasp on social matters can see that the system is still skewed towards the rich and the powerful, despite the claim of being a government of the people, which includes black women.

Critical analysis

While affirming the fact that there has been change in the political sphere, comparisons with the former homeland system are helpful to make people realise, for example, that to have black leaders does not automatically bring about a perfect and caring society. Black leaders are prone to corruption and abuse of power as much as white leaders, and it is only through vigilance by civil society that the gains of democracy can be translated into meaningful economic and social changes for all people of the country.

Organising

The community leader has to help the community to analyse the socio-economic and political conditions of their lives and suffering in order to raise their awareness and to advocate for changes. The next challenge is to mobilise other sectors of society for protest, action, and meaningful change within the working class. Organisational skills become crucial, and the moment there is a crisis, for example, water is cut off by the local council, a meeting is called to analyse the problem and see what can be done to restore water supply. In communities where there is weak leadership, water can be cut off for weeks, if not months or years. Competent leaders can bring such a crisis to the attention of the media quickly and effectively.

Courage

It is up to critical community leaders to point out the inconsistencies and empty promises that help to improve the lives of the elite at the expense of the working class and the poor. Some community leaders find it helpful to debate with and challenge elected political leaders in public meetings, pointing out their empty promises and self-enrichment. This calls for courage and political tolerance, as there is so much anger and impatience among the ordinary community members, who just want to beat up political leaders, especially during community meetings.

Goal-setting

At such meetings contradictions raised between promises and delivery can be used to point out the strategic orientation of political parties, orientation copied from the previous regime and prescribed by the IMF, and which has failed.[16] Community leaders then have to point out that true alternatives are possible, but they come with a lot of sacrifice and community building, including raising of awareness, advocacy, and mobilisation of the whole community. The ultimate aim is to set common goals, and review them together with the community, with the aim of building a genuinely inclusive and caring vision of society, and realising it.

To persuade the community to think in this direction is not easy, and many community leaders can become despondent and impatient. Here, it is demonstrated that those who trust and have faith in the beliefs of the community and can respect them can persevere in their dreams of building caring and committed communities.

Stories of these kinds of community leaders are not well known, as the mainstream media have often shirked their responsibility towards them and have labelled them 'rabble rousers' or troublemakers.

The following section introduces a community leader who exemplifies the competencies discussed above.

The Case of a Community Leader

Bricks Mokolo of Orange Farm has worked selflessly for change for many years, and now relates his story in his own words. He starts off by acknowledging others, admiring them, as they remained strong and did not change by joining the governing party or the private sector in order to enrich themselves, but remained with their people.

My Models: A Case Study by Bricks Mokolo

One of my models is **Oupa Lehulere**, a man of his word and who qualifies to be anywhere in government, but he prefers, through his work in Khanya College, to work with the marginalised, helping people to understand the politics of the working class and the poor. Khanya empowers communities around the country to analyse, understand and work for change, and I am one of the community leaders.

Another leader is **Sam Radebe** – he works in the rural areas around Harrismith in the Free State, with very meagre resources. He loves to mobilise as many people as possible, and he wants people to stand on their own. I was inspired about his leadership style – he believes in consulting and planning together with the people and not imposing his own ideas on the people during any campaign. He has gone through a great deal, and many of his comrades have been jailed, tortured, and even killed by the state in the process, yet he persists.

Yet another is **Trevor Ngwane**, who started as an ANC councillor, but since he opposed the privatisation policies of GEAR, he was expelled by the ANC. He formed the Soweto Electricity Crisis Committee to oppose GEAR and the installation of pre-paid electricity meters. He differs from us, as he thinks one can change the system from within, but he himself did not stand; he encouraged his comrades to stand during the local elections. There was an opportunity for 'floor crossing', and some of his comrades joined the DA party. The other members remained, but they only attended the meetings and voted with the opposition parties. I believe that this strategy of Trevor is not effective, as the ANC is too strong and may remain strong through various strategies and means, even in the future.

My story

I will focus my story on the Orange Farm community. However, my situation is true for many other townships. As a community leader, I have seen myself as a servant, and this was long before the talk of *servant leadership*. Whenever there was a major community crisis, I would be approached to be part of resolving the matter, which I see as a service to the community. I do not get paid or rewarded for it at all, and that is how I grew up, like many other leaders in our communities all over the continent, not thinking about money.

My roots as a community leader

I reflect on how, when I was a youngster in Evaton township, other children appointed me to lead, be it on the school playground, or in the streets during soccer matches, as their captain. That is where I got the nickname of 'Bricks' as defender in the team: "You are like a brick wall and nobody can get past you!" This kind of recognition was part of my formation in Evaton, a black township in the Vaal Triangle, an industrial area with places such as Vereeniging, Vanderbijlpark and Sasolburg near the Vaal River. The Vaal River brings water from the Lesotho Highlands Water Scheme to Johannesburg.

Township life, in the late 1950s and early 1960s, was characterised by hardship and oppression, tempting many a youngster to a world of crime, gangs and drugs; but it could also impart very rich leadership skills. The hardship was particularly cruel to black women – my mother was one of them – who had to raise many children (we were nine), while being excluded from formal employment. Work was reserved for their husbands to keep the industries of steel and oil production going under the names of Iscor and Sasol. According to the laws of the land, women had to wait for their husbands to visit them once a year in the black homelands, or 'Bantustans.' Officially blacks did not belong to South Africa!

The painful experiences of my mother and those of most of the working class and the poor have continued after apartheid, although under different forms. Then people used to say: "There is nothing we can do to change the situation; look at Sharpeville (March 1960). They will only kill us if we talk of changing apartheid. Better keep quiet," was the refrain back then.

Fortunately for me, my mother was one of those who did not agree with such sentiments. I was inspired by her example of fearlessness and dealing with the hardships of apartheid, as well as her concern for the suffering of others; but most of all, how she wanted things to be different, and the way she spoke out against the wrongs of the government. "Free yourselves," she would remind us time and time again.

There were other people who also were part of my formation as leader. Following the example of many Catholic priests and nuns, I became an activist in the church, though I didn't see myself as a 'leader', while others did. The priests in our church had a lot of faith in me.

One such priest appointed me as the youngest funeral leader in our parish:

- I had to lead political mass funerals that some of the church leaders were afraid to conduct during the States of Emergency of the 1980s. For me, it was service to comrades who gave their lives for our liberation, and I saw it as my work to defend the dignity of fellow Africans, even at their funerals. That made me a servant of the people and an instrument of peace and justice, more than a leader. At that time we would not use the word 'servant' because of the negative connotation in the kitchen and workplace. Since public meetings were banned, I could speak out against the oppressive regimes during such funerals. That pushed me to a different position, on that I would not normally have had.
- More and more community members came to me with their problems, be they regarding pass laws, retrenchments, detention without charge/trial, or even family problems, with the hope that I would attend or help to solve them. At times they were general problems: children who were too lazy to go to school, or couples with marital problems. However, social justice and political issues were the pressing ones. People who were 'not into politics' were also detained when they happened to pass by a protest march, and we had to bail them out. Several became more politically minded as they saw that one could not remain neutral under apartheid.
- I assisted people, with the aid of other leaders, to stand up and fight all injustices, at great cost to myself: detention and torture by the security police. At one time I was left in a mortuary for several hours. It was only my faith that saved me from bitterness and hatred towards whites and which has allowed me to continue the struggle today in a different spirit of openness to all people. The example of Jesus of Nazareth helped me to see what kind of struggle we need to wage in order to bring about real change in the world. "An eye for an eye is going to make us all blind," is what I learnt from Jesus, Gandhi and others.

- In the church and Khanya College we were taught: "Read the signs of the times", and also "Think globally, act locally", which I'm still trying to put into practice after the demise of apartheid and the continued suffering of my people today.

Today, the struggle continues

After the euphoria of 1994 and seeing how things developed in South Africa, I started the Orange Farm Water Crisis committee and was elected as the chairperson in 2002. Under the policy of GEAR, the new government privatised basic services such as health, education and water – the kind of policy others and I myself knew would not help the poor people, as many are unemployed or live on meagre state pensions.

With others we agreed that to opposed the neo-liberal policy of the government we needed to focus on one issue and therefore we started by opposing the installation of pre-paid water meters in Orange Farm.

At the beginning we called for consultations with the government officials, who refused to meet with us and to scrap this new policy called GEAR. We realised that the only way to get their attention was to organise protest marches. When the government still did not listen, we then decided to block the Golden Highway, a major route that connects Johannesburg to the rest of the country across the Vaal River.

Many people were surprised and even unhappy that we could embarrass our newly elected democratic government in such a way after 1994. Several of the governing party leaders came to me and offered me positions of leadership and telling me how I could help the community 'to advance'. I refused as I saw that the suffering of the people would not stop. I knew deep down that the problem was with the policies of the government, as prescribed by the World Bank and the IMF, and not so much the government officials.

I learnt about these policies and western influences when I attended workshops organised by the Justice and Peace department of the Catholic Church and by other civil society organisations, such as Khanya College. Through the church network I was invited to places such as Canada to speak out against the privatisation of basic services, and recently I was invited to Budapest. I was even invited to the South African parliament to speak out against their own policies and yet, they did not listen or change!

It is for this reason that I decided to remain with the people I had grown up with instead of moving to the former white suburbs. I stayed on in the dusty and dirty township, with the people helping me to see what we really needed to liberate ourselves from: "Free yourselves!" as my mother used to say. However, I realised that I also needed new skills and training, even as a community leader, in order to be an effective leader and to bring about meaningful change.

I trained as a paralegal and assisted on setting up an advice office in the parish where I attended church in Orange Farm

Organising for change and liberation

When we arrived in Orange Farm in 1992 from Evaton, there was no infrastructure – for example, no running water, no toilets, and poor roads. We had to build our own toilets, which were pit toilets.

When I visited the clinic, I saw long queues, and that worried me. I conducted research and asked: "Why are there such long queues, and mostly women?" I discovered that women were more affected by these pit toilets than men. Then I approached the Cancer Association of South Africa, asking them how they saw the problem. CANSA replied: "People need to use clean toilets."

"Who must build these toilets?" I asked, and was told: "The local municipality."

I also discovered that when women went to the clinics they were harassed by the nurses, blaming their husbands for not being faithful. It might have been true that some were not faithful, but we knew there was more to the story – that the basic problem was lack of proper sanitation. We started demanding a proper toilet infrastructure – this was one of the first major struggles after 1994.

A lot of our struggles were very localised, but then there were international events, such as the World Conference on Racism in Durban in 2001. Some of us attended as we could see racism persisting in South Africa after 1994, especially in the socio-economic sphere. When we got back, I started organising workshops against racism and xenophobia, raising awareness around these social issues and educating people as to what could be done in order to bring about change.

Many townships are still rife with tribalism and other forms of discrimination against persons from other African countries or with disabilities. We made people aware that apartheid was not only between blacks and whites, but also among us. Even today they use hurtful names and labels according to ethnic backgrounds. These brought back memories of apartheid, and I saw that we must learn from our mistakes. One of the lessons I have learnt is to work more closely with others, even if there are disagreements, and to look beyond the superficial differences, be they race, ethnic background, gender, or political orientations.

You find strength when people agree with you and see value in your work as a community leader. People's poverty, retrenchment, or being laid off after a strike do not deter them from coming to meetings, even when their stomachs are empty, or they have to walk from far away, or pay taxi fares they can hardly afford.

People come to voice their support for the community struggle against privatisation and corruption. It is then that you feel humble and say: "If these people can sacrifice so much, what stops me from carrying on the struggle?"

Spiritual strength does not make things easier in the community struggles, because you also need resources – material resources. You need to make phone calls and write letters to the magistrate to organise a protest march or public meeting, which you know will be denied. But you do it anyway as it is required and you want to obey the law. They will deny you permission to march at the last moment and at times not even give you the reasons for the denial. At times they do not even acknowledge that they have received your request. As a leader you have to go back to the community and explain to them things that you have no control over, and the community gets cross with you.

At times you need a hall to conduct the community mass meetings, and sometimes the churches will help. However, many church leaders are still afraid to be associated with us, owing to the stigma of being labelled 'troublemakers'. They are afraid it will tarnish the name of their church, or that the collections will go down, or that the well-to-do parishioners will join the prosperous churches. In these churches people are told: "We do not mix politics with religion," yet you see their leaders mixing with government and political leaders when they make deals, or during elections.

At times those with resources, such ase funding or donor organisations, will support you and ask you to set up community projects, after which you have to apply for funding. It is not easy, as you may not even have a writing pad, let alone a computer, and so you borrow and beg. You have to attend many workshops in order to write a funding proposal, and then have to supply three years' audited statements. If you are lucky and can manage to get access to resources and fulfil all the requirements, then you have to wait and wait.

Suddenly, without warning you are told you you have been granted the funding, but not all of it, and you need to report within the next three months. Then you have a dilemma: Do we take the money and run around conducting many workshops, including awareness campaigns? Or do you refuse the funds as there are so many strings attached to the money, and evictions and retrenchments are more pressing? There are, however, some donor agencies that are genuinely in true solidarity, and they try to support you all the way.

In these community projects, with the limited funds and time constraints, you are also burdened with the issue of group dynamics. You are no longer just a community leader who has to listen to others and support those who are vulnerable; you are now a 'manager', and you are required to supervise your comrades, who now feel like employees, and you are their 'boss'. At times the people you work with feel threatened, as you have to make decisions with which they do not agree – but this was in the funding proposal, and they were not consulted because of time constraints.

At other times your colleagues do not like your leadership style as a manager. Teammates hold different views, and you do not have the comfort of long meetings. During the anti-apartheid struggle you could hold long meetings during the night, but after 1994, people did not like to attend long meetings; they wanted to go and watch soap operas on the TV.

In the meantime, the donors want a report, and they don't want to know about matters such as electricity cut-offs or colleagues who are stubborn or lazy. You yourself are not familiar with how to deal with such conflicts, but you hang in there, knowing it is for the good of the community. Again it would be so easy just to walk away or to take up on the offer to work in the local government structure or win a 'tender' to build RDP houses or pavements. At least you would have some income and could put bread on the table for your family.

Your own family also comes with lots of challenges when you are a community leader and it feels more painful, because you live with them every day. Even though during the anti-apartheid struggle we used to agree a lot about our involvement in the community struggle, and it was clear who and what the enemy was, as well as the goal, namely, the end of apartheid. Things changed after 1994; in our family, we now have different opinions and views regarding the goal and what kind of society we want.

Some family members are still afraid to criticise the new government and are aware of the threats, so they would prefer us to co-operate with the government and would rather not oppose the government and its policies. At times they feel that I'm too vocal in criticising the new government. As a family, we have not spoken enough about the times when I was detained and tortured, and I believe they do not want such things to happen again – it was also very painful for them.

On the other hand, when you have your own family, with a house and some assets, you have to start prioritising your family, protecting your family against criminals, as burglaries and robberies are rife in the townships. There are the expenses to maintain a family; this is not easy as you do not have a 'normal' salary like other citizens who work for the government or companies, or run their own business. In the back of their minds, your family must be wondering: "When are we going to have a normal life?" At times you can share your concerns and try to help them understand that the 'struggle continues'; that a normal life should be for all people, including the so-called 'poor'; and that it should not be just the elite who should benefit from the new South Africa. But most of the time you cannot share these ideas and insights, as you are so busy running up and down with community matters and so relationships with your family become difficult.

> As you are so busy with community matters, you do not have enough time to support them, and they may not support you, especially when things are tough, such as when a colleague is detained or retrenched. You wish you could spend more time with your family and children, but the community comes with so many demands and request for help, and your family have to sit back and wait. Deep down you wish things to be different. When you arrive late at night from your community work, they may be sleeping, or you are too exhausted to listen their stories. Then you feel bad for wishing that things could be 'normal'.
>
> You also know that other people have different understandings, and this is also a challenge. These differences arise not only in the family, but also in the Church and the community; and deciding how to live with them is not easy.
>
> There are not many places where you can go as a community leader to find support for your convictions and ideals. At times I am invited to speak or be part of conferences, seminars and public hearings – yes, even by the government.
>
> I attended a leadership conference at North West University in Potchefstroom when the Public Protector invited me to be part of a discussion as to how we could translate the South African Constitution into the lives of ordinary citizens. She spoke about her experiences and the opposition she faces by the ruling party, and how they see the Nkandla scandal differently. She explained that people will oppose your position and they do not want to promote the Constitution into the lives of people. They see the Constitution in isolation, as some people see the Bible, and they will oppose you. But you should not feel threatened. If you are afraid, you become a weak leader, and you cannot promote social justice. She said that other people will support your position, but the first thing is to believe in yourself.
>
> The Public Protector's words remind me about those of my mother: "Free yourselves! First of all, you have to make sense of the importance of fighting for social justice, driven by your conviction that apartheid was wrong, and socio-economic injustices, even in the new democratic system, are wrong and need to be addressed."
>
> I was inspired by her example and her courage in standing up for social justice and for promoting the Constitution. It helped me to see the solidarity that we are building, whether coming from Orange Farm or from the national level, where the Public Protector works.
>
> To be a community leader is not easy; nor is working for social justice in today's world. However, we are called on to bring about change, not only in the Bible, but also by our conscience, when we see so many people suffering in the new South Africa.
>
> I feel honoured that I can walk in the footsteps of my mother and alongside somebody like Thuli Madonsela.

A Future Perspective

To date, people have trusted current leadership too much, and leaders have messed things up: not only in the area of corruption or the financial crisis or climate change, but, more importantly, with regard to social relations, be they on the political, financial, economic, or even the religious and spiritual front.

All these and other factors will influence the relationships between leaders and the people with whom they are working, the results of which may be seen only in the future.

Leaders will have to show more than oratory or persuasion skills, and will not compete and run for positions. Instead, the communities and society at large will take charge of the process. They will examine the track records of potential leaders, who will be nominated by their groups, be those environmental interest or conservation groups (especially water, yes, even oxygen and air), or even the elderly, or migrants. This process will first be introduced on the international and perhaps regional (or continental) levels, and slowly filter through to nations and communities. Those leaders who are willing to sacrifice and even work on a voluntary basis, albeit for limited periods, will be asked to lead communities and larger groups.

At the community level, people will know each other much better via social media platforms, cutting across language and cultural barriers.

In the future, leaders will be made to account to the people more and more. There will be more challenges for community leaders, as people will ask more critical questions about the way in which they operate. As more and more people start reading and understanding their situation and can compare it to progress or regress, and come to understand more fully the need for social justice in their lives, they will start taking charge of change – with leaders who can work with them, rather than just 'lead' them. And there will be retaliation against leaders if they cannot account for their deeds or if they try to manipulate situations to their own advantage.

A leader will be leading with the mandate of the people, not being elected and then carrying on by him- or herself, as in the past. The mechanism of recalling elected leaders will be used more often, until leaders start showing their worth and their true commitment.

Many leaders will start living a more simple and spiritual life (not necessarily religious). In fact, religious leaders will find it harder to build communities, partly as a reaction to the abuses of the previous decades, where religion has been commercialised unacceptably.

People now understand their constitutional rights and duties, and they have access to large communities and assistance via social media and other forms of communication.

Conclusion

Working as a community leader in the past, today, and the future has never been and will never be an easy task. Whether one experiences torture by the apartheid regime, the apathy of the community today, or working with couch activists, community leaders need to learn from the mistakes and successes of those who have gone before them. With technology, organisation and mobilisation may become easier, including access to information and communication with the broader community and those in government, and I hope it will help young leaders to be more effective.

It appears that our focus in the apartheid struggle was rather 'easy', as it was a 'clear cut enemy'. Today and in the future, social issues will be more intertwined with global matters such as climate change and financial economic structural systems. Community leaders will have to learn to balance the different kinds of focus while trying to show 'impact' on a local level. This is not an easy task. Because of the better education of some young community leaders, I hope that they will be able 'to read the signs of the times' better than we did, and will build on our mistakes.

Our hope is based on the faith of people towards overcoming suffering and building solidarity across class and group distinctions on a local and global level. I hope and pray that the cry of my mother will be joined to those of Jesus, MK Gandhi, Dorothy Day, Martin Luther King Junior, and Steve Biko, and with those of the young leaders of today and in the future.

Endnotes

1. Lodge & Nasson, 1991.
2. Ibid.
3. World Bank, 2015.
4. Busitech, 2015.
5. News24, 2105.
6. Callinicos, 2014.
7. Union of South Africa, 1923.
8. African National Congress, 1994.
9. Mandela, 1994.
10. Bond, 2005.
11. Ibid.
12. Southern African Catholic Bishops Conference, 1999.
13. Makhanya, 2009.
14. See endnote 10.
15. Ibid.
16. Turok, 2008.

References

African National Congress, 1994. *The reconstruction and development programme.* Johannesburg: Umanyano Publications.

Bond, P (ed). 2005. *Fanon's warning: A civil society reader on the new partnership for Africa's development.* Trenton, NJ: Africa World Press.

Busitech. 2015. 12 March. [Online]. Available: http://businesstech.co.za/news/general/82287/how-many-bee-millionaires-are-in-south-africa. [Accessed 16 April 2016].

Callinicos, L. 2014. *Gold and workers.* Johannesburg: Khanya Publishers.

Lodge, T & Nasson, B. 1991. *All, here, and now: Black politics in South Africa in the 1980s.* Cape Town, RSA: David Philip & Ford Foundation.

Makhanya, M. 2009. *Sanibonani.* [Online]. Available: http://consolatasa.blogspot.co.za/ [Accessed 27 April 2016].

Mandela, N. 1994. 'Speech by Nelson Mandela announcing ANC Election victory. 2 May 1994. [Online]. Available: http://www.anc.org.za/show.php?id=3658 [Accessed 16 April 2016].

News24. 2105. 29 October. *Is South Africa the protest capital of the world?* [Online]. Available: http://www.news24.com/MyNews24/IS-SA-the-protest-capital-of-the-world-20151029. [Accessed 16 April 2016].

Southern African Catholic Bishops Conference. 1999. *Economic justice in South Africa: A pastoral statement.* Pretoria: SACBC.

Turok, B (ed). 2008. 'Wealth doesn't trickle down. The case for a developmental state in South Africa'. *South African Journal of Social and Economic Policy*, Cape Town, RSA: New Agenda. 159.

Union of South Africa. 1923. *Natives (Urban Areas) Act 21 of 1923.* Bloemfontein: AC White & Co.

World Bank. 2015. *Overview: South Africa.* Last Updated: Apr 12, 2016. [Online]. Available: www.worldbank.org/en/country/southafrica/overview [Accessed 16 April 2016].

Chapter 7

SPORTS LEADERSHIP[i]
Wim Hollander

The sports industry contains three segments, namely sports participation, sports production, and sports promotion. The *sports participation* segment refers to all the consumers of sport, that is, athletes, coaches, administrators, technical officials, and spectators. The *sports production* segment refers to those sectors that deliver to the consumers in the participation segment. Examples are the education and training (= the training of coaches, administrators and technical officials), facility and event management, merchandising (= sports equipment, clothing, and memorabilia), fitness (= sports sciences), and health (= sports medicine) sectors. Lastly, the *sports promotion* segment contains the marketing of sport (= television, papers, and social media), and marketing through sports (= sponsorships) sectors.

In this chapter the focus will be on leadership in the sports participation segment, seeing that this is where products/services are developed and consumed. Sports participation is delivered through social/recreational participation (for example, leisure activities such as walking, fishing, and cycling) on the one extreme, and elite participation on the opposite extreme of a continuum. In between the two extremes, competitive sport is positioned: organised league and/or event sports competitions.

The purpose of my chapter is to discuss contextual trends that provide challenges to sports leadership in the sports participation segment of the industry, for example the increased differentiation of sports participation. Sports leadership challenges are next explained with regard to these trends, followed by a discussion of the resultant sports leadership requirements. The chapter is concluded with a future perspective on leadership requirements within this sector.

Contextual Trends and Dynamics in Sport

Over the last fifteen to twenty years sport has transformed into a context of competition, on and off the field. Where the ultimate goal of sports participation on the competitive and elite levels is to win, competition to develop sustainable business performance; access to sponsorships; media exposure; and a fan base have grown rapidly. Sport is an industry where organisations jointly develop competitive opportunities, yet they compete for the same sponsors, media exposure, athletes, coaches, and to some extent for the same fan base. To do this, leaders in sport need to be able to understand the trends in the sports industry. I would like to highlight at least five major trends: differentiation, professionalisation, commercialisation, globalisation and transformation.

Differentiation

Perhaps the biggest change in sport over recent years has been the shift of focus away from amateur sports into the realm of professionalism. Where the responsibilities of sports clubs was amongst others to develop talent that can represent provincial and national teams, clubs are currently seen as providers of mass participation and competitive sport. Their role to develop sports talent has gradually fallen away. It has been taken over by professional setups of sports academies with development programmes, agents, scholarships, and contracts for athletes from an early age.

---
i   Invaluable assistance by Wilhelm Crous in putting this chapter together is gratefully acknowledged

Over the last ten years a new initiative and movement in sport has been established, namely, 'sports for development'. This is a phenomenon where sport is utilised as a vehicle to deliver on human and community development outcomes through mainly advocacy, education, and health programmes. This trend evolved through a process where non-governmental organisations (NGOs) positioned themselves, accessing funds from national (GIZ – the Deutsche Gesellschaft für Internationale Zusammenarbeit) and international (UNICEF – the United Nations Children's Fund) development aid agencies and other organisations, in order to deliver programmes on their behalf through sport.[1] This new development came about as a result of the educational gap caused in communities on aspects such as HIV/AIDS and other health issues. Another aim of sports for development is to deliver on both the Millennium Development and the Sustainable Development Goals.

Today, NGOs in South Africa are also moving into schools, where the delivery of physical education and coaching of extramural sports lacks as a result of limited or no training of teachers in these fields.[2] This is to supplement the reluctance of teachers to engage in after-school sport as they are already overburdened with teaching and administrative responsibilities. Extramural sport delivery does not form part of their employment contracts.

Sport participant numbers have further migrated from team sports to individual sports. Different reasons could be provided for this. Perhaps one reason is that the 'big sports' in South Africa such as athletics, soccer, netball, rugby and cricket did not ever consider the need to market their sport 'because South Africans love sport'. And this is not just a South African, but a global one. Today, parents are encouraging their children to become involved in individual sports, which leaves team sports with a challenge. Where will they find the next generation of elite participants?

A further development regarding sports participation is the evolution of individual sports into extreme sports, also called action sports and adventurous sports. This is where certain activities are perceived as having a high level of inherent danger which involves speed, a high level of physical exertion, and highly specialised gear. Examples of such activities are caving, mountain biking, skateboarding, cave diving, white-water rafting, snow skiing, base jumping, bungee jumping, and wing suiting.

The development of the computer and the Internet further resulted in eSports, also known as electronic sports, which include competitive (video) gaming or pro-gaming. This is a form of sports where the primary aspects of the sport are facilitated by electronic systems. The input of players and teams, as well as the output of the eSports system, are mediated. Games fall into a few major genres, of which the titles of the vast majority fall into fighting games, first-person shooters, real-time strategy, sports games, and multiplayer online battle arena (MOBA) games.

Increased differentiation has left the leader in sport with challenges around the focus of the sports business. Where international, national, regional and local sports structures are mainly the custodians of a particular sport, the question arises as to how the organisational structures can deliver on these differentiated opportunities, if they will ever be able to. A business decision has to be taken on the focus of delivery of sports products and services. In most instances, professionalisation of sport has provided some degree of resolution, but to the detriment of social/recreational and competitive sport.

Professionalisation

Professionalisation is discussed in literature from an employee/participant and a managerial perspective. For decades sports purists were of the opinion that the essence of sport is to compete against each other on a voluntary basis after daily work has been completed. It was seen as an activity by amateurs, who should not be paid to participate in sport.

In 1890, rugby football was in a crisis in England when players were remunerated to play, seeing that they had to take time off from work to compete in sport. This was the year when the game of rugby was divided into an amateur and a professional stream. However, interest in professional rugby dwindled over time. In 1995, after the Rugby World Cup, professionalism in rugby surfaced again and was accepted as the norm. This included professional coaches, administrators, technical officials, and players.

From a systemic and management perspective, the first white football club in South Africa was established in 1879, with the first African and Indian clubs in 1880. Football became professional in South Africa in 1959, utilising the Professional Soccer League (PSL) as a basis for competition. Similarly, in 1971, the International Olympic Committee accepted professional athletes for the first time to compete at the Olympics. It was only in 1978 that the United States of America sent their first professional players to the Olympics, a basketball team named the 'Dream Team'.

Professionalisation has changed the face of competition and athlete preparation. Training programmes for today's professional athlete mean far more than getting fit. Both athlete and team preparation now includes elements of sports science (= conditioning, prevention of injuries), physiotherapy and biokinetics (= rehabilitation), nutrition, vision and psychology (= motivation, being in-the-zone). Conduct and ethics (including the use of performance-enhancing substances) has also become a major issue, with sports stars constantly in the public eye. This is a real issue for leaders to manage. In Canada the use of 'performance coaches' was implemented in order to integrate information of all scientific components; to monitor the individual's progression; and to inform the coach on expected performance of athletes. Not only physical signs of athletes are monitored, but also emotional, nutritional and visual aspects.

In South Africa a process has been established whereby coaches in all sports will be able to register with a professional body for coaches. Training programmes are aligned with the requirements of the South African Qualifications Framework (established in terms of the South African Qualifications Act 58 of 1995 (SAQA)) and registered on the National Qualifications Framework (NQF). This is in line with countries such as Australia, England and Canada.

Commercialisation

Professionalisation of sport inevitably had an impact on the commercialisation of sport. Professional sports clubs are bought and sold. In the case of Chelsea in the UK, the new owner spent nearly two hundred million pounds after a takeover to align its brand with business initiatives. Sport changed in form and dimension during the commercialisation process. It has not only become a form of entertainment but has also gained commercial recognition.

Different streams of income have been developed, such as television and broadcasting rights, sponsorships, supporters' merchandise, supporters' communication through social media, special seating, and season tickets. Sport is viewed throughout the world on television, listened to on live streaming, and heard on radio. Players of the likes of Sachin Tendulkar, David Beckham, and Ronaldo have become billionaires through endorsement of products, and have signed contracts with clubs.

Along with this development, commercialisation is helping to sustain other business sectors such as television networks and sponsoring companies. Big sporting events such as the Olympics, World Cup competitions, Indian Premier League cricket, and English Premier League soccer competitions are broadcast. In some cases these rights are sold for billions of pounds.

Commercialisation has also had a negative impact on different levels. One such impact has been on the attitudes of athletes. They now play to a great extent purely for the salary that they earn. The thrill experienced through love of the game is missing. Match fixing, the use of performance-enhancing substances, and bad behaviour on and off the field have become the order of the day. Similarly, supporters are guilty of hooliganism, the burning of stands at sports stadiums, and chanting 'warlike' slogans.

Some unfolding trends in respect of the commercialisation of sport to be discussed next are: sportainment; gamification and the role of social media; smart stadiums; whether global events are becoming too costly; volunteerism; and athletes as investors.

Sportainment

Event days also become an experience that is sought after which brings sportainment into play. Sportainment is a new word in sports marketing vocabulary. It means the total experience at the stadium, where the supporters will have an experience that will bring them back – time and again – irrespective of the performance of their team. Results of games are inconsistent and no team can always win. However, supporters require a consistent experience to draw them back to the games. Examples are Real Madrid, who fill their home stadium even in difficult times, and the International 7s Rugby event offered in Hong Kong.

The Varsity Cup League SA is an idea that came from the United States, with their massive American football varsity games. It was a former CEO of First National Bank who came up with the idea of starting this league with South African university rugby teams, utilising a former Springbok captain to implement and further develop the programme. Based on the success of the Varsity Cup, other sports followed such as athletics, beach volleyball, soccer, hockey, netball and 7s rugby; their success speaks for itself. Within hours of opening ticket sales for the Varsity Cup, students at the University of Stellenbosch had bought them out. Why? Pure sportainment. Students not only enjoy seeing their favourite teams play but also enjoy the 'vibe' that goes with it. The future of ticket sales, sponsorship acquisition, and increase of fan base will be guided by the success of the sportainment offerings.

Gamification and the role of social media

Gamification is all about fan engagement through social media for fan loyalty purposes. It sees supporters participate in activities through social media and other platforms, mobilising them to go to the games and be part of the system. This not only provides an opportunity to increase the fan base, but also to sell merchandise, programmes and memorabilia. Combined with social media, gamification also offers different platforms, with the newest trend being to utilise social media through content strategies and reach different segments of the market effectively. These are possibly the older generation, with emails or Facebook, and the younger generation through Twitter or Snapchat. It is all about packaging the media to suit the market.

Smart stadiums

To go one step forward into the future, the newest trend is 'smart stadiums', where fans have a virtual reality experience. Seats with their own small screens allow playback of parts of the game, while drinks can be ordered via a computer or an iPad waiter. This development is still in its infancy, but is fast becoming a trend.

Making stadiums pay is not always easy, as we know from the white elephants from the South African 2010 Soccer World Cup. But some countries got it right. The Otago Highlanders' very successful Forsyth Barr home stadium in New Zealand was specifically designed as a versatile community venue to host different events, with changeable seating allowing for a large entertainment area where they host successful music festivals as a further stream of income.

And when it comes to sponsorship, it is no longer just talking banners lining the sides of fields. Today it is all about activation. Sponsors require activation of sponsorships by providing opportunities to increase sales. Where Steers is a sponsor at the SA Varsity Cup, all food being sold at the event will be bought from Famous Brands. During the SA 2010 Soccer World Cup, Budweiser as sponsor had the sole right to sell their beers inside the stadiums, including in suites.

Costs of global events

A trend that is becoming apparent is apprehension around hosting global sporting events. Although Durban has been awarded the 2022 Commonwealth Games, the government is seemingly not prepared to support the event. It is reluctant to allocate funding for this purpose, which leaves Durban as the host city in an impossible financial position. Canada withdrew its bid for the same reason. Although countries and cities often see little advantage in hosting these events, an opportunity exists commercially if someone is able to take advantage of such an event to generate funding.

When the 2010 Soccer World Cup was awarded to South Africa, facilities were upgraded and many new facilities were built which were directly financed by sponsorships or the government. The organisations behind these events had no financial commitment. Add to this the cost of other infrastructure and aspects such as security, transportation, accommodation, and others on such a massive scale, and it is easy to see why taking on such a venture is losing its lustre. It could, however, be argued that infrastructure development, job creation, tourism and entrepreneurial initiatives could add value to the economy of a host country.

Volunteerism

The very word 'volunteer' indicates doing something for nothing other than the goodwill attached to it. Today, with the commercialisation of big sporting events, volunteerism has taken a whole new turn. In South Africa, because of the economic situation, volunteers have been paid for the past 20 years. This is a concept that is not in line with global understanding. There is generally a small stipend to cover transport and possibly food. Questions are being asked by volunteers internationally as to why they should volunteer to do the work for no financial reward when the hosting organisation potentially generates a profit if the event is managed successfully. This raises an ethical question regarding the commercialisation of sport. Meanwhile volunteers will perhaps increase their profit margin to their own detriment.

Athletes as investors

An increasing trend today is that athletes are starting their own non-governmental organisations to develop athletes. A good example is the Youth Development Fund started in 1995 by former professional basketball player Michael Finley after visiting South Africa to mentor and coach kids in the townships. Today he has taken this into 15 African countries. With the SA Department of Social Development, he has helped to develop and teach a substance abuse prevention programme called 'Ke Moja: I'm fine without drugs'. The money to fund these workshops comes from a professional basketball league around Africa. This is a perfect example of athletes becoming investors in part of the structures around the sport they played.

Globalisation

Professionalisation of sport resulted in globalisation. Professionalisation provided coaches, athletes, administrators and technical officials with an opportunity to dedicate their work time to prepare for and participate in sport. This again resulted in an opportunities for globalisation in sports competitions and tournaments. Good examples are the IPL (Indian Premier League) and the Super Rugby franchise systems, both being commercial enterprises competing on an international platform. In the case of the IPL, professional players from around the world compete together in franchised teams and not as nations against each other. Apart from signing highly remunerative contracts, the IPL also reimburses the cricketers' provinces. This is a win-win business deal for all concerned.

Some of the major emerging trends regarding globalisation to be discussed in greater detail are: the global migration of athletes; global sponsorships; and global supporters.

The global migration of athletes

Apart from the IPL attracting international top-level cricketers and officials, globalisation of sport has generally seen a migration of all types of athletes, coaches, technical officials, referees, sports scientists and managers within their countries to participate for different franchises or from their home countries to abroad. In some instances athletes and coaches adopt citizenship of the country they migrated to and play for the national team against their previous country.

This is seen in the Super Rugby teams of franchises such as the Sunwolves (a rugby franchise in Japan) and America (national rugby team) where the coaches are New Zealanders, commonly called 'Kiwis'; the England rugby team with Eddie Jones, an Australian, as coach; and the current Springbok Assistant Coach (Mathew Proudfoot), who played for the Scottish national rugby team.

Global sponsorships

Along with globalisation of sport come major global sponsorships, perhaps the biggest being Coca Cola as the consecutive sponsor of the Olympics from the 1928 Olympics, to be replaced by Visa from 1986. The World Cup Soccer sponsors are Coca Cola, which has displayed stadium advertising at every World Cup since 1950; Nike manufacturing kits for the world's biggest clubs such as Manchester United and Barcelona; and McDonalds emulating Coca Cola in being a long-term sponsor for both the FIFA World Cup and the UEFA European Championship, as well as the English Football Association's grassroots coaching efforts. It is therefore clear that sport has become a perfect platform for global brands to reach their market.

In the South African context, the Free State Cheetahs, a South African Rugby franchise, are currently sponsored by Toyota, with a direct link to Toyota's head office in Japan. In Japan, rugby is fast becoming an important sport. Emirates Airline sponsors the stadium of the Lions, another South African Rugby franchise.

Global supporters

Globalisation is also evident in different ways in the context of supporters of various sports and sports franchises and clubs. As an example, Manchester United Soccer Club supporters are found on almost every continent. A club such as Real Madrid has websites in different languages for supporters in different countries in order to satisfy a number of specific international fan bases. With so much franchised sport, it is not unusual to see a South African sports team playing overseas with a dedicated local fan base of ex-patriots turning out to cheer them on. That is where the marketers know their business lies, making sure they cater for their brand.

Globalisation of supporters is also combined with sports tourism. Supporters can travel and support their favourite team wherever they play. Tourism packages are designed and marketed to supporters to enable them to travel the globe with their team. An example is the well-known group of supporters of the England cricket team, the Barmy Army, which travels the globe with their favourite team.

Transformation

Two trends will be discussed here: the racial transformation of sport in South Africa; and the increasing participation of historically marginalised groups in sport.

Racial transformation of sport in South Africa

Transformation in sport is a subject that has been debated at length since South Africa became a democracy in 1994. Although there is agreement that transformation should take place, different opinions exist on the way it should be achieved. One of the ways suggested to speed up the process was to implement quotas in sports teams at the national level. After 20 years this has not resulted in a change towards transformation in national teams. A second approach advocated was that change had to take place from the ground up, meaning that it has to start at school level, building up to club, and then provincial level. However, from the 2014 Eminent Persons Group (EPG) Report[3] it is clear that this process has not been implemented. Money spent on provincial level did not impact on the transformation of club sport.

For true transformation to take place, there has to be access to resources. This is where school sports and club systems fail. One of the main challenges facing transformation in schools is that no budgetary allocation is made by government for school sport. This leaves principals and teachers without resources for implementation and development of sport in schools. Quantile three (= no fee) schools have no money to support sport, because they have to supplement feeding schemes at schools. This need is for obvious reasons higher on their agenda than sport.

However, there is a range of schools in South Africa that could be seen as sports schools. These schools originated from the apartheid era and maintained their position with regard to sport. Although a limited number of talented black athletes are recruited by these schools, this is not even close to an ideal situation for total transformation of school sport. When transformation is implemented from the top down (= national and provincial teams), it is evident that those with the financial ability to participate in sport will inevitably be in a better position to develop their sporting talent. This again is counterproductive to the concept of total transformation in sport.

Another challenge around the governance of school sports is that, although the National Department of Basic Education and the Department of Sport and Recreation signed an agreement on school sport delivery,[4] no clear results are evident with regard to changes and progression. There is nowhere to draw funding from for these no-fee schools. They cannot request funds from parents. So currently many are using funds from their maintenance budgets.

Participation of historically marginalised groups

The 2012 London Paralympics acknowledged the position of sport for people with disabilities and granted disabled persons the right to stand on the winner's podium. For the first time the Paralympics was a global event that millions of people watched on television, and thousands attended the events. Para-sport is one of the most exciting areas of growth in sport. In 2018 the

Gold Coast Commonwealth Games will have the most events ever for people with disabilities, an example of continuing with the trend. Another less well known arm of sport today which is also growing exponentially is Special Olympics for people with mental challenges.

Women are also taking their rightful place in the world of sport, as participants as well as coaches, administrators, and technical officials. Sports where this is evident on an international level are cricket, rugby, and soccer. There is a global drive by women in sport which will create more opportunities, not just in playing and coaching, but in management structures.

Sports Leadership Challenges

Five major challenges facing leaders in sport will be discussed: running the re-inventing business of sport; managing the complexity of sport in an increasingly connected world; sustainable performance of athletes and teams; managing ethics; and transformation.

Running the re-inventing business of sport

Running and transforming the business of sport is probably the major challenge leaders in sport are facing. Where the majority of leaders in sport are volunteers with a limited number of professionally trained managers, it is a daunting task. In a study on the effectiveness of governance of Commonwealth Games Associations,[5] 78% of the Presidents and Secretary-Generals were volunteers. Of the present incumbents, 52% have been in these positions for seven years, and 37% for more than 10 years.

This is due to the understanding in amateur sport that coaches and administrators 'earn' their positions through their time involved in sport, and are not necessarily appointed based on knowledge and competence levels. This is also true for the majority of organisations in professional sport worldwide. This situation leaves leaders without the required knowledge and skills to manage differentiation, professionalisation, commercialisation, globalisation and transformation.

Leaders further grapple with understanding commercialisation. They are challenged to the changing face of sport from an amateur organisation to a professional, business, and profit-driven organisation. Generating income from selling tickets and recruiting sponsors has become the norm. A mindset shift is required to change an amateur sports organisation into a profitable business enterprise with sustainable income streams.

Managing the complexity of sport in an increasingly connected world

A second major challenge for leaders in sport is to manage the complexity of sport in an increasingly interconnected world. This is evident in the differentiation of sport, where a National Sports Federation is involved in professional and amateur sport. In addition, moving into the domain of sport-for-development seems to be inevitable. This is particularly the case in Africa, where there is a dire need for advocacy on health issues through sport. Leaders will have to make a decision on how to manage this complexity and provide for the needs of its consumers.

Sustainable performance of athletes and teams

Sustainable performance of athletes and teams in sport is a third challenge faced by leadership in sport. This requires technical and tactical knowledge and understanding in order to manage the demanding context of athlete development and performance sustenance; the contracting of athletes and/or players; and the ethics of participation. Dealing with the pressure from globalisation, attracting, engaging and retaining athletes and/or players and coaches as a workforce is mission critical. With the exchange rate of the rand against other currencies, this has become a significant challenge in South Africa. This challenge is intensified by global professional competitions, as well as the possibility for players to sign more than one contract, in particular in seasonal sport. For today's athletes and/or players the world is their oyster, and therefore attraction and retention become major problems.

Managing ethics

Managing ethics as the fourth leadership challenge in sport necessitates the leader in sport to juggle with metaphorical balls; increasing pressure for performance; and abiding by generally accepted values for sports participation, sponsorships and management. One of the biggest challenges in sport worldwide is putting in place a shared value system for sports participation and management across culturally diverse countries and nations. Doping is one such area. Cases in point are those of the women's tennis player, Maria Sharapova, testing positive for a banned substance, and the Russian athletes being found guilty of doping during the Sochi Winter Olympic Games. Also in the global spotlight is sports management, with FIFA and soccer being at the forefront of bribery and corruption, and facing criminal prosecution globally. This leaves leaders in untenable situations, with dilemmas which should be carefully managed and balanced.

Transformation

To keep up with transformation as the fifth challenge, it is required from leadership not only to understand the challenges that go with transformation, but also to develop strategies to curb these. However, this is a complex issue that needs not only to address access to resources, but also to enable more people of both genders, as well as people with disabilities, to participate regularly in sport at all levels from an early age.

Resultant Sports Leadership Requirements

Given the above challenges, what are the resultant sports leadership requirements? A discussion of the major required leadership attributes and competencies follows.

Required leadership attributes

What are the attributes needed to be a great leader in sport? Excellence in sport starts with leaders of *good and strong character with the will and commitment* to leadership in sport. Furthermore, sport requires leaders who show *drive, energy, determination and self-discipline, willpower, and nerve*. A leader should be a person who knows what he/she wants, and has a strong vision. A person who comes to mind is the late Dr Danie Craven. He was well known for his charisma, knowledge of rugby, and his visionary ability. He was moreover determined, had exceptional will-power, and knew exactly what he wanted.

Effective leaders in sport should furthermore have sound *ethics and values* and *be trusted* by followers. A leader in sport should be someone espousing sound values and empathy, and upholding an ethos that is lived daily. The name of the late Nelie Smit comes to mind. He was known as a leader with sound values, who upheld the ethos of sport and lived accordingly.

The sports industry requires leaders with *presence*. This includes leaders with a blend of appearance, communication and gravitas. Presence entails confidence, resilience, and the ability to focus on the task at hand and not be distracted by unrelated incidents and/or other detractors. It requires leaders who can focus on what they have to do to make a success of their commitments to sport.

Lastly, the sports industry requires leaders with *intellectual capacity*. This implies that sports leaders should be cognitively intelligent in order to learn, and be able to adapt, create and innovate. At the same time, they have to be able to focus on detail with logic, good sense and wisdom. This requires making the right decisions; generating future-directed good ideas; and designing plans and strategies to make these ideas a reality in order to take the sports organisation to the next level. It therefore implies leaders with mental agility, sound judgement, innovation, interpersonal tact, and sound sport and business knowledge. The name that comes to mind in the South African context is Kitch Christie, the coach of the Springbok team who won the 1995 Rugby World Cup. He had the intellectual capacity to develop the players into a winning team with his mental agility, innovation, and personal tact.

Required leadership competencies

Leading change

In order to be leaders of change in sport, it is imperative to be visionary. It requires leaders who are open to new information on professionalisation and commercialisation of sport, have an ability to make predictions of the future based on the current situation, and have persistence to fulfil their plans. They should in addition be strategists who can develop business strategies that have a greater chances of success, based on past experience. They should also have external awareness of trends in the sports industry. This should be coupled with creative and innovative thinking supplemented by flexibility to adjust when required.

Leading people

The sports context is one where services are delivered through and with people. One of the competencies leaders in sport should have is the ability to work with people. This refers to leveraging diversity of staff and managing conflict in the workplace. In the sports industry, there is currently tension between volunteers and professionally trained managers, based on the different approaches to amateur and professional sport. Sports leaders should be able to address this tension and acknowledge diversity. They should manage diversity to the benefit of the sports organisation.

Leaders in sport need to develop others in the sports organisation by creating a positive setting through valuing diversity and differences; building and maintaining relationships; and creating and maintaining effective teams and work groups. Good leaders always lead by example and influence others positively.

Being results driven

The sports context *per se* is a context that is results driven. Sports teams and athletes compete to win, while a sports business is required to perform commercially. To obtain results, entrepreneurship competencies are required from sports leaders, with a strong focus on customer service. Because sport is a service-orientated enterprise with fans and partners, customer service plays a significant role in achieving results. A service strategy and approach should therefore focus on outcomes such as customer satisfaction.

Having business acumen

Business acumen refers to competencies to manage human capital, finances, and technology. Sports leaders are required to have competencies in these areas because the effective and efficient utilisation of people, supported by financial competencies, inevitably leads to positive results in sport. Aligned with these two competencies, the application of technology supports the business context of sport.

As an example, Rowing South Africa (RowSA) introduced a person with business acumen as president, with a view to implementing business principles in the organisation. This resulted in two boats qualifying for the Rio Olympics and one for the Paralympics, with a limited budget and the best coaches in rowing in South Africa. Human and financial capital were effectively and efficiently utilised to obtain these results.

Building effective coalitions

Sport is a context where organisations have to work together in order to be able to sustain and develop the industry. Sports organisations have to structure competitions, access sponsorships, partner with broadcasting companies, work with governments, and build a fan base in order to compete. As an example, Varsity Sports SA, which incorporates the University Sports Company (USC), was structured by universities through building coalitions between universities, sponsors, sports federations, and the media. Through building a coalition with these partners, the vibrancy and relevance of varsity sports competitions were developed and sustained. In order to do this, sports leaders require the ability to influence people, partner with potential stakeholders, and understand the political context that goes with sport.

A Future Perspective

As in the case of other industries, there is a growing need in sport for global leadership development. Where sport has become a global commodity, leaders in sport will increasingly have to *understand different cultures, know how to do business in other parts of the world*, and *be entrepreneurial in an intuitive way*. This is required in order to foster growth through thinking like the customer and staying abreast of all developments that concern them. The future leader should also be a complete leader with the ability to adapt, connect with different types of employees, be flexible, and have interpersonal relationships.

Agility is another emerging competence required by leaders in sport. The speed of change will require leaders to be more flexible and have the foresight to spot change on the horizon, and strategise accordingly in order to comply with the future demands. Leaders in sport with this competence will inevitably stay abreast with changes in the market place and will be in a position to assure sustainable development of the sports organisation. This competence should be transferred to employees in order for them to be agile in their domain in the sports organisation, which will establish a stronger employee value proposition.

Change in the sports industry is inevitable. The future leader in sport will be required to institute *progressive change* in the sports organisation, which means going forward with clear purpose, meaning and resilience. Managing change requires innovation of not only the products and services that comprise the value proposition of the sports organisation, but also the processes, communication, and employee engagement, to name only a few. Changing a sports organisation run by volunteers into a dynamic commercial business will require the implementation of a variety of processes, skills and tools. The leader in sport will have to acquire knowledge and competencies in this particular domain in order to sustain future performance.

Conclusion

The sports sector is undergoing rapid, radical changes subject to the trends in differentiation, professionalisation, commercialisation, globalisation, and transformation. Resulting from these changes, leaders in sport will face a number of major challenges: running the re-inventing business of sport; managing the complexity of sport in an increasingly connected world; controlling sustainable performance of athletes and teams; managing ethics; and transformation.

It appears that these emerging trends and challenges will demand leaders in sport with a strong character and presence, who are able to engage in the entire process of leadership across the whole domain of sport. These persons must show drive, be ethical, and have strong business acumen. They will need to be visionaries with a strong sense of the global sports market. They must be able to lead change through forming effective coalitions. This will inevitably have an impact on the re-invention of sport from an international competitive approach into a global commercial industry.

Endnotes

1   Burnett & Hollander, 2010.
2   Burnett & Hollander, 2008.
3   Department: Sport and Recreation South Africa, 2014.
4   Burnett & Hollander, 2005.
5   Burnett & Hollander, 2014.

References

Burnett, C & Hollander, WJ. 2005. *Facility audit for Siyadlala (Mass Participation Sport and Recreation Programme)*. Research Report prepared for Sport and Recreation South Africa. Johannesburg, ZA: University of Johannesburg, Department of Sport and Movement Studies.
Burnett, C & Hollander, WJ. 2008. *The pre-impact assessment of the School Sport Mass Participation Project*. Johannesburg, ZA: University of Johannesburg, Department of Sport and Movement Studies.
Burnett, C & Hollander, WJ. 2010. *The impact of GTZ/YDF on selected African Countries (GRZ/YDF Annual Report)*. Johannesburg, ZA: University of Johannesburg, Department of Sport and Movement Studies.
Burnett, C & Hollander, WJ. 2014. *Commonwealth Games Federation (CGF) Development Framework*. Johannesburg, ZA: University of Johannesburg, Department of Sport and Movement Studies.
Department Sport and Recreation South Africa. 2013. 'Pilot Evaluation, Rugby, Cricket, Netball, Athletics, Football, A Transformation Status Report'. The Minister of Sport and Recreation officially received the Report from the EPG on 25 March 2014. [Online] Available: http://www.srsa.gov.za/MediaLib/Home/DocumentLibrary/SRSA%20EPG%20Interim%20Report_LR.pdf [Accessed 4 July 2016].

Chapter 8

LEADING PROFESSIONAL FIRMS
Jenny Greyling in association with Ajen Sita

This chapter looks at the leadership demands and challenges which are often specific to professional services firms. While the expectations of leaders across industries and sectors are very similar, this chapter aims to explore the professional services context, and compare emerging versus mature markets. The leadership approaches, principles and insights from one of the big four global professional services firms are shared in order to enhance the understanding of leader expectations and the challenges they face when entering and working in these professional firms.

In this chapter we will first look at some of the unique characteristics of professional services and consulting firms as described by Maister.[1] We then explore leadership practices at EY (previously known as Ernst & Young) and how the EY Leadership Framework is used as a model for developing leaders in this professional services firm. We end the discussion by sharing the perspectives from Ajen Sita, Regional Managing Partner for the EY Africa Region, on leadership in professional firms.

Unique Characteristics of Professional Services and Consulting Firms

According to Maister professional services firms differ from other business enterprises in two distinct ways: "Firstly, they provide highly customised services and secondly, they are highly personalised, involving the skills of individuals. Such firms must therefore compete not only for clients but also for talented professionals."

One of the interesting discoveries that Maister made in his consulting work with professional firms, was that almost every firm in the world has the same mission statement, regardless of the size, specific profession, or country of operation of the firms. This similarity does not necessarily detract from the value of such mission statements. However, it does pose a challenge for leaders of professional services firms who need to delicately balance the demands of the client-and-people marketplace against their firms' economic conditions.

He then goes on throughout the book to describe some of the characteristics of such firms. A few of these are described below.

The leverage model

Maister recognises that a critical factor in bringing the demands of clients, people and economic conditions into balance is a firm's leverage model. A leverage model refers to the required shape of the organisation or each unique business unit. This shape is primarily determined on the one hand by the skills requirements of the work against the profitability requirements of each client assignment on the other hand. An inability to recruit or promote according to the right leverage model could result in the risk of the poor utilisation of resources; non-profitable accounts; poor client service; and delivery and quality risks.

According to Maister professionals join professional services firms for a career rather than a job. They have a strong expectation of progressing through the organisation and up the ranks, typically to partner level. For many, the way in which professional services firms operate is often compared to that of acquiring a trade as an artisan via the apprenticeship model. In these instances, senior people would reward the hard work and assistance of more junior staff by teaching them their craft and extending their skills base.

A professional services firm's leverage is central to its economics. The 'rewards of partnership' come partly from the high hourly rates that top professionals can charge for their own time and from the firm's ability to leverage the professional skills of the seniors and juniors.

Maister highlights a number of unique features of professional services firms which all have an impact on leaders within this context when compared to other industries. Such characteristics will next be discussed in some detail.

- *Lifecycle of a professional services firm*

    This refers to the extent to which clients seek expertise, experience and efficiency from their service provider. This need varies depending on the size and complexity of the client. The recognition of the distinction between these three needs is critical for the success of building the right professional services organisation.

- *Profitability drivers*

    In a partnership, the ultimate measure of profitability is profit per partner, which is driven by three main factors: margin, productivity and the right leverage model.

- *Building human capital*

    Professional services firms have to focus as much effort on marketing the firm's services as they do to extending and polishing the knowledge and skills of their people. The true added value of a professional lies less in what they know and more in how they can apply such knowledge to address client needs. Such professional skills can be enhanced only through practice.

- *The partnership model*

    One defining characteristic of professional services firms is the expectation by professionals that with time, experience and personal development, they will proceed through the ranks to be considered for partnership. Individuals will therefore seek better opportunities elsewhere if they do not progress to this elite role.

From his research and work with professional services and consulting firms, Maister identifies a number of success factors for such leaders. With the most successful firms success had little to do with their creative strategies, unique management systems, IQ, or professional talent. What is noticeably different at the best firms are characteristics such as energy, drive, enthusiasm, motivation, morale, determination, dedication, and commitment. While many factors appear to play a role, the one which stands out above all others is the *skills and behaviour of the practice leader*. The EY Leadership Framework (described below) looks at the skills and behaviours required of a leader operating in a globally integrated professional services firm.

The sections which follow look at leadership in practice at one of the big four, global professional services firm, namely EY.

Applying the Leverage Model – the EY Case

Against the backdrop of Maister's work, at EY we develop our leaders to understand their unique role within a professional services firm and the expectations of leaders in our firm. The rest of this chapter will look into leadership practices and challenges specific to our organisation against this departure point. We will begin by unpacking leadership at EY in more detail by looking at: the challenges of being a 'producing manager'; and the complexity of managing multiple roles.

The challenges of being a 'producing manager'

Leaders in professional services firms are often referred to as 'producing managers' or 'producing professionals'. The nature of their profession means that professionals need to continue to practise their craft at some level. By pre-selecting to work in professional services or consulting firms, individuals often excel as consultants and client service providers, but at some point they are expected to manage and lead people. If individuals did not want to practise their craft, they would be more likely to sign up with large corporates such as Unilever, Proctor and Gamble, and other similar organisations, where they would have learned the skills and arts as practising general managers heading up business units.

Roles of producing managers include maintaining their professional practice of accounting, law or other specific chosen discipline, client service, business development, project leadership, organisational leadership, coaching and mentoring, plus specific firm duties. Each of these roles requires different skill sets and managing of potential conflicts.

One of the major stressors at work for individuals in professional services firms is role conflict and ambiguity. The producing manager's role set is loaded with these anomalies. This is often one of the reasons many professional services and consulting firms suffer with senior staff that are burnt out at a young age. They therefore leave their profession for what they refer to as better work/life balance.

The question arises as to why firms need producing managers. The answer is threefold: the credibility of the profession requires it; clients expect a high level of expertise from the partners with whom they interact; and involvement in the practice is required in order to make good business and organisational decisions. Individuals themselves often also have a high personal need to practise their profession and become known as experts (or specialists) in their field.

Harvard Business Best Practice Research conducted in the 1990s[2] has shown that better-performing professional services firms had a greater intensity of producing manager roles. They promoted more 'producer managers' to more senior roles than the lower performing firms in their sample. Conversely, the lower performing firms had more discrete professional managers in their senior ranks. Thus, there seems to be empirical evidence to support the idea that producing managers know how to run their own businesses to better effect than professional managers do.

The challenges faced by a professional typically in the role of a producing manager means that there is:

- *Constant tension* between practice/client service needs versus management needs
- *Ongoing tension* between short-term execution and client development versus longer-term strategic and developmental needs
- *Time conflict* over technical aspects versus people aspects.

A comparison of the expectations of professionals in contrast to those of leaders and managers is shown below in Table 8.1.

Table 8.1: A comparison of expectations

Professionals	Leaders and Managers
• Get quick and visible results, including client feedback • Tasks are involved, intellectually challenging, and fun	• See results gradually, over months and years • Deal with details and human problems which are complicated, intangible, and frustrating

Thus, the temptation to focus on the 'profession' is highly appealing, but very dangerous to the firm's results. The consequences for a leader in a 'producing manager' role are: the feeling of never having enough time; being less fully in control in at least one of two roles; a high potential for 'ongoing guilt'; the danger of abandoning one of the two roles; and stress and health issues. The implications of this is that leaders need to learn to: work more smartly; develop an internal sense of direction; utilise opportunistic behaviour; create an agenda as a producing manager; build a network; delegate more; and get help.

Intellectually, it may seem simple to address the challenges of being a 'producing manager', but skill in doing these things well and consistently is difficult. The result is that many leave the profession for a role in another organisation which does not necessarily offer fewer demands, but is rather one that has less potential for role conflict and ambiguity. Professionals then feel that they can contribute and make an impact. Leaders in professional services firms need to understand the importance of the dual role of partners in being a 'producing manager'. They also need to have insight into the human and economic impact of multiple roles on themselves and their business units.

Managing the complexity of multiple roles

While leaders need to understand the importance of being a 'producing manager', they also need to have some strategies for managing the complexity inherent in the dual roles. We now look at some of the strategies suggested above in more detail.

- *Strategy 1: Develop an agenda*

    The concept of an agenda is based on some of John Kotter's early work in identifying why some general managers were more successful than others. The notion of an agenda is most useful in 'overload' situations. Being a producer manager is an overload situation in that there are always more things that could be done than there is time for. The successful general managers in Kotter's study all had an agenda and had organised a network to help them achieve their priorities. An agenda is a list of four to seven items or issues that effectively are a personal business plan, related directly to the organisation's and the individual's long-term goals. Agenda items should be time framed, and individuals should differentiate between short-, medium- and long-term goals.

    In order to develop a personal agenda or strategy, professionals need to have:

    - A clear idea of their long-term goals;
    - An understanding of what they must accomplish in order to get there;
    - A screen to judge which activities are most important: what can be deferred and what do not matter; and
    - A means to make choices about how to spend their time.

    In developing an agenda, leaders in professional services ask themselves four questions:

    - What sort of practice are they going to build?
    - What do they want to be known for?
    - Why should anyone want to go there with them?
    - What are they going to **DO** to be famous for something?

    One issue that leaders face is the lack of time to undertake all these activities. How does one increase the amount of time that is available to do the important things expected as a leader in a professional services firm with multiple roles and expectations while keeping the whole operation running smoothly? Time is the one resource that professionals cannot expand, whereas all of the others (for example, people, cash and technology) can be accessed for a price. Kotter found that successful general managers were adept at using their time and opportunities as they presented themselves, such as during elevator conversations, brief meetings at coffee machines and water coolers, and so on.[3]

The skill needed is how to use time as effectively as possible and find ways to work more smartly rather than harder. We all know leaders who calmly seem to manage leading a large business unit and a client portfolio very successfully while focusing on being fit and healthy and safeguarding their time with friends and family. Most leaders do not portray such finesse at balancing all their roles, but are constantly late for meetings; unresponsive to important e-mails; send important requests at the last minute; work late nights, early mornings and over the weekend; and superficially seem to thrive on the constant pressure and demands of their busy roles.

An individual's agenda is a means to make choices about how to spend their valuable time. The Important/Urgent Time Management Matrix used by many organisations is based on *The 7 Habits of Highly Effective People*, by Stephen Covey.[4] He reflected on how to distinguish effectively which tasks lack importance and urgency. He defined *Importance* as an activity one personally finds valuable if it contributes to your mission, values, and high-priority goals. *Urgency* was defined as an activity one or others feel requires immediate attention.

- *Strategy 2: Opportunistic behaviour and time bonuses*

Opportunistic behaviour combines managerial, leadership and professional activities. It refers in this context to the ability to make the best use of available time and potentially expand the finite time available. Some examples of this could be: using travel time to think about longer-term issues; coaching younger professionals when meeting clients; and using team meetings to 'sell' a new strategy.

Leaders need to avoid the trap of multi-tasking by learning to 'compartmentalise' issues, and dealing with each in relation to their agenda. They need to remain as focused as possible. They must succeed in doing a few things well rather than being distracted by multiple requests and opportunities. This means being able to say 'No' to things which do not fall within the leaders' agenda.

- *Strategy 3: Effectively managing your network*

Effective leaders make extensive use of their network and delegate to the maximum, given the capabilities and potential of their teams. There is a critical need to access help and support from a wider network. Effective leaders use their network to consult with, to access resources, and to expand visibility of what is being worked on.

In summary: the effective 'producing manager' uses at least three strategies to manage the complexity inherent in their dual roles: having a clear work agenda setting out priorities; opportunistically utilising his/her time smarter; and set up an effective network to get the work done.

The EY Leadership Framework

Research shows that organisations with a clear articulation of leadership behaviours select and develop better leaders who, in turn, drive better performance. A leadership model provides the anchor for alignment and integration across all ranks and roles within a professional firm.

Over the past year EY has recognised that to build the leaders of tomorrow – for EY and for the world – we need a clear definition of leadership behaviour. Without a shared vision and language of leadership, professional services firms run the risk of communicating mixed messages to their partners and people. Having multiple models creates confusion and inconsistency across processes and programmes.

Achieving our 2020 strategy requires strong leadership. The EY leadership definition describes the distinctive shared qualities of our leaders. It aims to do so in a way that can be communicated, replicated, and developed consistently throughout EY and across all ranks. The EY Leadership Framework© consists of four dimensions, each with three competencies as shown in Table 8.2.

Table 8.2: The EY Leadership Framework©

Leadership dimensions	Associated leadership competencies
Personal leadership	• Presence – Communicates with confidence, humility and integrity to build trust and support of others • Vitality – Actively maintains personal well-being, energy and enthusiasm • Agility – Exhibits curiosity and self-awareness to adapt behaviour and connect in diverse contexts
Team leadership	• Shared vision – Articulates a bold, clear vision that engages and inspires everyone • Right mix – Selects, respects and develops a diverse mix of talent with the right skills at the right time • Quality results – Sets the high standards expected of our profession, and enables each individual and team to deliver quality results
Client leadership	• Connected – Brings all of EY to our clients with the right people in the right locations, building trust and enriching relationships • Responsive – Is proactive, visible and timely • Insightful – Shares EY experiences and a point of view tailored to our clients, thereby advancing their thinking
Business leadership	• Business acumen – Applies financial, operational, risk, sector and global insights to make business decisions in dynamic global markets • Business development – Leverages EY's business development practices in order to achieve market leadership responsibly • Innovation – Collaborates widely within EY and externally to bring new ideas, talent and services to build a better working world

These leadership competencies capture the essence of leadership at EY. They are aligned to EY's purpose statement of 'Building a better working world'. Strong and distinctive leadership sustains the EY culture. It inspires our leaders to seek answers that help our clients and EY to work better. When business, governments and communities work better, the world works better.

Leadership in Practice

The next question to address is how leadership in professional services firms may be different from leadership in other contexts such as those of our clients or even EY in other regions across the world.

Leadership of professional services firms is both similar TO and different FROM that of leading other firms. From his perspective, he says that what is similar for all leaders is that leadership happens in the domains of yourself, the organisation and the context. But within these three domains, the challenges and expectations are different. This framework of reference is important background to understanding how leaders are selected in professional service firms and the characteristics expected of people in the leadership talent pool.

Leadership with respect to Self

Leaders need to have a strong ability to lead themselves prior to being able to lead others. This requires leaders to have presence, be adaptable, and be agile. Leaders need to be able to deal with a lot of change, ambiguity, and understanding of the global context in which they are operating in order to lead their people. From a change perspective, leaders in emerging markets are continually challenging their strategy to see if it is responding to the complex context in which they are operating. Embracing change and being able to manage change needs to be core to one's personality and DNA as a leader. This means that leaders need to be able to change and lead at the same time. Emerging markets are faced with increasing competition from global entrants. Leaders therefore need to be agile enough so that they can move with enough speed to be able to transform the organisation as needed. Simultaneously leaders need to acquire the new skills they need to respond to market demands.

Leaders face the challenge of having to inspire and motivate their people who in their daily lives may be experiencing difficult problems and poor living conditions. One just has to open the newspaper to read about the ongoing crime and poverty being experienced. Leaders, and the people making up their teams, are constantly experiencing corruption, increased prices, and load shedding, among others. Families are impacted on by unemployment and crime. People bring these stresses and challenges with them to work every day. This means that leaders in emerging markets are expected to inspire and motivate employees for a longer term purpose and strategy while being conscious of their daily living conditions. This harsh everyday reality versus the hope one tries to create as a leader is a complete contrast.

The average age of employees in professional services firms is very young compared to mature markets. In mature markets people are more established in their roles. The depth of experience of these leaders is stronger. There is a shortage of leadership depth in professional services firms as we struggle to find successors to fill key leadership positions. The potential is there amongst many of the firm's people. But at the time when they have to step up and fill a strategic leadership role, most often they have not had enough time in the role. This means that they often have not had the time or opportunity to get enough varied and global experience in order to lead with the same level of expertise and competence as their global counterparts.

Emerging markets and professional services firms in particular feel the impact of leadership gaps more strongly, given the nature of the services being provided to the market. Leadership development is a critical focus area for our organisation, but we are challenged by both cost and time pressures. In emerging markets, leaders in professional services firms often find themselves in senior positions at a young age in comparison with mature markets. The initial core competence which resulted in their being employed and noticed, is not enough in order for them to succeed.

Leaders have a short time in which to build up their expertise, develop industry experience, C-suite client relationship skills, and international market experience, and to have the ability to develop and motivate people. There is not enough mentorship locally by the traditional 'grey-haired', experienced leaders. Most organisations would say they aspire to high performance. However, the reality of building a high-performance culture in the context of the challenges mentioned above and current economic conditions is not easy.

From a client perspective, they require advisers with strong business acumen skills and expect leaders to be able to advise them within a global context. From a Pan-African perspective there is an even greater lack of skills, which makes it even more difficult to get a cross-border assignment done according to the same standards. Both professional services firms, and global organisations, are faced with the challenge of outsourcing or off-shoring key skills to countries where skilled labour is cheaper and where there are greater efficiencies for standardising routine processes. Organisations experience an increase in efficiencies, turnaround time, and quality of deliverables by off-shoring. However, the costs for emerging markets are more significant when converting to local currency. The efficiencies of consistent processing across global operating units comes at a higher price.

When comparing operating costs at a regional or country level in a global professional services firm which operates as an integrated partnership, one needs to take cognisance of how long it takes for a partner in a mature market to generate $1 of revenue as opposed to a partner in emerging markets. When developing a recharge model, finance leaders need to factor in how many hours of sold revenue it takes to generate enough profit to buy, say, one iPad in a mature versus an emerging market. Practically, leaders in mature markets are able to generate $1 of profit on an engagement more easily than their counterparts in emerging markets.

Leadership with respect to the organisation

Leadership with respect to this domain refers to dealing with and relating to the unique culture, strategy and operating model applied by an organisation. This in turn influences the leadership style and behaviours expected.

From an organisational perspective, leaders within EY need to be able to deal with ongoing 'corporatisation' of the traditional 'partnership model'. Making partner therefore does not necessarily mean being able to influence or vote before decisions are made. Collaboration and influencing skills become more important. To run an integrated business, leaders cannot succeed without a good understanding of our African business and the need to have the ability to lead and connect with cross-border teams on a virtual basis.

Leadership with respect to the context

If we move on to consider the third domain, we have to accept that the context is not just the local context but rather one that is impacted on by the ongoing volatility, uncertainty and complexity experienced worldwide. In the news currently, it has become hard to find positive stories about Africa and even the globe. Global unrest is magnified by these three aspects in the context.

- *Volatility*

    As a leader in emerging markets, one is constantly faced with highly volatile exchange rates which affect the local economy, as well as ongoing social unrest. Leaders are not afforded the luxury of stability and predictability in the same way as many of their colleagues in more mature markets.

- *Uncertainty*

    Unpredictability is a major problem. The level of volatility in exchange rates, the economy, and social unrest means that leaders are unable to predict the future. Locally, people are focused on the short term because of the levels of inequality and high unemployment rates. Organisations are constantly asking themselves whether our economy will continue to grow. Also how changes in mature markets will impact on emerging markets. The big question is whether Africa can sustain its growth.

    Leading a professional services firm in emerging markets is also complex. Growing globalisation means that one is affected by crises in China or Greece. Leaders can never look at our business in a local context. They need to have a strong market focus, especially with regard to how the factors mentioned above are impacting on not only our own business but also those of our clients. This creates an added responsibility for leaders in emerging markets to be aware constantly of global issues and to enhance their business acumen skills continually.

- *Complexity*

    Complexity arises from globalisation, multi-locations, diversity, language, culture, and race. In emerging markets, skills are constrained. Leaders need to be adept at finding the right skills to serve the emerging needs of global clients. They need to be consciously aware of their role in the balance of our ecosystems by challenging themselves as to their role in education and how this could positively impact on the availability of skills. Organisations therefore need to take an active part in schools, universities, and professional bodies so that there is a positive change in the output of education across Africa, in this way increasing the skills pool. Organisations need to invest significantly not only in learning and development, but also in the upliftment of education.

In order for leaders to be effective, they therefore need to embrace this shared value concept by giving back to the system of which they are a part. This is different from mature markets, where one can leave the development of critical elements of the ecosystem to the government and institutional bodies responsible for education and the development of skilled resources.

Given the level of globalisation of our clients and their demands for global expertise locally, professional services firms are always in need of new skills. Our education system is not geared to generate a sufficient number of people with the new skills which are required.

These then are the three aspects of our context what leaders of organisations struggle with across Africa and in the world. So what does this mean for us at EY, and how do we respond to our clients? With regard to *volatility*, people often react to change and become very short-term focused. In the case of *uncertainty*, people wait until the last minute and then react and hope it works. When we are confronted with *complexity*, planning and prioritisation become difficult.

To respond to these challenges, EY uses a framework to guide leaders in their daily behaviour:

- In response to *volatility* we advocate *concentration*. This implies being present in the here-and-now; knowing what is under our control; and making sure we do those things well. As an organisation, our purpose, vision and strategy are our guidelines. Our leaders need to concentrate on building high-performing teams who deliver exceptional client service and have a relentless focus on winning in the market.
- In response to *uncertainty* we advocate *consistency*. This implies not pulling in different directions. Leaders need to deliver on the pillars of our strategy in a consistent manner, using these pillars as a compass to determine what to focus on and what to say no to.
- In response to *complexity* we advocate a spirit of *co-operation* and simplification. Leaders need to remember that they are not alone. We need to collaborate with our governments, businesses and clients across Africa. As we shape their thinking, they shape ours. Together we build a better working world.

In volatile, uncertain and complex contexts, leaders need to make decisions based on clarity, as opposed to certainty. Leaders can apply the 3Cs of concentration, consistency and co-operation as a means to better decision making.

A Future Perspective

In taking stock of the unfolding future regarding professionals firms, three topics will be addressed: expected future mega-trends that will be shaping the world, and hence professional firms; the impact of these mega-trends on future professional firms; and the profile of leaders in future professional firms.

Expected future mega-trends

At least three future mega-trends will be shaping the world, and hence professional firms, namely globalisation, technological innovation and demographic shifts.

Globalisation

The world has become, and will increasingly become, a global village. Many, if not most boundaries restricting the movement and flow of information, knowledge, people, stakeholders, products/ services and resources across the world are disappearing/will disappear rapidly, though at varying paces over time. For example, increasing trade barriers are disappearing and trade relations are shifting, like in Africa where inter-country trade and trade with Asia are growing. Current and future organisations will operate globally, through a physical and/or virtual presence and reach. Customers (or clients) will be globally connected, aware and informed. In accessing products and services they will make global comparisons in deciding who to go with.

Technological innovation

Digitisation, Big Data, and automation are, and will, create a significantly different future world. Firstly, digitisation will invade and re-invent everything we do in future. It refers to the technology enabled, ability to be present and deliver on an ongoing basis, anything, anywhere, anytime, anyhow, for anyone by means of technologies such as the Internet; social media in the form of Google, Facebook, LinkedIn, Blogs, Twitter; smart phones; and Cloud-enabled connectivity.

Digitisation will force existing organisations to rethink from first principles everything they do: from their products and services – where products and services increasingly will converge to become seamless wholes – to the ways they connect and interact with their clients. Everything will become digitised. A one-stop service and contact point of clients with organisations will be the client expectation. Digitisation will also enable high levels of customer centricity allowing customers to self-design and specify completely individualised, unique products/services matched to their own needs, liking and preferences: "This is what I want on my terms."

The digitised, connectivity infrastructure also will also lower the entry barriers for completely new, start-up, 'garage-based' businesses with a global, virtual reach. These businesses will either take on established businesses, forcing them to radically re-think their business models, for example Uber in the taxi sector and AirBnB in the accommodation sector. Or, open up completely new application- enabled businesses, offering new products/services to satisfy client needs – existing or new – in better and/or different ways.

Secondly, the continuous ability in real time to rapidly generate, mine, analyse, interpret, make predictions from, and act upon Big Data will be mission critical to businesses in the future. This implies amongst other things, the ability to generate predictive insights from each and every customer encounter, for example, through Wi-Fi customer connectivity in a shopping mall, and then shaping in real time or in future the information a customer is exposed to in the mall. Access to and an in-depth understanding of customer biometrics will be the name of the game in the future.

Thirdly, automation. Virtualisation is about having a virtual presence and connectivity at all times, in all places with all persons on anything. Automation entails the means used to conceive, produce, deliver and maintain products/services. We are in the throes of the Fourth Industrial Revolution, characterised by an exponential rate of change in and merging of multiple technologies, for example, Artificial Intelligence (AI), robotics, DNA sequencing, the Internet of Things (IoT), autonomous vehicles, 3D printing, nanotechnology, biotechnology, and algorithms to mine Big Data. Increasingly it is all about people working in tandem with and alongside robots with growing AI, being able to do increasingly higher-level tasks. There is the growing fear and anxiety amongst people that the machines have come to take them over, destroying jobs and rendering skills and expertise obsolete.

Technological innovation as typified above in terms of digitisation, Big Data and automation are creating an insatiable, exploding demand for professional experts such as actuaries, data scientists, and IT engineers.

Demographic shifts

Significant demographic shifts are occurring. In the Northern Hemisphere, in particular North America, Europe and Japan, populations are aging and contracting. China with its past one-child policy will be in a similar position soon. In contrast, the population of Africa is getting on average younger. It is estimated that one out of four workers in future will be/come from Africa. Immigration or accepting exiles fleeing from conflicts from the Southern Hemisphere to extend the shrinking populations of the Northern Hemisphere will become normal ways of doing things.

Globalisation and digitisation will also enable and accelerate the global mobility of the future work force, at present the generation of millennials. Future workers will be well informed about work opportunities globally, and in a discerning and critical way match them to their career needs and aspirations. Workers will want to move where the jobs are that meet what they want, regardless of where the jobs are located in the world. Recruitment and head-hunting firms will also seek out and hunt attractive, prospective talent wherever it is found in the world, and alert them to and entice them to consider new job prospects.

The impact of the expected mega-trends on future professional firms

It is believed that the expected mega-trends will impact in at least the following ways on professional firms: the criticality of the ability to anticipate; changing client needs; adopting a global, ecosystem mindset and approach; automated, digitised solutions and delivery; and ongoing innovation as the DNA of firms.

The criticality of the ability to anticipate

The hyper-turbulent, hyper-fluid world of tomorrow with its associated unpredictability, ambiguity and uncertainty will be make the ability to anticipate what the future is going look like for clients and one's own firm an imperative not only to survive but to thrive in a sustainable, relevant way. Anticipation will enable one to engage with the future pro-actively. Anticipation will require working in three interdependent time horizons simultaneously:

- *Incremental time horizon.* The day-to-day, continuous improvement in products/services, ways of servicing and interacting with clients. It is about transactional anticipatory future engagement but in the present.

- *Adjacent time horizon.* Finding new permutations of the existing in new and different ways, both internally in the firm or externally in enhanced value-adding servicing of clients. For example, combining disparate products and services into an extended, integrated total solutions, delivered through a one-stop service.
- *Disruptive time horizon.* Future-directed to conceive and craft totally new products/services and means of delivering them to satisfy existing or newly anticipated client needs and expectations.

Changing client needs

Future clients will have three dominant needs: digital connectivity; cybersecurity; and Big Data analytics. Digital connectivity is about the need to establish a competitive global, digital footprint, presence and brand in terms of products/services and delivery. A cybersecurity need because of the security risks of operating in the Cloud and of shared digital infrastructure. The enhanced protection of data security and privacy will become critical. Satisfying the need for Big Data analytics will require strong real-time data mining, algorithmic and predictive skills and expertise.

This implies that future professional firms will need to move beyond the traditional Accounting/Finance expertise base into the actuarial, mathematical, data scientist and gaming expertise spaces, altogether new expertise domains for firms. Cybersecurity and risk will give rise to the need to employ 'ethical' hackers to test clients' and firms' digital platforms to conduct vulnerability assessments.

The adoption of a global, ecosystem mindset and approach

Future clients will expect end-to-end solutions offered by a single service provider in a one-stop manner. Future professional firms will have to create and manage an ecosystem of different alliance parties offering separate products/services that the firm will mould and fuse into integrated solutions matched to client needs.

The future professional firm will increasingly move away from being merely advisory, entering into the client space by designing and managing client 'back office', transactional delivery and support activities, enabling the client of the firm to focus on their 'front office', customer-facing activities where value is created for their clients. For example, the professional firm will provide to clients the digital infrastructure on which to run their business. So a second client ecosystem consisting of the firm in interaction with a client will emerge, next to the first above ecosystem consisting of the firm with its own service providers contributing to integrated client solutions, delivered in a one-stop manner.

Automated, digitised solutions and delivery

Future professional firms will move away from a 'time and materials' business model. Services and people tasks at the 'lower end' of professional firms will be digitised and automated. The solutions delivered will be much more automated and ditigised through technology, and less people-delivery intensive. Examples are of digitised solutions running on the firm's digital platform sitting in the Cloud; fully real time, automated audits using full data populations, and not samples, enabling one immediately to pick up patterns, deviations and exceptions in real time; automated, real time, continuous self-auditing by clients through block chain; robots performing mundane transactional auditing tasks, like stock taking; drones doing stock takes of physical sites like mining reserves; and automated, real time Big Data analyses and reporting.

Professional client-serving teams will also work much more virtually, being globally distributed but digitally connected in real time, integrated around client needs and integrated solution delivery. Expertise and skills will be accessed and mobilised physical location free from anywhere at any time. These teams will also be much more diverse in terms of skills, expertise and nationality, as well as gender, race and age.

Ongoing innovation as the DNA of professional firms

Ongoing innovation in the anticipatory fashion described above will need to become a way of life in the future professional firm in all of its business areas/units. This will embrace all facets: from products/services through to client interface and delivery. Outward facing this innovation will be triggered by and driven by innovative ideas arising out of daily client interactions and shifting needs, and internally by formalised innovation hubs with the firm.

This would imply engendering an innovation and learning organisational culture where everyone learns from everyone else in real time. In tandem the firm's organisational design will have to become much flatter hierarchy wise, egalitarian, inclusive and participative, and functioning in a matrix manner. Rank and status will need to take a back seat. The move will be away from geographical organised service delivery to seamless, global delivery to industries and sectors founded on deep knowledge about them, drawing in the necessary services lines in an integrated solution way.

Profiling the leader of future professional firms

The given departure point of the leader of the professional firm of the future will be integrity, trustworthiness, vitality, agility and humility. From this non-negotiable foundation, the future leader will need at least the following integrated profile of being/ having, given in no particular order:

- a strong *personal identity*: who am I?; what do I stand for"; what difference do I want to make?
- *purpose-driven* ('why' leadership) bringing about lasting, worthy *legacies* benefiting multiple stakeholders and societal challenges/problems beyond the 'hollow' pursuit of mindless growth for the sole benefit of a firm and its partners
- imbued by a constant *future-centric anticipation*, from a short, medium-term perspective
- a high *tolerance for ambiguity, uncertainty and unpredictability*, and hence the ability to make decisions and take action to shape and direct the anticipated future
- *systemic, big-picture thinking and doing*, in this way bridging the future and the present
- a *networker and alliance builder and maintainer* in order to bring about thriving, value-adding ecosystems
- able to affect the synergetic *fusion of multiple disciplines and parties* into integrated, one-stop client solutions by operating beyond hierarchy, function and business units
- instilling a strong *shared organisational culture* of innovation, learning and diversity friendliness
- highly *people-centric*, constantly communicating and being highly visible and accessible in person where and when it matters
- building and growing *the upcoming generation of leaders*, fit for the unfolding, anticipated future

Conclusion

Professional services firms have some unique characteristics which have an impact on the challenges and requirements of leaders in these professions. Very often, leaders who succeed in these contexts are ones who have started their trade within such an organisation and have grown up through the ranks, influenced by the culture and unwritten operating norms. Joining as a leader from an external organisation and a different industry, is often a very difficult transition.

In a recent McKinsey article, the authors state that "great leaders complicate leadership development". In the organisational context, effectiveness depends less on the traits of any one leader but more on the competitive challenges of the organisation, legacies, and other shifting forces. They remark that if only we had a clear set of keys to effective organisational leader – a "decoder ring", which would help us to understand which practices produce the best outcome – all organisations would be in a position to strive for perfection.[5]

Endnotes

1 Maister, 2003.
2 Gabarro and Samantha Graff. 1998
3 Kotter, 1982.
4 Covey, 1989.
5 Bazigos, Gagnon & Schaninger, 2016.

References

Bazigos, M, Gagnon, C. & Schaninger, B. 2016. 'Leadership in context'. *McKinsey Quarterly*, January. [Online]. Available: http://www.mckinsey.com/business-functions/organization/our-insights/leadership-in-context. [Accessed 27 May 2016].

Covey, SR. 1989. *The seven habits of highly effective people: Restoring the character ethic*. New York, NY: Simon and Schuster.

Gabarro, John J., and Samantha Graff. 1998. 'Transformation at Ernst & Young, United Kingdom'. Harvard Business School Case 498-049, January 1998.

Kotter, JP. 1982. *The general managers*. New York, NY: Free Press.

Maister, D. 2003. *Managing the professional service firm*. London, UK: Free Press Business.

Additional reading

Gabarro, JJ. 1987. *The dynamics of taking charge*. Boston, MA: Harvard Business School Press.

Gabarro, John J. 2002. 'Tim Blanchard at Jones Mendel & Co'. Harvard Business School Case 402-052, Revised May 2002.

Lorsch, J & Mathias, P. 1997. 'When professionals have to manage'. *Harvard Business Review*, July. [Online]. Available: https://hbr.org/product/when-professionals-have-to-manage/an/87406-PDF-ENG [Accessed 27 May 2016].

Nohria, N. 2009. 'From regional star to global leader'. *Harvard Business Review*, 87(1), 1 January. [Online]. Available: https://hbr.org/2009/01/from-regional-star-to-global-leader/ar/1. [Accessed 27 May 2016].

Chapter 9

BUSINESS LEADERSHIP
Hixonia Nyasulu

"We live in such an exciting world if people are willing to embrace the challenges and not duck for cover and run from them. It's about turning these challenges into positive experiences..." – Hixonia Nyasulu

The purpose of my chapter is to explore the challenges facing business leaders who have to lead in what is arguably one of the most difficult and turbulent contexts of our times. It will address current and emerging challenges; how they have an impact on companies and leadership; as well as the leadership skills companies will need to attract and retain to navigate this volatile socio-economic context successfully. The following topics are addressed: the challenging trends business leaders are facing currently, and leadership demands arising out of these challenges, concluding with a discussion of current and future leadership requirements respectively.

Challenging Trends for Business Leaders

Some of the more notable contextual trends challenging business leaders today to be discussed are: the VUCA context; the digital revolution; sociopolitical and socio-economic factors; a shifting geopolitical focus; the talent grab; and disruption from competitors.

No end to the VUCA context

Leaders will continue to contend with a VUCA context (Volatile, Uncertain, Complex and Ambiguous), which we are told is going to remain with us for a long time still. "A long time" in this case could mean two years, which in today's conditions is like a lifetime. In two years, what a VUCA context can do to a company is decimate it completely, unless the leadership team is ready and able to roll with the punches.

The 2008 economic crisis, which first introduced us to the VUCA phenomenon, has eased up quite a bit. But there are definite signs of more volatility in the markets again. From a leadership standpoint, this means responding with speed and agility. The situation can perhaps be compared to playing tennis in the dark. You cannot quite anticipate where the ball is coming from until it hits you. But once it hits, how you respond, and the speed with which you respond, will determine whether or not your company will survive.

These conditions and challenges point to a different kind of leader, one who has his/her finger on the pulse of what is happening in and outside their company, and is able to react very quickly.

The digital revolution

Embracing the digital revolution, and all it has to offer, has the potential to leapfrog one's company onto a new growth trajectory. Today, leaders must ensure that their companies have the necessary capabilities, or at the very least form the necessary alliances and joint ventures, that

---
i   Invaluable assistance by Wilhelm Crous in putting this chapter together is gratefully acknowledged

will allow them to take full advantage of the digital revolution. This is not a trend that is about to disappear, but one that needs a particular kind of leadership: innovative, deliberate, flexible, and sharp.

As much as the digital revolution introduces exciting opportunities and a vastly different way of doing things, it brings with it new problems for leaders to contend with, such as cybersecurity and greater challenges around information security and privacy. Of course, no leader can be an expert on all of these areas, but they are expected to understand how the digital revolution will have an impact on their businesses, positively and negatively.

Shifting geopolitical focus

There is a clear trend that the world is moving east and south. This means that business leaders, more accustomed to doing business in developed countries, are suddenly moving into terrains with which they are no longer comfortable and about which they know and understand little. Moving east to the Far East, and south as in southwards to and in Africa, means that business leaders used to the western way of doing things find they are suddenly in over their heads. These different contexts where they have to navigate very different cultures are exacerbated by a shortage of skills and talent. It is also not as easy to move people around as they are used to doing in Europe and North America. Leaders find themselves grappling with totally unfamiliar terrain, not comparable to anything they know at present.

Sociopolitical and socio-economic factors

Sociopolitical and socio-economic factors will always play a role, whether we are looking at trends today or tomorrow. In South Africa, and the rest of the African continent, these issues centre around poverty, access to education, social justice, currency weaknesses, and, to a lesser extent, the environment. This can be compared to the situation in the western world, where the emphasis is on sustainability, organic foods, slowing growth, and being the conscience of global companies in their interface with the developing world.

Going back to the trend of the world moving east and south, the priority of the latter governments will be on growing their tax base and grabbing a bigger slice of that base. Developing countries are therefore focusing on growing the fiscus through very aggressive tax collection. Consequently, multinational companies will come under tremendous financial pressure and demands. Of course, this is not unique, as the OECD countries themselves are also switching the spotlight to BEPS (Base Erosion and Profit Shifting). So leaders are going to be facing quite an onslaught here.

The talent grab

With today's shortage of skilled and experienced talent, we see companies grabbing talent from each other. We are seeing the talent "musical chairs" phenomenon hitting companies significantly, particularly when a company is going through a succession race for a CEO. This introduces a period of uncertainty into the company. Frequently, this results in some members of the senior team, who may not even throw their hats into the ring, seeing this as an opportune time to exit. It is also a good time for the talent "vultures" to begin circling. Suddenly there is a focus on top executives of the company concerned, because everyone knows there is going to be a talent leakage once the final CEO decision has been made, opening the way for a huge talent grab.

Disruption from competitors

Adding to the challenges of leadership today is the necessity of a constant awareness of what one's competitors are doing. They are in fact one's best teachers in the VUCA context, because they are going to disrupt the way one has been doing business traditionally. Being able to anticipate trends; gather and use insights to refresh one's company's innovation pipeline and ideas; and going to market quickly and efficiently, will set companies apart. And if one's company cannot create its own waves, one may at least learn from what one's competitors are doing, and smoothly surf the waves they are creating.

Today's leader needs to have his/her finger on the proverbial pulse, as the trends highlighted above move consistently and constantly, and new challenges emerge with rapid speed. These trends have significant implications for how companies do business, and how "people decisions" will be made by Boards and their CEOs.

Leadership Demands Arising out of These Challenges

Four trends are discussed with regard to the leadership demands arising out of the above challenges: contextual understanding and sensitivity; the great divide – inequality of wealth; governance and responsiveness; and company agility.

Contextual understanding and sensitivity

With the east–south move, the understanding of and sensitivity towards different cultures become a top priority. Very few European and American leaders understand the nuances of working in these cultures. High levels of cultural and emotional intelligence by leadership will be required to learn and adjust to how to do business in these new contexts. This also requires being politically savvy. Leaders who have not worked in these cultures are advised to build strong local government and stakeholder relationship teams, and to heed their advice on how to engage politically. Cultural misunderstandings can have a devastating impact on a company's ability to work effectively with governments in developing countries.

This also requires an understanding of a whole new governance structure. For instance, the discussions that happen now around the issues of ethics and conflicts of interest are challenging. Companies which are ethical and aspire to do things the right way stand to lose out to others who are more willing to "adjust" to how business is done in these new contexts. It is important for global companies to lead by example. They should never allow themselves to submit to a different governance standard when doing business in developing countries.

It is crucial to understand the issue of "facilitation", for instance, which has spawned a whole industry around lobbying in the USA, based around the issues of paying for the facilitation of meetings and the opening of the "right doors". Most companies would find this very uncomfortable. They would shy away from using lobbyists, even in the USA, where this is an accepted practice. In the developing world, where this practice is more covert, it is likely to be seen as a bribe. Ethical companies should not compromise their ethical governance stance.

Consider a scenario where the people in control may say: "Unless you pay, your goods are not going to be offloaded from ships that have docked." So what do I do as a company: let the food rot, as no one will unload it until some facilitation fee has been paid? Or should I be saying to the government: "Is this a fee for doing business, in which case, should I be paying it, and to which authority?" It is a very difficult world for leaders ethically as they to try to manoeuvre around right now, in their east-and-south move with its ethically different way of doing business.

My response to the above leadership demand is clear: you just say no! Companies that are really good at taking such a position should ensure that they have strong relationships with the government. In this way they would be able to call for intervention from the government. I do not know how smaller companies would fare. I am fortunate enough to have worked only with companies that have the stature and gravitas to say: "Unless our goods are offloaded and given free passage to wherever we need them, there will be negative consequences for your country, which may include disinvestment." For me, the issue is black and white, with no greys in between.

Boards need to be aware of and speak openly about these issues, and have a code of ethics in place that reads: "Under no circumstances would we agree." Most companies would have a matrix that tells the person at the coalface that if one is facing such an ethical problem, escalate it to the next level, and the next level, up to the point where the CEO becomes involved, if necessary. If it reaches that point, then a government interface and intervention would probably be necessary.

The great divide – inequality of wealth

There has been a lot of discussion around the gap between CEOs' pay and that of the lowest workers in organisations. The debate is so emotionally charged that key issues are often lost in the heat of the discussion. To be clear, I am in full support of everyone being paid a living wage which allows them to provide food, shelter, and a good education for their children. I also believe that the salaries of the world's CEOs have grown out of control.

But the solutions being suggested are totally irrational. In the context of a skills shortage, CEOs will always be able to "sell" their skills and experience for significantly more than a factory worker or miner could. The debate and the solution require a joint effort and the co-operation of the world's major corporations, as well as a few brave men and women to take the lead. No company will walk this path alone, because they see the CEO's remuneration and package as a point of competitiveness.

Let us be fair, though. There is a vast difference in the responsibilities a CEO carries, compared to various levels in the structure of the company. Most have 18-hour days. Even the six hours they are at home are not really free, as they are on permanent call. They have pressure on them to deliver results and unlock value for shareholders, regardless of the economic climate. They face tremendous risks, including jail, destruction of reputation, and, in extreme cases, physical harm. They need to be available, sometimes at short notice, to activist shareholders, and various other stakeholders. They are accountable to Boards and regulators with regard to the health and safety of employees.

This is as it should be. But it all comes at a price. This in no way minimises the role other workers play, but seeks to demonstrate that this is not a simple debate, but a multifaceted topic. Boards, governments, corporates, and labour will all need to work together if we are to close the income gap in a fair, equitable and ethical way.

Governance and responsiveness

The question is sometimes asked: when it comes to big corporations, especially listed ones, can leaders be quick to respond while buried under a mound of governance issues, in comparison with start-up companies, which are not shackled in this way?

Corporations can respond with speed. The difference between them and a start-up in terms of governance is that they have an array of people able to deal with such issues. This frees up the CEO and his executive team to move quickly, making sure the company responds quickly to the VUCA context in which they find themselves. Let us take, for instance, listing requirements.

There is a whole "army" of experts within the company's secretarial services division who deal with those types of issue. So if a corporation has to comply with the Sarbanes-Oxley Act of 2002 (SOX), or King III, it is the responsibility of the company secretary and the legal people to make sure that the compliance forms are filled in and all relevant disclosures made. No CEO or executive leader in a big organisation would have the time to deal with this.

What they have to worry about is understanding what impact such governance requirements and issues will have on their company; making sure their board is apprised with regard to changes in governance; ensuring that their company complies by delegating responsibilities appropriately; and then overseeing the processes and the people who are responsible. Even start-ups such as Uber are not immune. In most countries, including South Africa and the UK, small companies have to comply with the same laws as big ones. Often, the only difference is whether one's company is listed or not.

Company agility

It is possible for major companies to be agile, too, given the VUCA context. It depends on how the company is structured to allow for an effective interface between the CEO and his/her subordinate teams, affecting the level of agility of the company. The deeper the hierarchical structure, the more difficult it is to be agile. So it really is about flattening the structure and cutting out layers. Traditional hierarchical structures have made it difficult for leadership as a collective to be agile and respond quickly. Previously, it took too long to convey messages, decisions and solutions up and down through the vertical structure. If one looks at today's modern company structures, deep hierarchies largely do not exist.

Most leaders and new CEOs in the last seven years have focused on their company structure to see how they can contribute to quicker decision-making through better delegation of powers and empowerment of roles. They have started by making sure that the structure is flat so that the CEO is close enough to his/her fellow leaders and organisation to understand what is happening. In a flatter structure with no silos, he/she can delegate and empower more confidently, knowing everyone is tuned in to everyone else and fully aligned on goals and direction. If one is operating in silos, one person may be unaware of something that is happening in a context that may threaten the company. He/she would have no way to appreciate its full impact on the company as a whole, and will be unable to feed his/her observations into the brains trust and war room of the company.

Today's leaders hold regular townhouse meetings which go deeper and deeper into the organisation. It is no longer the leaders speaking to only 20 people in their direct line of reporting. Instead, CEOs are reaching out to 2 000 and more employees in one go at these meetings. They can thereby ensure that a unified message goes out as quickly as possible, and reaches into the very belly of the company. Communication technology, like social media, also helps the CEO to communicate with every employee of the company, no matter where they are based. Technology has really been a game changer for communications in the 21st century.

Digital connectivity also helps companies to pick up on what is happening much more quickly, even from a disruptive competitor's perspective. Nowadays it is not as easy for a competitor to surprise one as in the past. Companies can now pick up market intelligence easily, merely by using what is available in the public domain. For instance, one can now see what a company's competitors are doing thanks to Twitter, Instagram and other social media platforms such as Facebook. People today will sit in a company conference or meeting and excitedly Tweet the slides being shown on the screen, inadvertently sending pictures of their company's future strategy or tactics as they try to "capture the moment". How easy it is to Tweet: "Tired, but going for 10-hour stretch as we prepare for the launch of a new *xyz* variant in 2 months…" And suddenly, the cat is out of the bag!

Today's digital world makes it very difficult to steal a march on your competitor. Therefore companies have to put certain measures in place to sensitise employees about being discreet. They have to be very careful what they post on social media platforms, or even what they communicate to family and friends regarding the company.

Leadership Requirements Today

It is quite difficult to separate the requirements of a leader today and the leader of the future, because we are living the future now. What is required of a leader today is basically a demonstration that we are already living in the future. Knowledge, skills and expertise we thought would be required in 2020 are now required today. We live in a dynamic and ever-changing world.

It is my contention that at a minimum today's leadership requirements, and going into the future, are composed of the following: listening, acting and facilitating; ethics, political savviness; collaboration; and strategic risk taking.

Listening, acting and facilitating

A leader today *needs big ears* – the ability to listen not only to what is happening within and outside the company, but to have the *skill to respond appropriately*. The leader needs to have "*long, sensitive fingers*", so he/she can have his/her finger on the pulse of what's happening. Furthermore, the leader has to understand how *to facilitate both individual and collective learning* in his/her company in order to really enable his/her company to grow. He/she has to turn his/her company into a learning organisation.

Ethics

It should go without saying that a leader needs *to be ethical* and set the right moral tone at the top. The saying that "[t]he fish rots from the top" has never been truer than in business and government contexts today. One can detect virtually immediately that the decline started right at the highest level when one reads stories of companies that have gone astray ethically. Enron and Fidentia come to mind. The ethical decay seldom starts with employees. It almost inevitably starts at the top.

Political savviness

Another key leadership requirement is having *political savviness*. This means understanding and being sensitive to the political context and issues in which one operates. For example, the gap between the Haves and Have Nots comes to mind as a worldwide debated sociopolitical issue. I do not know of any CEO today who is unaware of the pressing challenges associated with this gap. At issue is how to correct it. One will have to uplift people in monetary terms significantly and/or redistribute the wealth of the super-wealthy; this was the key theme at the 2015 World Economic Forum. It is a matter of who is willing to compromise and sacrifice what. CEOs know that they have to face the myriad issues attached to the gap debate head-on, and not shy away from this challenge or the ongoing debate regarding CEO pay.

Being politically savvy enough to understand these issues against the backdrop of today's broader VUCA context means that leaders cannot isolate themselves from whoever governs at that given point or the stakeholders, who have the social media at their fingertips to influence, steer and guide public opinion and views with regard to these issues. Another example is the degree of industry regulation in force. Whether one is in a highly regulated industry or not is not the issue. The vital issue is being close enough to understand the dynamics of the context together with the stakeholders in the areas in which one's company operates and into which it is moving.

Collaboration

Unless one sets up *the right partnerships*, particularly within the digital context, it will be hard to move one's company forward and take full advantage of the opportunities that are currently available in the world of tomorrow. Companies such as Unilever, Procter and Gamble, and GE recognise that, while they can hire people who possess good ICT skills, the pace moves so fast that collaboration with people whose main purpose and job is to understand the digital space while one is taking care of other issues, such as innovating and launching consumer products, is a must.

One cannot spend all one's time as a leader trying to keep up with trends in the digital space and making sure that one has the necessary skills to do that. It is impossible. Collaboration is essential. Collaboration through alliance formation will come into even sharper focus for the leader of the future.

Strategic risk taking

It goes without saying that a leader today has *to be results-orientated*, and able to unlock shareholder value, while understanding and responding to the socio-politico-economic issues of the day confronting him/her. Strategic risk taking forms an inherent part of his/her engagement as a leader within the VUCA context. South African companies have frequently been criticised for being too risk averse and not investing enough in our country and beyond. But a closer look shows that South African companies are investing significantly in other high-risk countries, because these countries are easier to do business in; have good incentives; and provide higher returns than South Africa. Countries such as China, Nigeria and Angola come to mind in this regard.

I would contend that South African companies are not risk averse as such. However, there could be issues in the investment context of a particular country that makes it more difficult for these companies to invest there. Shareholders generally know and understand the strategy of companies they have invested in. So they would understand that if a company is sitting on a pile of cash, it is not because they are risk averse, but that they had possibly already identified assets they want to go after, which may not even be in the country where the company is domiciled. They are possibly only waiting for the right timing to make their investment move.

A Future Perspective

Gazing into a crystal ball at where we will be in five or 10 years from now, what will we see? I believe that at a minimum, future leadership requirements will embrace the following critical abilities: meeting the aspirations of the millennials to be led; clarity of purpose accompanied by radical innovation; fit-for-purpose alliances; balancing conflicting demands; and demonstrating the leadership attributes of adaptability, agility and resilience.

Meeting the aspirations of the millennials to be led

Millennials are the future generation to be led by leaders. What they probably would like to see is clarity of purpose in the companies with which they associate themselves. They are no longer interested in companies which are just out to make profit. They want to associate themselves with companies that are not interested only in making money but also in driving corporate social investment (CSI). They will demand to be led by leaders who are committed among other things to reducing our environmental footprint, and improving the lives of the poor.

Unilever has set the standard for such leadership. When Paul Polman became CEO of Unilever seven years ago, he put together a "Unilever Sustainable Living Plan" (USLP). This was so compelling that he was able to mobilise his whole company and the Board behind it. He has driven his company to make sustainable living commonplace. I think he is succeeding today because USLP has become the global yardstick and benchmark against which other companies are judged from a sustainability perspective. That is a step in the right direction for the world and humanity, and meeting the needs and expectations of the millennials.

Clarity of purpose accompanied by radical innovation

Essential to future leaders is to have complete *clarity of purpose* translated into a clear, compelling vision which is meaningful to people, inter alia millennials. This purpose must be compelling not only to the public but also to the people who have to make it happen, the employees of the company. Everyone has to say: "Count me in. This is what I want to do." It has to be so inspiring that when people in, for example, Research and Development are thinking of an innovation, they are thinking: "How will this contribute to the company's greater purpose?"

Returning to Paul Polman of Unilever, his clarity of purpose was so compelling because he not only presented it as a "paper" statement, but also translated it into hard, tangible numbers: the billions of people whose lives Unilever needs to improve through better health; the number of small farmers whose livelihoods Unilever needs to uplift. He stressed the impact on the environment by boldly stating that by 2020 Unilever will double its revenue but halve its environmental footprint. The company's annual report tracks progress against these objectives. Where they have not been met, it is acknowledged openly and publicly and corrective actions are indicated.

If one looks around one, one sees countless other examples of innovations that contribute positively to the context. A further good example of a sustainable innovation is around waterless shampoos that allow one to wash one's hair without using water. There are multiple areas into which future leaders will need to look in order to bring future sustainability through innovation linked to a clear purpose. These innovations can also involve administration: for example, developing paperless offices, and offices designed to use only natural light. These types of initiatives are amazing, compelling, and very courageous. They demand leaders with a clear purpose translated into a compelling vision, as well as demonstrating the courage of a pioneer.

But one company cannot do it alone. Companies today are under tremendous pressure to follow Unilever's example and clearly declare what their purpose going forward will be. Clarity of purpose is a non-negotiable for the leader of today, and for the leader of the future. Having such a purpose focuses people's minds on how they can do things differently in order to make and leave the world a better place for future generations.

Fit-for-purpose alliances

It will become increasingly difficult for companies to operate in isolation. This means a greater need to build alliances at various levels. These alliances will be with people and companies who have the same purpose as they do on issues such as sustainability within the framework of anti-trust rules.

Again, Unilever provides the perfect example. When sourcing palm oil, an ingredient that goes into soap products, it is required for them to certify and verify that the palm oil was not produced on farms created through deforestation. They are willing to pay a premium to farmers not to devastate forests, in this way procuring palm oil that does not in its production compromise sustainability. Other companies need to copy this model and follow this example, if they are to have a positive impact on the sustainability of the environment. Sustainable procurement is costly, so companies do this at the risk of being less competitive. However, their reward comes in the growth of the credibility of their brand. Today's modern consumer, particularly the millennials, love such initiatives so much that they are willing to shift their loyalty to products that have a greater purpose than just tasting, looking or smelling good.

Cost should also not be a factor when one is endeavouring to reduce child mortality to almost non-existent levels. The challenge in India for Unilever was that most children do not live past the age of five. This is due to diarrhoea and diseases caused by hygiene issues such as the non-washing of hands. Through Lifebuoy soap the company built alliances with India's Department of Health, and runs huge campaigns with schools to make sure there is enough education around washing hands to save lives and help children grow. The loyalty to Lifebuoy through this campaign has grown tremendously.

Balancing conflicting demands

Going forward in the VUCA context, leaders will need to make very difficult decisions. Balancing socio-politico-economic issues and ethical considerations simultaneously with shareholders' expectations of returns, as well as investing money in the execution of strategic plans while focusing on a greater purpose, will see future leaders having to make really tough decisions on what they support and how to support it.

They will need to structure their business carefully to make sure that they not only survive a tough future but thrive sustainably over the longer term. For example, making tough decisions about what divisions/product lines to focus on, and which ones to curb or terminate, will be major areas of concern. Furthermore, the countries in which they wish to do business, and which countries to exit, will be crucial. They will have to look at a country and assess whether the investment context is conducive, restrictive or worrisome, and whether exiting a city, town or village will mean its downfall. They must still have the courage to make the right decision. Being a leader in the future will require guts in abundance.

Adaptability, agility and resilience

The VUCA world will remain with us going into the future, and may even intensify. Critical leadership attributes to make leaders future-fit under these conditions would be adaptability, agility and resilience. Adaptability is essential because things will continue to change at a pace most of us cannot even contemplate. Agility will be needed in order to find new answers and solutions quickly as the context changes at the speed of light. Resilience, the ability to bounce back regardless of setbacks, wrong decisions, failures and crises, is also extremely important in the fight for economic survival.

The knocks – the tennis balls in the dark (see above) – are going to be with us for a long time to come. So leaders will need to drive their companies to take the knocks; dust themselves off, perhaps saying, "What just hit us?"; and then move forward very quickly.

In summary: tomorrow's leader is not just someone with the right degrees and connections. He/she will need to be the person who is "lion" enough to lead an "army of sheep" to victory.

Conclusion

Every challenge invokes opportunities. The ones highlighted in this chapter are no exception. The east-and-south shift will encourage business leaders to delve deeply into and immerse themselves fully in these regions in order to understand new cultures, explore new markets, and nurture fresh talent. They will have to harness the digital revolution of anywhere, anytime, anyone and anyhow in order to leverage exciting innovations that will lead to growth. Disruptors will bring new life into old industries and markets, forcing leaders to act with speed, adaptability and agility, seeking value-adding alliances.

The socio-politico-economic context will remain volatile into the foreseeable future, as the consequences and full impact of events such as Brexit become clearer. What is important for leaders to understand is that after these challenges will come further waves of change, which explains the need for constant research, analysis and fresh insights. The concept of "learning organisations" will not only take on a new meaning but become the way of doing business. Successful leaders will be those who are able to articulate a clear purpose and translate that into an inspiring vision and competitive strategy for their companies; build a rich pipeline of talent; make courageous decisions; and with agility quickly adapt to a rapidly changing world.

Chapter 10

POLITICAL LEADERSHIP[i]
Chris Landsberg

Prior to the independence of Tanganyika, I had been advocating that the East African countries should federate and then achieve independence as a single political unit. I had said publicly that I was willing to delay Tanganyika's independence in order to enable all the three mainland countries to achieve their independence together as a single federated state. I made the suggestion because of my fear – proved correct by later events – that it would be very difficult to unite our countries if we let them achieve independence separately. Once you multiply national anthems, national flags and national passports, seats of the United Nations, and individuals entitled to a 21-gun salute, not to speak of a host of ministers, prime ministers and envoys, you would have a whole army of powerful people with vested interests in keeping Africa balkanised.[1]

Works and analyses on leadership abound. More than that: they are overwhelming. But scant attention is paid to questions of political leadership: leadership in the context of struggles for power and control of resources in society, whether in democratic or non-democratic contexts. This is surprising, given that in Africa, we are dealing with a highly politicised context. Much more attention should be given to notions of political leadership in the context of Africa's continental interstate system.

Any assessment of Africa's interstate leadership challenges should start with the contextual continental complexity factors and dynamics. The African context is characterised by conditions of complexity, and dynamics of ongoing tensions and conflict. It is a fluid and dynamic context; in a state of flux, constantly unearthing shifts and starts, dilemmas and paradoxes; and forever in a transitory mode. Convergences are as much a part of the landscape as divergences. In short, the African context is at best a complicated one, and at worst a complex-chaotic one in which African leaders need at least to engage, let alone survive.

This chapter endeavours to advance the new idea of collective continental African agentic leadership, covering a number of topics and challenges, namely the complex African terrain; advancing a multidimensional notion of agency; making a distinction between transactional, visionary and democratic transformational leadership approaches; zeroing in on the pivotal decade of 1998–2008 as an example of proactive agentic leadership; dealing with the decline on African agency; and, finally, posing the need to restore the continent's collective agentic leadership.

The Complex African Context

Unlike the macro-internal contexts of China and India, which are huge individual states with populations of more than 1.4 billion each, the macro-internal context of Africa reveals the third largest continent in the world, with about 1.1 billion people, but made up of 54 states, if western Sahara is included. This reality results in the perpetual challenge of having to sing from the same political sheet, and needing to speak with one voice. This is the challenge of creating harmony among the disparate African voices.

---

i I am grateful to Dr. Ademola Araoye from Nigeria for his invaluable comments and critiques of an earlier draft of this paper.

Africa is a highly fragmented and atomised continent. The Pan-African interstate leadership challenge is therefore that of getting a vast plurality of states – some mega, some medium size and some micro – all with their own political, economic social and political challenges. Speaking with 'one voice' tends to elude the continent more often than not.[2] At times the different states on the continent come across as disjointed and even split pieces. Added to this variable is the fact that Africa has to find its voice and assert 'a' strategic agenda in the context of a fluid and vast changing post-apartheid, post-Cold War continental order.

This is a global order in which Western triumphalism reigns supreme. New powers like China and Russia, Brazil and India are emerging, often displaying the same imperialistic economic tendencies *vis-à-vis* the continent, even though the continent and its leaders would not readily admit this. As Mommo Muchie and Demissie Hailemichael[3] express it, "Africa is now in a situation reminiscent of the olden days. It is caught between old and new powers vying for their own spheres of influence in yet another edition of the 'scramble for Africa'".

A third variable in the macro-African context is that, while Africans in the main profess to believe in a supra-national United States of Africa (USAf) – the idea that the African nation-state as we know it, will be transcended – state sovereignty still is a vital socialising factor, as not all states are eager to cede their sovereignty.[4] Thus, whereas the rhetoric is pro-Pan-African paradigms, the reality is of African political elites who glorify national interest, as opposed to continental interest. The talk of commitment to Pan-African supra-national schemes notwithstanding, the Africa of the early 21st century is one in which leaders cling to narrow sovereignty and self-interests, and typically compete with each other instead of co-operating.

Highlighting another variable here, and added to the problem of being fragmented and patchy, Africa is struggling to come up with an agentic formula that would help it speak with one voice, and act upon the basis of a common continental agenda. In practice, prevarication and dilly-dallying characterise African responses. The African Agenda may very well be in jeopardy. This is mainly due to a lack of leadership and implementation of, and compliance with, that Agenda on the part of Africans, and undermining of the continent by the international community in general, and by Western powers in particular.

Drawing on my engagements of African interstate bodies, and contacts with diplomats and politicians throughout the continent, and my reading of a wide range of literature on the subject, this paper will examine the fragmentation of Africa. It will be argued that the latest failure to organise itself into a credible union, with a voice in its own dealings with the rest of the world, has largely been the result of poor leadership among Africans on the one hand. On the other hand, there has been concerted sabotage by the very powers who have claimed to have Africa's interests at heart, whereas it is actually only its resources they want.

This brings us to the compliance variable which reminds us that individual and collective agency and leadership in Africa matters. This begs the question: how do we get African states in general, and leaders and governments in particular, to behave in a manner that is befitting of a society or community of states on the basis of common norms, values, principles, and vitally, institutions? Indeed, during the apartheid and post-colonial decades, the major preoccupation of African states was to rid the continent of apartheid, colonial rule and white minority domination. It was only in the post-Cold War, post-apartheid era that the continent's states and leaders could give their attention to the question of building a community or society by which the continent's 54 states could negotiate common institutions, norms, principles and policies on which they could agree to subject themselves to and live by.

However, their project is often undermined by the tardiness and political gimmickry of some states within their own ranks, and also by the overt and covert efforts of external powers who would like to see this project of building a community of African states fail. This process of building a society of states – or a community of states – could be referred to as *continentalism*.

As a project, it would take the independence of African states as a reality and seek ways for them to co-operate more effectively and build common approaches to addressing problems.[5] But the major responsibility rests on the shoulders of African states to assert their agency and influence in order to meet their objectives. Foreigners will not offer them autonomy and development on a silver plate.

African states should realise that, during the anti-liberation and anti-colonial struggle decades, the major strategic question that needed to be answered was: "Who should govern over Africans?" Today, the major thought leadership questions that Africans need to confront are: "How do Africans wish to be governed?" and "What should be done to secure the economic emancipation and restore the human dignity of African people?"

Towards a Multidimensional, African Agentic Leadership Approach

Leadership is not a unidimensional, linear event. It is a dynamic, multidimensional, ephemeral and transient process and phenomenon. The very idea of leadership speaks to agency, influence and actorness. Gary Yukl defines leadership as "the process of influencing others to understand and agree about what needs to be done and how to do it". Yukl goes on to assert that leadership is "the process of facilitating individual and collective efforts to accomplish shared objectives".[6]

This raises the question of whether and how African leaders have gone about trying to mobilise individuals and groups in an attempt to realise the continent's strategic objectives. Oates also makes the link between agency and leadership when he contends that leadership is the art of helping, guiding and influencing people to act towards achieving a common goal. Oates rightly observes that leadership covers the entire spectrum of human aspects, such as intellectual, social, economic, political, behavioural, physical, spiritual, psychological, biological and environmental dimensions. All these factors certainly pertain to the African context.[7]

A collective agency approach

Finding solutions to the multiplicity of challenges faced by the African continent will not come about through unidimensional and single-factor solutions. As such, Africa requires a new and multidimensional political agentic leadership approach that would make it possible for this kaleidoscope and proliferation of states to speak with one voice in addressing the question of how Africa is to become a part of the proliferation of states, and simultaneously respond to the economic emancipation challenge.

Africa has to address the challenge of what Francis Kornegay and I have called "the one and the many" – how to construct one coherent voice among many.[8] The leadership approach at the interstate level that could be explored is what I would like to call the collective agency approach.[9] By agency we mean enhancing the voice, influence, interest and power of Africans by means of African states forming collective coalitions, networks and associations that would allow them to act in concert to attain their important strategic goals.[10] Indeed, agency refers to actorness, action-ness and manoeuvrability on the world stage. Actorness and action-ness require what I would call actionists. You need states to act as agents. In turn, agents need to act, because agency derives from actorness, and those actors who can shape and direct events in order to achieve certain outcomes.

Agency, or agentic leadership, refers to the ability to shape and change processes, events and outcomes, and even to have an impact on structures in human life.[11] Agency refers to exerting influence and driving events and processes. It comes about from deliberate and calculated acts seeking to influence events and actors in ways that would serve your own interests. When an actor displays agency, such an actor is able to influence, sway, control, direct and impel.

Although the African Union (AU) has in recent years toyed with the idea of a 'Union Government', that is, transforming the AU Commission in Addis Ababa into an authority on a par with that of independent African states, the reality is that it is not going to happen.[12] There is no continental government in Africa that can speak on behalf of the collective, and there will not be one for many decades to come. We will therefore not be able to realise the Pan-African ideal of a United States of Africa (USAf).

Furthermore, there is no one state powerful enough to lead any sub-region, let alone an entire continent. There are no hegemons in Africa. The closest we have to influential states that could exercise regional leadership are pivotal states in the form of South Africa, Nigeria, Senegal, Kenya, Algeria, or Egypt. But all of them have challenges with other states accepting their leadership roles, on top of the many domestic challenges that they face.[13] Again, we should stress that, as a continent inhabited by this plurality of states, Africa faces a unique leadership challenge of having to weave together collective agency or leadership in order to advance not just the narrow selfish interests of any one state, but the common interests of a vast community of states.

Given the vast and often competing interests harboured by different African states, a 'big-brother', 'hegemonic' leadership approach would not suffice.[14] Such an approach would only ferment alienation and antipathy among African states, and possibly even outright conflict and deadly wars, just as a 'big-brother' approach continentally would not suffice. So a "Big Man of Africa" stance within individual states would also negate chances of progress on the continent as it seeks to address the vast social, economic, developmental and peace and security challenges faced by the continent.

The "Big Man of Africa" model as well as the "big-brother" model would amount to what Angus-Leppan, Metcalf and Benn[15] called "authoritarian leadership". Leaders, usually powerful and domineering individuals, would make decisions and adopt policies on behalf of groups by dishing out instructions and demanding compliance, and lead by *diktat* and fiat. In this model, the leader positions him-/herself as the central commander. The leader is one who is not to be questioned, and is the embodiment of all wisdom. The entire organisation or state machinery is made dependent and subservient to such a leader. This individual regards himself as the extension of the African state. We have many examples of this leadership on the African continent: Robert Mugabe of Zimbabwe, in power since 1980; Yoweri Museveni of Uganda, at the helm for 30 years; Eduardo Dos Santos of Angola, who has been in power for more than 36 years, since 1979; Pierre Nkuronziza of Burundi, who in 2015 insisted on running for a third term as president of Burundi, and literally took his country to the brink of civil war, which may verge on potential genocidal conflict.

These "Big Men" of Africa often resort to "autocratic" leadership tendencies to impose their wills. Ademola Araoye refers to "one man states" which operate on the basis of "illegal and dubious constitutional elongation of constitutional term limits" and abuse of privileges in the neo-patrimonial state.[16] Garth le Pere echoed the sentiments expressed here when he opined that "prominence of personal rule and 'Big Man' politics account for real and latent authoritarian tendencies often accompanied by corruption and the ubiquitous appropriation of public resources for personal gain and aggrandisement".[17]

The other extreme is the approach that seems to be displayed by leaders such as South Africa's President Jacob Zuma and former Nigerian President Goodluck Jonathan during his term in office. Salman et al call this the "*laissez-faire*" leadership approach, which would also not work in the African context.[18] This approach would amount to a unilateral go-it-alone approach, a free-for-all scenario in which states simply fend for themselves and disregard the interests of others. Leaders engage in zero sum politics instead of a win–win approach in which the common interests of sub-regions and the broader continent are promoted. There seems to be a *laissez-faire* approach in South Africa currently. In the African context, '*laissez-faire*' would also mean that individual states could do as they please and undermine common African institutions and programmes.

As discussed above, agency refers to 'actorness': the power to act and influence. It is about leaders coming together to act in unison. The collective agentic leadership approach advocated here could accommodate a multitude of different leadership styles and approaches. As a multidimensional approach, it could include elements of inspirational and visionary leadership; transactional leadership; democratic leadership; and transformational leadership. Agency literally means influence and the ability to bring about change in prevailing structural conditions. We are therefore dealing here with a structure–agency problem.

Visionary direction

The collective agency, or continental agentic leadership model, suggests first and foremost that, in order to exert influence abroad, Africans must first show responsibility and assume responsibility for their destiny internally, or exercise endogenous agency within the continent. It could start, for example, by taking ideational responsibility for the continent's emerging governance, peace and security, development and co-operation agendas.

As such, the continent is in need of what we could call "visionary thought leaders",[19] those leaders with the capability of exercising strategic analytical capacity in order to dissect the continent's challenges and then offer innovative African solutions for African problems. There is no gainsaying that, in the African context, Mbeki displayed the quality of ideational and thought leadership.

Transactional leadership

But the continent also needs transactional leaders who can constantly build ties and form networks with different state leaders, interstate bodies and actors in the private sector and civil society, including international governments together with state and non-state actors so that all of these could support Africa's and not their own narrow self-interests. This presupposes that the visionary thought leaders and transactional leaders would have a clear grasp of the continent's challenges and would be willing and able to take ownership of the continent's agenda.

Democratic transformational authority

The continent would also be able to benefit from democratic transformational leaders who would be willing to embrace and strengthen the continent's emerging development, peace and security, governance, and co-operation architecture based on strong norms, values and principles which states should appropriate, internalise and domesticate. They should be willing to engage the continent's sovereignty-obsessed governments to inculcate these values and principles at home and abroad, including in their personal lives.

Democratic transformational leaders should augment capable functional leaders within continental institutions, most notably the AU and organs such as the AU Commission, the Peace and Security Council (PSC), the Permanent Representatives Committee (PRC), and Regional Economic Communities (RECs) such as the Southern African Development Community (SADC), the Economic Community of Central African States (ECCAS), the Common Market of East and Southern Africa, the East African Community (EAC), the Economic Community of West African States (ECOWAS), and others.

While the democracy and democratisation questions have been placed firmly on the continental agenda since the end of the Cold war, African states and leaders remain ambivalent about democracy promotion and state society relations. Notwithstanding the African Charter for Democracy, Elections and Governance (ACDEG) which was drafted and came into force in 2012 in order to foster democratic governance in Africa, the domestication of constitutional democracy remains a challenge on the continent (EISA, 2015).[20] Countries like Senegal, Angola, Zimbabwe, Burundi, Algeria, Burkina Faso, the DRC, Uganda, Rwanda and others have grappled with presidential term-limits in their countries (EISA, 2015).[21]

Also, in spite of the ACDEG's promulgation, or the AU Constitutive Act's doctrine "from non-interference to non-indifference", the continent has continued to struggle with "unconstitutional changes of government" or *coups d'état*. Since 2012, the problem revealed itself in Burundi, Central African Republic (CAR), Egypt, Guinea Bissau, Mali, Madagascar, and Sao Tome and Principe (EISA 2015).[22] The frequency of these episodes of unconstitutional changes of government shows that the norm of "from non-interference to non-indifference" did not really consolidate at national, regional or even constitutional levels. Some have referred to a practice of "constitutional dictatorships" in some parts of the continent, in which constitutionalism is used as a hindrance to democratic consolidation (EISA 2015).[23]

The Renaissance Decade 1998–2008: Key Moments in African Agentic Leadership

It is important to consider examples of African agency and agentic leadership in action, and look in particular at how personal, institutional and interpersonal and interstate leadership was being considered previously. Indeed, Africa's political leadership narrative "… has revolved around the notions of Pan-Africanism and an African Renaissance, as philosophical underpinnings to its endeavours".[24] There are many examples of collective agency moments we could point to, including post-liberation Pan-Africanism; the Renaissance moment; and, of course, Agentic African leadership.

Post-liberation Pan-Africanism

The partition of Africa turned the continent into the most fragmented, and what the 2007 African Union Audit Report called an "atomised" continent. In response to this partition, many Pan-Africans in the diaspora such as Sylvester Williams, WEB du Bois, Marcus Garvey, Joseph Casely-Hayford, George Padmore, and others engaged in plurilateral diplomacy and ideational leadership as they started organising Pan-African Congresses to campaign for the liberation of African peoples. Key points were the Pan-African Congresses of 1900 and 1945.[25] From the onset, these individuals stressed the idea of a Pan-Africanism that would speak to liberation, independence, unity, autonomy, and African agency.[26]

Another pivotal moment was the creation of the Organisation of African Unity (OAU) in 1963, when Kwame Nkrumah and others accelerated the fight for African independence. During this time, actors such as Nkrumah himself, of Ghana, Prof. Cheikh Anta Diop of Senegal, President Modibo Kaita of Mali, and President Sekou Toure of Guinea organised under the auspices of the Casablanca Group, pushed for the idea of a United States of Africa (USAf) to be formed. For them, African agency could be realised only through forging a grand scheme of a federalist, united Africa. This group advocated for the idea of immediate and total integration of the African continent.

Contrasted with this group were the Brazzaville and Monrovia groups, who favoured a gradualist approach to the concept of African unity, starting with regional and cultural integration. This group consisted of Nigeria, Sierra Leone, Liberia, Togo, Ivory Coast, Cameroon, Senegal, Chad, Gabon, Ethiopia, Tunisia, and Tanzania, among others. The Brazzaville group included the former French colonies of Central African Republic, Ivory Coast, Mauritania, Gabon, Chad, Madagascar, and others. These two groups favoured progressive economic integration, and strong technical and economic co-operation, as opposed to political unification.

The differences among these states notwithstanding, they did agree on a number of important goals: the rapid de-colonisation of the continent; the unity of and co-operation among African states; advancing collective self-reliance; and defending the sovereignty and territorial integrity of African states.

During the 1970s we saw Africans taking the lead in establishing continental sub-regional bodies in a devolutionary bout of Pan-Africanism. During the 1980s, Adebayo Adedeji, described by Adebajo[27] as an African "Cassandra ... scholar–diplomat ... most renowned visionary of regional integration", and the African Economic Community (EAC) developed the African Alternatives to Structural Adjustment Programmes. They proceeded to adopt the Lagos Plan of Action of 1990, setting out details about how Africa's integration was to be achieved. This is another example of Africa's determination to set its own agenda and challenge foreign *diktats* and impositions. By the late 20th century, Africans had taken the time and effort to work on the transition from the OAU to the new African Union – a continental body with executive, judicial and legislative authority – with the aim of taking Africa into the 21st century.

African Renaissance – the golden epoch?

In my professorial Inaugural Address at the University of Johannesburg in August 2013, I invoked the notion of "Afro-centric diplomacy" and "African agency" during the Pivotal Renaissance decade, 1998–2008. I have elsewhere described this decade as the "golden decade".[28] For purposes of this analysis, I would like to zero in on a vibrant moment for African agentic leadership during the end of the 20th century and the beginning of the 21st century. Just on the scores of democratic, transformational, transactional and visionary thought leadership, one could point to what I have described as the "golden decade" of Africa's collective agency, the years 1998–2008, when the continent adopted many institutions, plans and programmes based on strong cosmopolitan values.[29]

Co-operative, co-ordinated and conjoint action

During this Renaissance decade, continental agency was exercised through strong "concert diplomacy". Many states, including South Africa, Nigeria, Senegal, Algeria, Mozambique, Tanzania, and Ghana, organised themselves into what I called a "concert of African states" in which states from the continent acted co-operatively and conjointly. This is what Gilbert Khadiagala called a "Renaissance coalition".[30] They were determined to articulate their own continental revival and international resurgence agendas that for once were to be crafted and owned by Africans, not outsiders.

They sought to put in place the building blocks of continental order. Concurrently, they were articulating a clear African outlook that prioritised political, economic, social and developmental renewal, backed up by genuine partnership. This was instead of the apparatus of patrimonial neo-colonialism that characterised its relations with the outside world, the industrialised powers in particular. These African states and many others, spearheaded by the "new" continental leadership coalition, demonstrated renewed agency and leadership as they sought to take responsibility for, and ownership of, the continent's future. Key members of the African agency network, or African agenda coalition, including Thabo Mbeki, Olesegun Obasanjo, John Kuofor, Joachim Chissano, Benjamin Mkapa, Meles Zenawi, and others, had left a void in agentic leadership, and the African Agenda had started to drift.

Bilateral interpersonal relationship

Thabo Mbeki and Olesegun Obasanjo cemented their bilateral relationship. They also engaged in an example of a network (or fellowship) style of leadership in which they came to appreciate the importance of their own inter-personal relationship, and the need to connect constantly with others. Some scholars refer to this kind of engagement as a "stakeholder model" of leadership through which leaders constantly build coalitions and partnerships. The bilateral relationship between them, they realised, was pivotal. They elevated their relationship to that of strategic partnership. They made a point of expanding their network (or association) to include other continental strategic partners in general, and showed a great deal of ideational leadership – the power of ideas. In addition, they demonstrated that with their brand of soft power and African diplomacy, under the banner of "African solutions for African problems",[31] they could help to influence international relations thinking.

It was Thabo Mbeki who was instrumental in articulating a vision for the continent. His was in essence an attempt to put on the agenda a vision of African political, economic, social and cultural rejuvenation. Obasanjo in turn crafted the idea of the Conference for Stability, Security, Development, and Co-operation (CSSDCA) in Africa, based on a belief that Africa needed its own variant of the Helsinki Initiative that stressed stability, security, development and co-operation. Mbeki and Obasanjo himself married their plans to come up with a new continental Renaissance vision.

Agentic extra-African influence

Members of the "African Renaissance" association did not merely try to influence the macro-African continental environment. They also set out to display agency by trying to change the complex extra-African environment. They set out to take Africa "to the world". One way in which they tried to do this was through ideational power, or the power of ideas.[32] They constantly worked on concrete policy proposals, and sought to lock partners into deals. They therefore often resorted to transactional leadership tactics.

They did so often against the backdrop of a hostile and inhospitable external environment that was dominated by Western and increasingly Asian and South American powers. Yet this did not deter them from seeking to put African concerns firmly on the international agenda, and trying to extract commitments from external powers that would help address the continent's vast political and socio-economic challenges. Driven by a second generation of Africans desiring to end centuries of humiliation and colonial domination, in which they were treated as second class citizens, they wanted a relationship with former colonial masters and outside powers, not of paternalism, arrogance and neo-colonialism, but of genuine partnership.

South Africa's President Thabo Mbeki, described by Adekeye Adebajo as "Africa's philosopher king" and "most influential Pan-African leader of his generation", was a key player during this golden decade.[33] At least since 1998, African states, spearheaded by Mbeki – arguably Africa's most engaged and assertive agentic, visionary and transformative leader – engaged the G8 and other international actors in favour of a new paradigm and relationship, namely strategic partnership, based on mutual development. Indeed, in 2000, during the annual G8 summit in Okinawa, Japan, history was made when African leaders first engaged the G8 leaders in search of this new post-Cold War development model.

They showed real leadership when they proposed a move away from a historical paternalistic and dependency relationship to one of genuine partnership, based on the principles of mutual respect, equality, responsibility and accountability, responsiveness, and an equitable world order, advocated under the AU/NEPAD framework. Accordingly, African expectations were that the new partnership would be – in the true sense of the word – a relationship based on equality. In such a relationship both sides – Africa and the rest – had something to contribute. This would be in contrast to the one-sided donor–recipient relationship that had characterised past interactions. No longer could agendas be imposed on Africa. Its own identified needs and priorities would instead be addressed.

The new partnership framework was supposed to draw on existing arrangements, while bringing strategic consolidation, coherence, expansion and result-orientated focus to the new architecture. It would therefore need to forge relationships with strategic partners willing to engage in its development agenda. Imbibing the core partnership principles was considered vital as a result of a growing sense of realism among a new generation of Africans that development partners had to adhere to such evolving norms and standards in order to redress the injustices of the past.

In particular, given the need to underpin African ownership and leadership of Africa's development agenda and process, the G8 offered – at Africa's insistence – the possibility of establishing a political process that could translate political will into mutual accountability, as well as an effective monitoring of commitments, vital to translating them into effective strategy and policy. Indeed, through NEPAD, African leaders sought to bring about a new strategic partnership between Africa and the outside world, and to help address the North–South divide, while also advancing South–South co-operation. These leaders showed vision by preparing positions on debt, free and fair trade, and accelerated and unconditional development finance. Very importantly, given the age of technological advancement, NEPAD's architects stressed the importance of information and communication, and the need to address Africa's poor position regarding technology.

In short, the African Renaissance was more than just a vision. It contained core priorities, as well as plans of action, and most importantly, a crop of leaders working on turning plans into outcomes and measurable results. They took upon themselves the responsibility of taking this to the foreign community for endorsement on the basis of the principles of mutual accountability and mutual responsibility. Through these principles Africa would be expected to account to international partners as much as they should account to Africans.

NEPAD as modernisationist plan

Some leaders exercised assertive ideational leadership by drafting the continent's own modernisationist development plan: the New Partnership for Africa's Development (NEPAD). NEPAD is a visionary plan and aspires to bring about "an integrated Africa, prosperous and peaceful, and driven by its own citizens, and a dynamic force in the global arena".[34] As a real demonstration of a commitment to agency and a clear agenda, NEPAD was dubbed by its architects as a "quest for a new partnership in Africa and between Africa and the outside world".

NEPAD envisaged a two-way partnership. It wanted to see a move away from paternalistic and parasitic relationships based on exploitation and subjugation. It wanted to ensure a genuine new paradigm of equality.[35] African leaders prepared positions on debt relief, free and fair trade, accelerated and unconditional development finance, and bridging the information and technology divide. The idea was for Africans to develop their own plans and agenda and gain buy-in from external partners, not the other way around.

NEPAD made linkages between "development, democratic governance, peace and security, and economic growth". These leaders stressed the importance of owning the agenda which had been drafted by them. Some of the items and emphases stressed economic and political modernisation, including education, health, infrastructural development, strengthening governance, and promoting democratisation.[36]

We should stress the emphasis on education and health care here, as these are suggestive of genuine developmental programmes. On the education front, it realised the importance of scientific and technological development. Some have even likened NEPAD to a "neo-liberal" scheme. But far from making the case for market fundamentalism, members of the African Renaissance league have not just made the case for the strengthening of the African state and its role in development, but have actually advocated for the transformation of African states into developmental states.[37] There is no gainsaying that NEPAD can be infused with more heterodox ideas such as the continent's leaders becoming serious about the continental free trade agreement (CFA), something that has enjoyed just lip-service to date without the requisite follow-through on these important ideas.

The African Peer Review Mechanism (APRM) as novel governance instrument

The establishment in 2003 of the African Peer Review Mechanism (APRM) was an example of this new dynamism on the continent. Post-independence Africa has long had an ambivalent relationship with democracy and governance, primarily because the continent's priorities during that period were to rid itself of the yokes of colonial rule and white minority domination.[38] South Africa, and some of its African partners, assumed key leadership roles. They displayed crucial agency in negotiating, and promoting a new political normative framework for the continent that included a governance and democratisation regime. Africans had learned bitter lessons from the structural adjustment years and did not wish to experience any forms of structural adjustment or foreign impositions. They decided to take responsibility for their own programmes.

In a clear commitment to agency, the promotors of the APRM were interested in bolstering "African ownership and leadership".[39] They realised that there was a need to "anchor the development of the continent on the resources and resourcefulness of the African people" by, *inter alia*, "accelerating and deepening of regional and continental economic integration", as well as "creating conditions that make the African countries preferred destinations by both domestic and foreign investors".[40]

The promotion of "good governance" in non-confrontational fashion – or in a quiet diplomatic manner – occupied a central position in the emerging African Agenda.[41] Africa wished to engage the industrialised and other powers on the basis not of neo-colonialism or neo-patrimonialism, but of genuine partnership based on the principles of mutual accountability and mutual responsibility.[42] If Africans continued to show seriousness about their own governance instruments, they should not be surprised if such vacuums started being filled by outsiders and normative frameworks began to be imposed on it from abroad.

The Decline of Agentic African Leadership

During the course of the past eight years or so, African agency has been on the wane. A palpable sense of vacuum started to reveal itself on the continent as leaders throughout the continent started to adopt an inward-looking posture and regime consolidation within their states. African leaders scarcely considered a common continental approach. Even programmes such as NEPAD and the APRM were allowed to drift and lost their strategic underpinnings. Because these programmes were (wrongly) associated with predecessors, leaders such as President Goodluck

Jonathan of Nigeria and Jacob Zuma of South Africa distanced themselves from the programmes.

There was a huge expectation that South Africa and Nigeria would continue to play pivotal roles on the continent. Some even suggested that these two regional anchors could come to play hegemonic roles on the continent. However, a sense of an insular approach has crept into the politics of these two states during the past decade. Added to this is the fact that great antipathy and tension crept into the bilateral relationship between the two. Their ties reached an all-time low by 2015. African agency among African states and leaders was set on the back-burner as there was little sign of states putting the notion of the common African interest on the agenda.

It is important that pivotal states such as South Africa, Nigeria, Kenya, Algeria, Ghana, Senegal, Egypt and others restore the sense of constructive solidarity between them. It is not all doom and gloom. President Jacob Zuma from South Africa has in recent years spearheaded the NEPAD Infrastructure Development Plan which seeks to mobilise over $60 billion in resources for continental projects. But here, too, we need concerted and co-ordinated continental action, and inroads to be made into the continent's vast development challenges. This will not come about through the efforts of one "Big Man".

Much more is needed. The post-2008 generation should step up to the plate and show responsibility and take ownership of the continental agenda. Joel Netshitenzhe[43] said in this regard: "The notions of Pan-Africanism and African Renaissance have not lost their relevance. But their inheritors," he continued, "are more than just fighters against what Africa does not like. Today's generations are – and should in their mindset act as – architects of a new socio-economic system in what should be an all-encompassing Continental Democratic Revolution".

A Future Perspective

Restoring African agency

Going forward and taking a peep into the future, we can categorically state that the African state system as we know it will not disappear. Fifty years from now, Africa will still be a continent made up of independent, sovereign, but not necessarily stable states. African agency will be as vitally needed as it is now.

The chief architect of the African Union's (AU) much-vaunted Agenda 2063, Dlamini-Zuma, argued that Africa's "most important priority is investment in people, including healthcare, water and sanitation, and education – in particular education in science, engineering, mathematics and technology".[44] Agenda 2063, she asserted, "prioritises Africa's industrialisation through value addition and beneficiation of the natural resources that the continent currently exports as raw materials – exporting jobs and raw material in the process".[45]

Akin to the international agenda set by the Renaissance Agenda, Dlamini-Zuma voiced the need for a partnership of "co-operation, based on mutual benefits and respect" that should continue to "evolve at bi-lateral and regional levels, and increasingly at continental level".[46]

Making Agenda 2063 a reality

If Agenda 2063 is to be more than just a pipe dream, then pro-active and individual African leaders, both in governments and within states, will become important. As such, critical leadership competencies will become more vital going into the future. Before Africans can expect outsiders to respect their agendas, they should first respect and take collective ownership of their agendas themselves, lest Agenda 2063's vision of a united and prosperous Africa is rendered a pipe dream. Agenda 2063 should be translated into a tangible set of actionable plans, with the emphasis on implementation. Africa has always been good at coming up with ideas and visions, but poor in turning such plans into tangible outcomes. Emphasis will have to be placed on common norms and values. But such common values will have to become "shared" values in which African leaders, states and regional organisations live by mutual and conjoint principles and ideals. Africans must continue to search for common ground, and it is in standards and tenets that such common ground could be found.

Functional leadership for effective institutions

But functional leadership will also have to be emphasised, as institutions matter. A big part of the continent's problem has been weak institutions at local, state, regional and continental level, and greater emphasis will have to be placed on functional and effective institutions if Africa is to tackle its 21st century challenges with greater confidence. Important AU structures and organs such as the AU Commission, the Peace and Security Council, the Panel of the Wise, the Permanent Representatives Committee, and the Pan-African Parliament have been under-funded and under-resourced, and politically undermined to the point that their political agency has been rendered almost ineffectual.

Without strong inter-state bodies, Africa cannot hope to achieve its political, economic and social potential. These continental structures and organs, together with Regional Economic Communities (RECs), must be strengthened and their capacities bolstered if we are going to realise the goal of 54 starting to act as one. So functional leadership will be as important as visionary and transformational leadership going forward.

In short, Africa cannot hope to claim the 21st or 22nd century as the African century unless it reasserts its agency through collective action, civic activism, and determined political will, anchored in thought leadership. In the words of one of Africa's foremost thought leaders, Joel Netshitenzhe,[47] "[a] Pan-African renaissance will not come of its own accord. It requires foresight in leadership, activism of society, and a renaissance of Africa's 'think industry' ".

Conclusion

At the present international juncture as we enter the second half of the second decade of the 21st century, African agency and leadership in world affairs are being threatened by a number of factors: lack of a common understanding on vision, mission and objectives; no common political ownership; and no display of collective leadership and sense of responsibility, among other things. African agency will always be undermined for as long as the continent's institutions, at national, regional and continental levels, remain weak, and are undermined by political and social elites.

All the talk about the "Africa rising" narrative notwithstanding, Africa therefore faces endogenous and exogenous challenges in leadership, and we should not adopt "either–or" approaches. It is important to be nuanced and stress both approaches.

During the past eight years or so, we have seen a vacuum emerging in African leadership. A lack of co-operation and strategising among African states appears palpable. This has grown to the extent that there is no real African concert of powers visible. Few African states embrace the AU or its institutions, currently rendering the continental project weak and rudderless. Gaps in policy-making leadership, and poor policy management, typically result in poor policy outputs and outcomes. Lack of policy or bad policy makes for bad policy implementation. The absence of strategic leadership in African continental policy and ownership of policy is conspicuous.

The breakthroughs of the early 1990s and first decade of the 21st century came about in part because of leadership and a "concert approach" to African diplomacy. At the current juncture, the lack of co-operation and co-ordination among African states, and the sense of fragmentation among them, means that the African Agenda is in jeopardy and the continent is both neglected and being undermined from abroad.

Indeed, there has been a high degree of policy discontinuity between the project as pursued by the first and second generations of African leaders, and the crop of leaders who came to replace them. In practice we have seen deviations and uncertainty creeping into Africa's continental posture, even a lack of political leadership. Continental policy in many senses appears to have become a victim of the fall-out between the crop of leaders who ushered in the turn of the millennium and those who came later.

Many of the new leaders and their supporters have tried very hard to distance themselves from the domestic and foreign policy projects of their predecessors. But this has triggered confusion, timidity and diplomatic coyness on the part of South Africa, Nigeria, Tanzania, Mozambique, and others. Western powers have responded to this with a new aggressive interventionism, coupled with a new aggressive cultivation and penetration of Africa by emerging powers such as China, India, Russia and others.

Many events and initiatives have the potential to destabilise, and at the very least deepen the continent's fragmentation. Pivotal states such as South Africa, Nigeria, Algeria, Ghana, Senegal, Kenya, in tandem with the AU in Addis Ababa, should show agentic leadership by combining transformational, transactional, democratic, visionary, servant, and thought leadership approaches. The many voices in African must be brought into harmony so that the continent can act as one and enhance its agency, influence and impact on world affairs.

Endnotes

1. Nyerere, 2006, p. 22.
2. AU Audit Report, 2007.
3. Muchie and Hailemichael, 2014, p. 27.
4. See endnote 2.
5. Landsberg, 2012.
6. Yukl, 2006, p. 8.
7. Oates, 2013, pp. 19–20.
8. Kornegay and Landsberg, 2009.
9. Kornegay and Landsberg, 2009, pp. 171–191.
10. Landsberg, 2013b.
11. Malope, 2016.
12. See endnote 2.
13. Adebajo & Landsberg, 2003.
14. Adebajo & Landsberg, 2003, pp. 11–26.
15. Angus-Leppan, Metcalf & Benn, 2010.
16. Araoye, 2013.
17. Le Pere, 2016, p. 19.
18. Salman et al., 2011.
19. Kondlo, 2014.
20. EISA, 2015.
21. Ibid.
22. Ibid.
23. Ibid.
24. Netshitenzhe, 2013, p. 21.
25. Bankie, 2007.
26. Ibid.
27. Adebajo, 2016b, p. 61.
28. Landsberg, 2013a.
29. Ibid.
30. Khadiagala, 2010, pp. 375–386.
31. Landsberg, 2013b, p. 14.
32. Ademola, 2013, p. 28.
33. Adebajo, 2016a.
34. Landsberg, 2015.
35. Rukato, 2013.
36. Ibid.
37. Edigheji 2007.
38. Ademola, 2013, p. 27.
39. Landsberg, 2013b, p. 15.
40. Ibid.
41. Sisulu, 2013, p. 9.
42. Mbeki, 2013, p. 14.
43. See endnote 24.
44. Dlamini-Zuma, 2015, p. 27.
45. Dlamini-Zuma, 2015, p. 29.
46. Ibid.
47. Netshitenzhe, 2013, p. 23.

References

Adebajo, A & Landsberg, C. 2000. 'Pax africana in the age of extremes'. *South African Journal of International Affairs*, 7(1):11–26.

Adebajo, A & Landsberg, C. 2003. 'South Africa and Nigeria as regional hegemons'. In M Baregu & C Landsberg (eds). *From Cape to Congo: Southern Africa's evolving security challenges*. Boulder, CO: Lynne Rienner. 171–203.

Adebajo, A. 2016a. *A Jacana pocket biography: Thabo Mbeki*. Auckland Park, Johannesburg, ZA: Jacana Media.

Adebajo, A. 2016b. 'A tale of three Cassandras: Jean Monnet, Raúl Prebisch, and Adebayo Adedeji'. In DH Levine & D Nagar (eds). *Region-Building in Africa: Political and economic challenges*. New York, NY: Palgrave Macmillan US, a division of Macmillan Publishers Limited. 53–67.

African Union (AU). 2007 (December). *High-level panel of the audit of the African Union audit report, Addis Ababa*. Addis Ababa, Ethiopia.

Andreasson, S. 2011. 'Africa's prospects and South Africa's leadership potential in the emerging markets century'. *Third World Quarterly*, 32(6):1165–1181.

Angus-Leppan, T, Metcalf, L & Benn, S. 2010. 'Leadership styles and CSR practice: An examination of sensemaking, institutional drivers and CSR leadership'. *Journal of Business Ethics*, 93(2):189–213.

Araoye, A. 2013. 'The African peer review mechanism in the context of the African renaissance'. *The Thinker*, 55:26–30.

Bankie, BF. 2007. Pan-African nationalist thought and practice. [Online]. Available: http://www.nathanielturner.com/panafricannationalistthoughtpractice.htm. [Accessed 26 May 2016].

Cilliers, J & Mills, G. 1999. *From peacekeeping to complex emergencies: Peace support missions in Africa*. Johannesburg, ZA: South African Institute of International Affairs.

Dlamini-Zuma, N. 2015. Evolving Sino-African relations prospects and opportunities. *New Agenda: South African Journal of Social and Economic Policy*, 58:27–29.

Dlamini-Zuma, N. 2015. Evolving Sino-African relations prospects and opportunities. *New Agenda: South African Journal of Social and Economic Policy*, 58:27–29.

Edigheji, O (ed). 2007. 'Rethinking South Africa's development path: Reflections on the ANC's policy conference discussion documents'. *Special Edition of Policy Issues and Actors*, 20(10), June. Johannesburg, ZA: Centre for Policy Studies.

Electoral Institute for Sustainable Democracy in Africa (EISA). 2015. *Recent trends in constitutional reforms in Africa: How do constitutions help or hinder democracy?* Concept Note, Tenth Annual EISA Symposium, 18–19 November 2015. Johannesburg, ZA.

Khadiagala, GM. 2010. 'Two moments in African thought: ideas in Africa's international relations'. *South African Journal of International Affairs*, 17(3):375–386.

Kondlo, K (ed). 2014. *Perspectives on thought leadership for Africa's renewal*. Pretoria, ZA: The Africa Institute of South Africa (AISA), a division of the HSRC.

Kornegay, FA & Landsberg, C. 2009. 'Engaging Emerging Powers: Africa's Search for a "Common Position"'. *Politikon*, 36(1):171–191.

Landsberg, C. 2002. 'The impossible neutrality? South Africa's policy in the Congo war'. In J Clark (ed). *The African stakes of the Congo war*. Basingstoke, UK & New York, NY: Palgrave Macmillan. 169–183.

Landsberg, C. 2010. 'South Africa's transformational approach to global governance'. *Africa Insight*, 39(4).

Landsberg, C. 2012. 'Afro-continentalism: Pan-africanism in post-settlement South Africa's foreign policy'. *Journal of Asian and African Studies*. [Online]. Available: http://jas.sagepub.com/content/early/2012/05/02/0021909612439741. [Accessed 26 May 2016].

Landsberg, C. 2013a. Afro-centric diplomacy: The golden decade 1998-2008 and Pan-African agency in world affairs. Professorial Inaugural Address, University of Johannesburg. [Online]. Available: http://www.uj.ac.za/newandevents/Pages/Afro-centric-Diplomacy-The-Golden-Decade-1998-2008-and-the-Pan-African-Agency-in-World-Affairs-Inaugural-address-Prof-Chris.aspx. [Accessed 26 May 2016].

Landsberg, C. 2013b. 'The African peer review mechanism (APRM): Afro-governance 10 years later'. *The Thinker*, 55(2):14–16. [Online]. Available: http://www.thethinker.co.za/resources/Thinker%2055.pdf. [Accessed 26 May 2016].

Landsberg, C. 2015. 'A "new" pan-africanism'. In C Villa-Vicencio, E Doxtader & E Moosa (eds). *The African renaissance and the Afro-Arab spring: A season of rebirth?* Washington, DC: Georgetown University Press. 157–170.

Le Pere, G. 2016. 'The African Union's agenda 2063: Building block or false dawn?'. *The Thinker*, 68:18–20. [Online]. Available: http://www.thethinker.co.za/resources/68%20le%20pere.pdf. [Accessed 26 May 2016].

Malope, T. 2016. *African agentic leadership: An inter-disciplinary analysis of Thabo Mbeki's political leadership*. MPhil dissertation. Johannesburg, ZA: Faculty of Management, University of Johannesburg.

Mbeki, T. 2013. 'Africa must unite – an imperative of our time'. *The Thinker*, 5:12–18. [Online]. Available: http://www.thethinker.co.za/resources/Thinker%2051%20full.pdf. [Accessed 26 May 2016].

Muchie, M & Hailemichael, D. 2014. 'Re-discovering and re-vitalising the neglected roots of pan-africanism, Ethiopianism for African renaissance and unity'. In M Muchie, V Gumede, P Lukhele-Olorunju & HT Demissie (eds). Unite or perish. Africa fifty years after the founding of the OAU. Pretoria, ZA: The Africa Institute of South Africa (AISA), a division of the HSRC.

Netshitenzhe, J. 2013. 'A pan-african renaissance in the next 50 years? Towards agenda 2063'. *The Thinker*, 51:20–21. [Online]. Available: http://blog.pan-africanparliament.org/wp-content/uploads/2013/05/AU-50th-Anniversary-Achievements-Challenges_EN.pdf. [Accessed 26 May 2016].

Rukato, H. 2013. 'NEPAD: Past, present and future'. *Africa Insight*, 42(3).

Salman, Z, Riaz, A, Saifullah, M & Rashid, M. 2011. 'Leadership styles and employee performance'. *Interdisciplinary Journal of Contemporary Research in Business*, 3(6):257–267.

Sisulu, L. 2013. 'Peer Review and the legacy of learning from each other'. *The Thinker*, 55(5):8–9. [Online]. Available: http://www.thethinker.co.za/resources/Thinker%2055.pdf. [Accessed 26 May 2016].

Yukl, G. 2006. *Leadership in organizations*. 6th ed. Upper Saddle River, NJ: Pearson Prentice Hall.

Chapter 11

RELIGION, SPIRITUALITY AND LEADERSHIP
Anthony Egan

This chapter will examine the dynamics of religion, spirituality and leadership. I shall argue that religious belief and practices influence leadership in a variety of ways based upon the structures of religious organisations. These structures mirror in many respects secular organisations – political, civil society, and corporate.

I shall suggest that there is a relationship between types of religion and their form of leadership, but that even within such types and forms there are subtle variations, generating organisational fluidity. Central to such variation is spirituality, which serves either to reinforce the pattern or subvert them. Generally, I shall suggest that spirituality has the effect of 'democratising' hierarchies, reinforcing networks, and moderating hybrid models.

Spirituality is somewhat simplistically (I would suggest wrongly) understood as religion in practice. It is also, I shall argue, a practice that moves beyond organised religion itself and looks at human core values and ultimate concerns. All of this has an implication for spirituality applied to leadership. Really effective leadership occurs where a leader's spirituality meshes with the organisational culture (and especially structure) of an organisation, with a resultant praxis that makes organisations effective.

I shall then explore how these forms can be applied to business, professions and public life. Drawing on the work of Chris Lowney and others who operate out of the paradigm of Ignatian spirituality, a tradition in which I am myself rooted as a Jesuit priest, I shall present the case for the *secular* application of spirituality to public life.

Unpacking the Term 'Spirituality'

The noted religious historian and spiritual director Philip Sheldrake has observed:

> *"Spirituality" has a more defined content when associated with historic religious tradition such as Christianity. In fact, Christianity is the original source of the word although it has now passed into other faith traditions, not least Eastern religions such as Buddhism and Hinduism. In Christian terms, spirituality refers to the way our fundamental values, lifestyles, and spiritual practices reflect particular understandings of God, human identity, and the material world as the context for human transformation. While all Christian spiritual traditions are rooted in the Hebrew and Christian scriptures and particularly in the gospels, they are also attempts to reinterpret these scriptural values for specific historical and cultural circumstances.*[1]

These observations help us to move beyond a narrow understanding of spirituality as simply prayer by setting it in a wider context: religion. I say 'a wider context' intentionally, because I contend below, with Sheldrake and others, that spirituality moves beyond religion itself. Later I shall also suggest that we need to interrogate the nature and structures of religions – which I see as a metaphor for organisations in general and types of businesses in particular – for us to see how a secular spirituality might assist the running and leading of organisations.

While spirituality may have begun within religion, and within Christianity in particular, it has today moved beyond its roots. Many who work in spiritual guidance now find that whereas fifty or one hundred years ago spiritual directees were practising religious believers, and more often than not ordained ministers within religions, this pattern has broken down. Many people outside the religious professions come for guidance and encouragement, along lines similar to those in psychotherapy. There has been a sometimes controversial but generally positive interaction between therapy and spiritual direction, often giving spiritual direction a new professionalism it had previously lacked. In addition, those engaging in a spiritual journey are no longer guaranteed to be adherents of one or other religious tradition or set of orthodox beliefs. Often spirituality appeals more to seekers after truth than the committed, to people who are on the margins of their faiths – or even to outsiders. A useful definition of spirituality (one among many) might be:

The deepest values and meanings by which people seek to live. In other words, "spirituality" implies some kind of vision of the human spirit and of what will assist it to achieve full potential.[2]

While orthodox religious believers may blanch at its dogmatic vagueness, this definition helpfully reflects the current state of spirituality and spiritual guidance in our era, an era where many are 'seekers' rather than adherents, and where the transcendent is found often in the secular, so much so that one sees today the emergence of what's sometimes called 'atheist spirituality'.[3]

In many traditions this levelled transcendence is viewed as a source of concern for organised religion but as an opportunity among those within the ministry of spirituality. For some it is an opportunity to lead seekers gently to faith; for others it facilitates ways for religious insiders and outsiders alike to negotiate for themselves a sense of meaning – however it is interpreted – and provide a reflective ground for ethical living. The latter, which recognises the ethical dimensions of spirituality, practical, affective and transformative,[4] is particularly relevant to our topic: spirituality for leaders and leadership.

The above observation serves not only as an outline of what is to come but also as a statement of limitation. My concern about spirituality (religious or secular) is not about the *personal* spirituality of a leader, but rather how spirituality as understood above may help a leader to lead. Similarly, while the question of spiritual counselling in organisations is a significant theme in itself, it is not my concern here. Rather my interest is how an organisational spirituality may contribute to the successful practice and overall ethos of an organisation.

Religions, Leadership and Spirituality

Just as in business and politics, so too in organised religion, varied structures exist with models of leadership that to a considerable degree accord with structure. Applying the political science theory of markets, networks and hierarchies (see, for example, Thompson et al 1991[5]) to organised religion, I would suggest that there are three basic models of religious (and secular) organisations, each of which tends towards particular forms of leadership. I would also suggest that organisational and leadership spiritualities, to be effective, need to be in synchronicity with structure – and if they are out of kilter, the organisation, and in particular its leadership, needs to decide what needs to change in order to make it effective.

Broadly, there are network/congregational religions, institutional/hierarchical religions, and what may be called a hybrid model of the previous types of religious structure, but within that, there is considerable variation. This may best be seen structurally as operating along a continuum between extreme poles of Network and Hierarchy, as shown in Figure 11.1.

Chapter 11: Religion spirituality and leadership

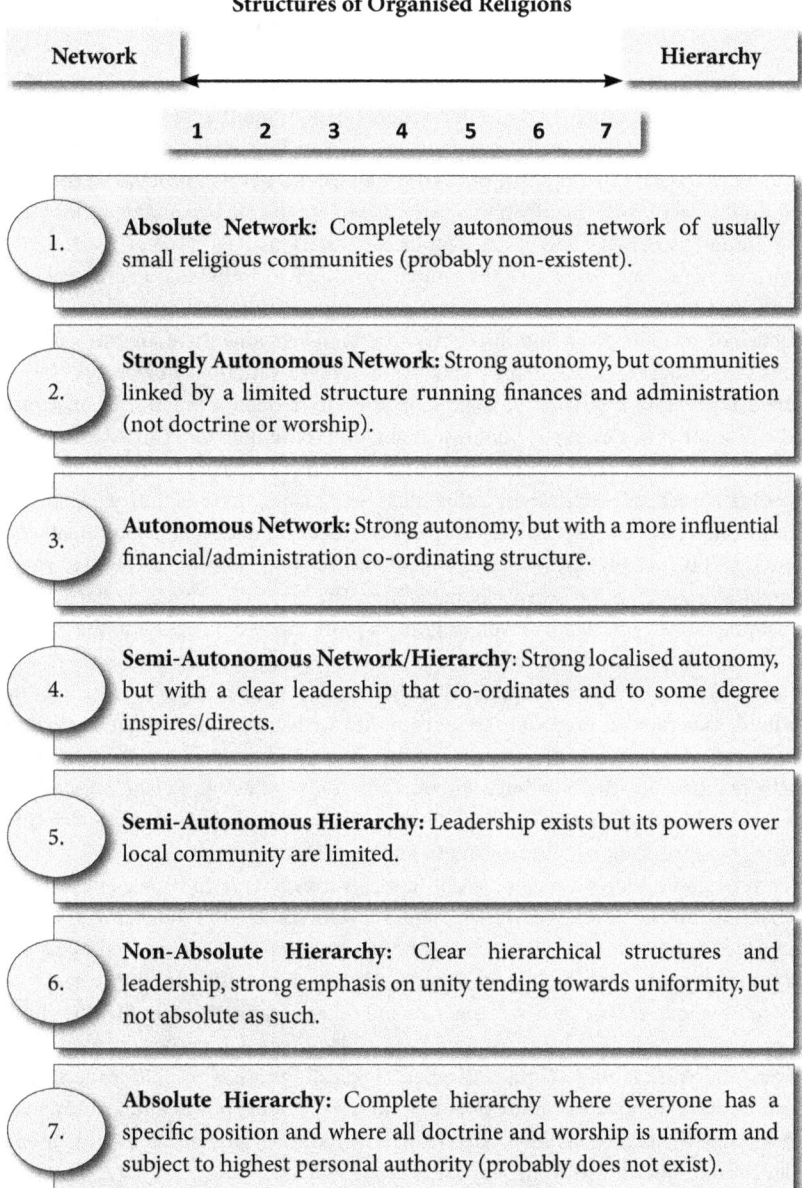

Figure 11.1: Poles of Network and Hierarchy

Most religions of any size or significance tend to be located between categories 2 and 6. An examination of ecclesiology (study of church nature, structure and governance[6]) of the Methodist, Presbyterian and Congregational churches would probably suggest they function somewhere between positions 3 and 4; the Anglican Church would be situated mainly around 5; with the Catholic Church at 6. Similar variation exists within other great faiths such as Islam, Judaism, Buddhism and Hinduism – though they are more likely clustered between categories 2 and 5, with co-ordination focused less on structure but more on agreement on core beliefs and religious practice.

There is a growing phenomenon of religions that fit into category 1: from independent 'storefront' communities to autonomous megachurches led by charismatic figures. These groupings within one or other of the great religions, or sometimes within traditional religions, tend to be aligned by shared basic beliefs or doctrines but without strong institutional ties. Occasionally one might call them broad 'movements' or communities of similar practice (such as the Emerging Church movement[7]). One religious tradition, Unitarian Universalism,[8] an offshoot of early modern radical Protestantism, bucks this trend: it has a visible structure of congregational affiliation and a very broad (mainly humanistic) statement of core beliefs, combined with nearly complete autonomy of belief and practice for its congregations.

Spirituality, the application of the content of belief to individual and/or collective life, is both affected by the particular form of religious organisation, and also affects the structure and practice of religion. Even within highly structured religions there are numerous internal variations of spiritual practice – many forms of prayer, even variations in worship. Nor are these variations fixed within a religion or denomination. Quite often a practice in one tradition is adapted into another (for example, Buddhist meditation techniques into Christianity, Pentecostal worship across denominations of Christianity, even Catholic forms of prayer into Protestantism).

Spiritual practices, adopted by individuals or small groups within a congregation or community often have the effect of de-centreing the focus on doctrine, institutional worship or clerical leadership. In many cases the latter has a 'democratising' effect on institutions at grassroots level, sometimes even up the organisational ladder. The reason for this is perhaps self-evident: a spiritual practice, by offering a person or group a more direct connection to the transcendent, is empowering. Any worthwhile spirituality makes its practitioner more self-aware while also more connected to the transcendent, the latter becoming less a matter of intellectual assent and more a lived, experienced reality for the person. Most effective and substantial spiritualities, I have suggested, also lead to a deeper sense of the ethical and a sense of personal responsibility within the practitioner. The individual discerns the course of action he/she must take, usually in dialogue – and sometimes in confrontation – with the values, laws and practices of his/her overlapping family, social, religious, business, and political communities.

These necessarily broad phenomena I have described serve to situate spirituality within its normal, but not necessarily exclusive, context: institutions. The inevitably political (in its broadest sense) structure of an institution is both a product of and produced by its structure, ideology and practice – including its organisational 'spirituality'. In this respect religious institutions of whatever type mirror businesses and other organisations, in that they both create worldviews/ spiritualities for their members, but are also affected, indeed re-created, by the same worldviews and spiritualities of their members. Logically those who hold leadership in these organisations have the greatest ability not only through personal power and institutional norms but also through their spiritualities to direct and influence their organisations and, by extension, the wider communities in which they operate.

There is another dimension to this, particularly when we move beyond religious organisations into the worlds of business or public life. Employees in most organisations espouse a wide range of religious or non-religious beliefs and practise a similarly diverse set of spiritualities. While some organisations may explicitly embrace or endorse a particular religious worldview, function according to a religious ethic, and even observe certain religious holidays, most are secular in outlook and function, observing only public holidays decreed by the state.

Most organisations, both secular and religious in outlook, whether the loosest of networks or tightest of hierarchies, are places of pluralism both across and within themselves. Members at every level adhere to different religious or non-religious belief systems, and even within a subgroup holding a particular set of beliefs, there is a range of ways in which beliefs are held and lived in practice. Inevitably power and leadership affects all of this. If diversity in organisations is not accommodated a number of things can happen. Across a spectrum of ills, this can vary from open dissent, resistance and fragmentation at one extreme to passive and resentful compliance without any zeal to grow organisationally. This is true no matter the structure or type of organisation, as the histories of fragmentation, heresies and schism attest in the religious world. No matter the structure, intentions, sincerity, spirituality or power of leaders, an organisation that does not accommodate its members will collapse.

An (Important) Aside: Secularity and Spirituality

The patterns I have described above highlight, I hope, not only the complexity of spirituality in the workplace but also the challenge for leaders who wish to apply their personal spirituality to leadership. With Hicks,[9] I support an organisational context setting that embraces what he calls 'respectful pluralism', "resisting company-sponsored religion and spirituality while allowing employees to bring their own religions to work".[10] Even in an organisation rooted in a particular religious or spiritual ethos, unless the nature of the work is itself explicitly religious in content,[i] the default should be a functional secularity of work and leadership. Values should be 'translated' into secular leadership, along lines similar to those proposed by philosopher Robert Audi in relation to religious engagement with politics.[11] And the spirituality of leaders and organisations should be phrased, with few exceptions, in secular terms.

Before we consider the relationship between secularity and spirituality and examine later how an explicitly religious spirituality can be applied to leadership, it is necessary to clear up what may seem like a provocation in the previous paragraph. We must distinguish between secularism (which I understand to be an ideological and often aggressive hostility to religion with a view to its abolition) and secularity, which is a condition that embraces tolerance of varied beliefs within a society that chooses not to enforce or privilege one religious or non-religious tradition over all others.

Philosopher Charles Taylor,[12] among others (including Audi, noted above), has argued that secularity is the natural and positive outcome of the collapse of Western confessional states since the Renaissance and Reformation. While not denying religion or spirituality a place in public life, the trend in most countries has been towards constructing a common discourse without overt reliance on religious argumentation.

Ignatian Spirituality and Leadership: Applying the Insights of Religion

There are many different spiritualities within religious traditions, too many to address here. Many of them have been applied to the practice of leadership. Within Christianity there have been attempts to draw on practices as diverse as the Rule of St Benedict governing the work and life of Catholic monastic communities,[13] to appropriations of biblical figures such as Moses, King David and Jesus Christ[14] as models for leadership. While all these traditions offer valuable insights, for the rest of this chapter I shall focus on the spirituality of St Ignatius of Loyola and how this can be applied to leadership.

I do this for a number of reasons. First, it is the spirituality with which I (as a practitioner, a Jesuit and spiritual director) am most familiar. Second, through an exposition of the spirituality, I shall suggest how it can be applied by any person, including those who are leaders. Third, by

---

i   For example if the organisation is a Catholic religious order of priests, it would be absurd to admit, ordain and mission a Hindu or a Methodist. Conversely, if the latter were employed in some supportive function, for example, a secretary, such exclusivism need not apply.

drawing on how Ignatian spirituality has been exercised in practice by the Jesuits themselves, I shall suggest how the praxis (reflective practice) can be fruitfully applied in organisations in such a way that they can make themselves more effective.

Ignatian spirituality in a nutshell

To understand Ignatian spirituality,[ii] we need first to understand its founder, Ignatius Loyola, and the Jesuits, the Roman Catholic religious order he established.[15] St Ignatius – Inigo Lopez de Loyola (1491–1556) – was a Spanish soldier who underwent a spiritual conversion in his thirties, founding a religious order, the Society of Jesus (or Jesuits), in the process. The notes he took during his rigorous process of spiritual self-examination – from repentance for his past sins, through reflections on the life, death and resurrection of Christ, to a commitment to a life of service to Christ and the Church – became what are now called the *Spiritual Exercises*.[16]

They frame Jesuit life: apart from making a full thirty-day retreat twice in his life-time, in addition to daily prayer, each Jesuit makes an annual eight-day retreat, normally a 'condensed' or adapted version of the long retreat. Prayerful discernment of what each Jesuit is called to do is made by the man himself and his provincial. Consultation is fundamental to the Jesuit 'way of proceeding', although decisions are made at various levels by superiors (local superiors of communities, provincials, and the head of the order, called Father General, in Rome) and are binding on those under them, at every level broad and thorough consultation with everyone in the Society is emphasised. This organisation under what resembles a military command structure, at least level 5 if not 6 hierarchy according to the model given in Figure 11.1, is mitigated by consultation rooted in the presupposition that all are not only thinking about options but also sincerely praying over them. This is in simple terms what one calls Jesuit Governance.

While said governance is rooted in Ignatian Spirituality, the Spirituality itself has taken on a life of its own, among ordained and non-ordained, Catholics and non-Catholic Christians, even occasionally among non-Christians and spiritual 'seekers'. There have even been attempts to apply the techniques and insights of the Exercises (but not, obviously, the Bible) in other religious traditions, and there have been 'secular' applications of the Exercises too. While the former experiment has largely been abandoned, the latter – secular – use of the Exercises has not, particularly in an age marked in many countries by people claiming to be 'spiritual but not religious', 'believing but not belonging'.

Some Ignatian authors (for example, Haight 2010, 2012)[17] are in fact developing their writings on spirituality overtly in order to address the needs and questions not only of 'seekers' but also of those concerned about ecology, ecumenism and interfaith dialogue. Their contention (which is not without some controversy) is that the Exercises need updating to Ignatius' fundamental intention in a new post-Reformation, postmodern, and even post-Christian era.

From our leadership perspective, based on my contention that any effective leadership spirituality must of necessity combine the transcendent with the secular, these developments are both welcome and encouraging. But what specifically in the Exercises can we use?

The meat of the Spiritual Exercises lies in a series of meditations on the life, death and resurrection of Jesus Christ – drawn from the four Christian gospels – inviting retreatants to engage personally in the scene, an act of 'being there', and usually ended with an imagined dialogue with key figures in the narrative, usually Christ. The exercitant (as he/she is sometimes called) is supposed to seek to identify with Christ and become more Christ-like. This is achieved by two meditations of significance for leadership, the *Call of the King* and the *Three Kinds of*

---

ii The most accessible introduction to this – and to Ignatius Loyola and the Jesuits – can be found in James Martin's *The Jesuit Guide to (Almost) Everything* (2010).

Person (discussed below). Before this, the retreatant is invited to review his or her life from the perspective of God's free grace and mercy. Though this first part (usually lasting around eight days) is sometimes misinterpreted as a week of penitence for one's sins, the more common approach today is to stress divine grace that helps the retreatants honestly (and without obsessive guilt) to face their sins, embrace God's mercy, and commit to a life lived in greater faith, hope and love.

Here and in the remainder of the full Exercises scripture-based meditation exercises are interspersed, inviting the retreatant to imagine how he or she can out of gratitude to God and love for Christ go beyond the normal 'duties' of faith to seek the *magis*, the more; and to decide how (realistically) to embrace a state of life that zealously seeks the greater good, for the greater glory of God.[iii]

Two sets of these exercises seem particularly relevant to developing leadership.

1. **The call to lead**

The first set focuses on being called to be leaders, the second, on how to make good decisions. Within the first set, the *Call of the King* invites the exercitant to imagine being called into service by a great leader ('king', in Ignatius' early modern language), ultimately the call for Ignatius by Christ himself. This call is to dedicated service; ultimately, it is a call to a kind of leadership. The *Three Kinds of People* (in original Ignatian terms the word is 'Men') meditation challenges the retreatant to consider further *how* one serves.

First, some keep the law, avoiding doing anything evil. This is good, but hardly inspiring leadership. Second, there are those who go beyond the minimum requirements; they do great things, but somehow fall short of doing what is needed for greatness. Finally, there are those who give their all, take chances, and strive for greatness. These would be the ideal leaders, those who make their mark on society.

While Ignatius' focus is on holiness in the service of God, such meditations can be adapted for business and political leaders who desire to lead. Note, too, that since all this is expressed within a call to serve God, the ethical dimension is fundamental. Great leaders must be good people; they must lead by serving God or the Good.

It is a myth that the Exercises are a form of brainwashing men into joining the Jesuits or, once in, enforcing the uncontested will of superiors over members. The fundamental point is inner freedom, connection to God, so as to make a free decision rooted not in fear or obligation, nor in a false sense of importance. Such inner freedom is essential to any leader, whether within or 'on top' of an organisation.

2. **Decision-making**

The second set of meditations of importance to leadership revolves around making decisions. *Discernment* in the Spiritual Exercises can be made both individually and communally.[18] Although the approach differs slightly in practice – communal discernment includes such elements as debate and even voting – the basic method remains essentially the same. This method has been summed up as nothing less than the prayerful application of See-Judge-Act: *seeing* the issue as clearly and objectively as possible; *judging* in the light of prayerful reflection on scripture and tradition; *acting* on a decision reached prayerfully and in conscience.[19]

---

iii At one point, if a person is trying to decide on a course of action, the ever-practical Ignatius actively encourages the retreatant to draw up what is effectively a spiritual balance sheet listing pros and cons of a decision – which then must be prayed about thoroughly so that one is not deluded or misled by what might appear to be good.

Good discernment is meant to be based on a disposition towards the greater good: careful reflection based upon reason as much as emotion, informed hopefully by the best available information, prayed over, and then confirmed in prayer. Crucial here is that discernment is about making a good decision that seeks what is good at least, indeed, what the best possible option available to us is. This is the way in which Jesuit superiors and men under their authority are supposed to (and generally do) make decisions about work assignments, new projects, and sometimes even whether a man remains in the Society or leaves. It is a practice that has worked for over 450 years.

Closely linked to, but different from, discernment is *Discernment of Spirits*. Here one tries to see what hidden forces influence our decision-making and actions. In Ignatius' 16th century these 'spirits' were considered real – the Holy Spirit, guardian angels, demons or the Devil. Today many people – believers or non-believers – prefer to see these as our inner psychological drives that either support or subvert our decisions. When one makes a decision, Ignatius counsels self-examination of our feelings before acting. Sometimes we make a decision in a state of desolation: emptiness, depression, perhaps desperation. This is a bad idea! Alternately, we may be carried away by an enthusiasm that is followed by a feeling of emptiness. In both cases, he would say that our deciding was influenced by the Evil Spirit. Better then to stop and to think again. We should make decisions ideally in a state of consolation – our consideration, prayed through ideally, but also considered rationally, should lead us to a state of calm and inner peace. This may even evoke sadness at times, but even sadness should lead to a sense of peace. This is, in Ignatius' terms, the working of the Good Spirit in us.

Ignatian Spirituality Applied Corporately: The Example of the Jesuits Themselves, including a Pope

While a number of authors and seminar leaders have applied the Exercises and Ignatian Spirituality to leadership, a distinctive new voice has recently been added: Chris Lowney,[20] a retired JP Morgan executive and former Jesuit seminarian, has taken not only Ignatian Spirituality but also the Jesuit 'way of proceeding' and argued convincingly that spirituality-based Jesuit governance offers an exciting and successful new way to lead. Drawing on (i) the history of the Society, in particular its innovation in mission (for example, promoting philosophical and theological inculturation four hundred years before it became acceptable); (ii) the adventurousness of some of its enterprises (such as being the first Europeans in Tibet); and (iii) the considerable scholarly contribution the Jesuits have made to almost every science and humanity, Lowney argues that the reason for such success lay in how governance was exercised.

Though a tightly run, hierarchical organisation, leadership was seen – through the spirituality of discernment and fraternal conversation between the Jesuit and his superior – as belonging to everyone. While under authority, each Jesuit was encouraged to show personal initiative in his ministries, rooted in prayerful discernment. The result, argues Lowney, is that four leadership principles stand out:

- *Self-awareness:* This implies a thorough understanding, rooted in the Exercises, of one's strengths, weaknesses, values and worldview. Remember that the Exercises focus on the person as a redeemed sinner, loved by God, aware of one's strengths and weaknesses.
- *Ingenuity:* With a firm basis in self-awareness, one has the confidence to innovate and adapt to an ever-changing world. Properly understood, the Exercises help one to see the divine working through the complexity of history.

- *Love:* Through the experience of love of God in the Exercises, one is able to engage with others in a positive, loving attitude. To know that the Creator loves the creature gives one the strength to love fellow creatures.
- *Heroism:* This principle encompasses the desire to seek the greater, and moves one from passivity to action and a willingness to take calculated risks in order to attain the *magis*. The Exercises invite the retreatant to ask: "What have I done, what am I doing, what will I do for God?", and should inspire one to seek the greater good.

In a later book (2013), Lowney[21] shows how this carefully discerned practice can explain the combination of tradition and innovation, collegiality and personal authority of Pope Francis. Born Jorge Mario Bergoglio, Francis is a Jesuit. To Lowney and most Jesuits (and anyone familiar with the way the Society operates), this would be self-evident even if one did not know his background: wide consultation, rigorous study, prayerful reflection, followed by decisive implementation. Similarly, Francis' personal style is witness to his Jesuit roots: simplicity, high toleration of ambiguity and human fallibility, warmth, plus a high capacity for work. He is a model Ignatian CEO, currently of Catholic Church Inc.

The beauty of an Ignatian spirituality of leadership, as Lowney and others (for example, Coghlan 2001; Darmanin 2005; Miles 2011) express it, is that it can be applied widely and ecumenically. Just as the spirituality itself has been adopted by Christians (and occasionally non-Christians) beyond Catholicism, it can easily be applied secularly. Moving outside its specifically religious language game, we find within it universally applicable motifs: the need for self-knowledge (and care of self, including at times self-forgiveness), a disposition to seek the greater good (*magis*), a willingness to imagine boldly and take (calculated) risks, yet with openness to constructive criticism and self-criticism, rounded off with a strong ethic of care for those one leads and serves.

Furthermore, Ignatian spirituality's 'spread' across religious and secular traditions manifests its applicability to almost every permutation of network to a hierarchy one might imagine, outside of the (possibly non-existent) category of absolute hierarchy. Lowney brilliantly demonstrates this in his interpretation of Jesuit history and the example of Pope Francis, while others offer us how it can be applied by individuals and small groups alike.

Application in South Africa: Spirited Leadership

Within South Africa, the Jesuit Institute South Africa (of which the author is a member) developed in the late 2000s the 'Spirited Leadership' Programme, based upon the Exercises. It drew in part on Lowney's work but expanded it, incorporating into the programme the works of leadership gurus such as Stephen Covey, Warren Bennis and Peter Drucker, the work of emotional intelligence scholar Daniel Goleman, and the values enshrined in the King III Corporate Governance report. The team presenting these workshops was varied. It included permanent members of the Institute and a number of its associates, Jesuits and non-Jesuits, with backgrounds from clinical psychology, spiritual direction, advertising and marketing, to one person who had helped to draft King III. The process has been applied in a variety of contexts – corporates, groups of school teachers, decision-making meetings of religious congregations, and even as an elective for MBA students.

A Future Perspective

Leadership for an elusive future

I am not sure what leadership in the future will look like. My suspicion is that leadership will take on a variety of forms in different places, in response to varied situations rooted in a multitude of organisational cultures. As one who recognises – and to a large degree embraces – postmodernity, I expect to see a number of culturally-mediated leadership styles: a western style, possibly subdivided into North American and European variants; an Indian style; and a Chinese style, at the very least. Depending on socio-economic developments, we may even see an African style, based upon some kind of *Ubuntu* ethos. Given that the trend is towards globalisation in business, these styles may enjoy considerable overlap and – if global business is to thrive without 'clashes of civilisations' – it will be up to leaders to develop a certain *multicultural intelligence* to avoid crises caused by cultural misunderstanding.

Parallel to that, religion and spirituality will need to adapt. Indeed, economic pressures will force adaptation. Religiously fundamentalist societies will find themselves isolated from the mainstream. Theologian Hans Küng's observation that global peace is impossible without peace between religions[22][23] should inform such a transition. Global economic necessity, spurred on by leaders who embrace a spirituality marked by tolerance of the *other*, will drive societies towards greater tolerance – initially to outsiders, but latterly to co-religionists within. Or, their societies will simply be left behind.

Religious- and spiritually-minded leaders in governance and business will probably spearhead a renewal that, while rooted in core beliefs, will re-evaluate the theory and practice of belief – in other words, theology and spirituality – in a manner that builds trans-religious/spiritual bridges in order to facilitate cross-cultural co-operation. Hopefully religions' theologians and leaders will follow. This must inevitably entail a 'postmodern turn' and a new, deeper understanding of truth.

The postmodern condition, as Lyotard[24] reminds us, undermines the possibility of an overarching world view or meta-narrative. Faced with this we are tempted – leaders and led alike – to adopt two unhelpful positions. *First*, there is the temptation to reject all world views but our own, adopting a hard-core realist understanding: "our truth is the Truth, our way of proceeding is the right way, and the rest must simply conform to it". In a multipolar global economy this is impossible. *Second*, there is a relativist view which holds all truth claims to be equally true. This results in a Babel of mutual misunderstanding, with global business – and politics – talking and working at cross-purposes. This is a formula for at best waste; at worst, all-out, mutually destructive conflict.

Leadership, a term often as elusive as the word 'postmodern', will need to steer the postmodern global economy in a way that embraces diversity while negotiating the complexities of multiculturalism. Religious people will need to do the same with spirituality – at very least in areas of governance and economics. In short, leadership itself must become postmodern.

But of what kind?

The philosopher John Caputo,[25] in a short book on the postmodern idea of truth, offers some concrete epistemological proposals that may be applied here. Rejecting both relativism and 'hard' realism, he proposes a way of thinking of Truth less as a Fact and more as an Event – where truth is negotiated – based upon three elements: hermeneutics, paradigm shifts, and language games. Hermeneutics, the art of interpretation, seeks to draw from an event the most relevant 'facts' –

themselves interpretations of an experience – that help us to create the truth of an event.

How a leader interprets the event helps him/her engage with those involved effectively. In a multicultural context this is essential. Reading the other correctly means engaging with the other in a way that reduces misunderstanding and conflict.[iv] Understood as an Event, religions must do the same. And some religions are already doing it, though it makes many adherents and ministers uneasy.

To further complicate matters, Caputo reminds us that "interpretations are not eternal beings", but change within frameworks or horizons of understanding (language games, to use Wittgenstein's[26] term) that frequently undergo shifts:

"Sometimes an event is encountered which the prevailing framework can accommodate, but sometimes it cannot and then things undergo an abrupt, discontinuous and holistic shift".[27]

Such a change is what Thomas Kuhn[28] called a paradigm shift.

We should note that in the postmodern condition there is no single, overarching language game that incorporates the local and particular language games of, for example, business or politics. We see this most clearly in the difficulty in defining and resisting corruption: what is corrupt in society A is simply natural in society B. One may not like this, but outside of a non-existent global monoculture, this is a brutal fact. Cultural anthropology helps us see this; it helps the good leader to negotiate between language games, and between the explicit and implicit rules of performance. It also helps religions to adapt to new paradigms of being religious in the world.

Yet these language games also change, sometimes gradually, through interactions and revisions of interpretation caused by shifting sociopolitical and cultural contexts. Occasionally, though, they move dramatically. A whole new way of proceeding emerges. Consider, for example, China's dramatic shift from state socialism to free market capitalism. China's paradigm of proceeding has changed, even as it maintains its Confucian-Marxist outer language. It requires a careful, culturally-smart leader – particularly those coming out of conservative religious language games – to negotiate in this new – and still quite unstable – paradigm.

To sum up, I suggest that effective leadership in the future will be determined by the degree to which we can embrace and negotiate the postmodern condition. Leadership motivated by religion and spirituality cannot stay out of this. We can no longer assume that when we meet and use the same words, these words have common meaning, as many scholars working between or within religious traditions already know. Nor can we assume the global nature of language games surrounding leadership.

We need, too, to be deeply aware of the paradigms governing the communities, organisations and countries we encounter. This is a tall order for leaders, but one that cannot be shirked. Clarity about one's own paradigms (including religious ones), the language games in which we live, and our capacity to interpret them well needs not only knowledge but self-knowledge – a self-knowledge which, I would argue, a healthy, dynamic personal and/or corporate spirituality can advance.

---

iv   Cultural anthropology teaches us that we live in a universe of symbols. Even ordinary words contain a whole symbol system behind them. Whoever uses the word, the way in which he/she understands the word is culturally conditioned. In a global economy, where economic language is suffused with differing and often particular cultural assumptions, the effective leader will need to be as well-versed in cultural anthropology as in economics and politics.

Conclusion

Having initially attempted to define spirituality broadly, as I believe it must both for itself and for the purpose of application to leadership, I have argued that religion itself is a form of organisation taking on different forms and structures. Religious organisation mirrors secular organisation. Lived religion, spirituality, mirrors the lived values and ways of proceeding of organisations.

From this I have concluded that spirituality itself can be applied to business and other organisations fruitfully and effectively, though appropriately not in a specifically religious form. To illustrate this I have used Ignatian spirituality as a case study showing how both Ignatian spirituality and (following Lowney) Jesuit practices of 'governance informed by spirit' can and have been applied, concluding with a programme in which I was a facilitator. Finally, I would emphasise that Ignatian spirituality is by no means the only form of spirituality that can be applied to leadership: it is the task of practitioners of other religious traditions to consider how their traditions can be appropriately adapted to develop other secular spiritualities of leadership.

Endnotes

1. Sheldrake, 2007, p. 2.
2. Sheldrake, 2007, pp. 1–2.
3. See Comte-Sponville 2007; Harris 2014.
4. cf. Spohn 2005, pp. 270–271.
5. Thompson et al., 1991.
6. See Dulles 1987; Küng, 1976; Mannion & Mudge, 2008.
7. cf. Sweet, 2003.
8. Greenwood & Harris, 2011.
9. Hicks, 2003.
10. Hicks, 2003, p. 2.
11. Audi, 2000.
12. Taylor, 2007.
13. Tredget, 2002.
14. Woolfe, 2002.
15. O'Malley, 1993; Caraman, 1990.
16. Loyola, 1951.
17. Haight, 2010, 2012.
18. Toner 1971; Futrell 1972.
19. Bernal Restrepo, 1989, pp. 16–22; Liebert, 2008, pp. 333–355.
20. Lowney, 2003.
21. Ibid.
22. Küng, 1991.
23. Küng & Kuschel, 1993.
24. Lyotard, 1984.
25. Caputo, 2013.
26. Wittgenstein, 1951.
27. Caputo, 2013, p. 219.
28. Kuhn, 2012.

References

Audi, R. 2000. *Religious commitment and secular reason*. Cambridge, UK: Cambridge University Press.

Bernal Restrepo, S. 1989. 'A methodology of discernment'. *Inculturation and Religious Life*, 79:16–22.

Caputo, JD., 2013. *Truth: Philosophy in transit*. London, UK: Penguin.

Caraman, P. 1990. *Ignatius Loyola: A biography of the founder of the Jesuits*. San Francisco, CA: Harper & Row.

Coghlan, D. 2001. 'Ignatian teamwork: An emergent framework from the instructions for the team at Trent'. *Review of Ignatian Spirituality*, 98, 33(3):65–75.

Comte-Sponville, A. 2007. *The book of atheist spirituality*. London, UK: Bantam.

Darmanin, A. 2005. 'Ignatian spirituality and leadership in organizations today'. *Review of Ignatian Spirituality*, 109, 36(2):1–15.

Dulles, A. 1987. *Models of the church*. Expanded ed. New York: Doubleday.

Futrell, JC. 1971. 'Communal discernment: Reflections on experience'. *Studies in the Spirituality of Jesuits*, 4(5).

Greenwood, A & Harris, MW. 2011. *An introduction to the unitarian and universalist traditions*. Cambridge, UK: Cambridge University Press.

Haight, R. 2010. 'Expanding the spiritual exercises'. *Studies in the Spirituality of Jesuits*, 42(2).

Haight, R. 2012. *Christian spirituality for seekers: Reflections on the spiritual exercises of Ignatius Loyola*. Maryknoll, NY: Orbis Books.

Harris, S. 2014. *Waking up: A guide to spirituality without religion*. London, UK: Transworld.

Hicks, DA. 2003. *Religion and the workplace: Pluralism, spirituality, leadership*. Cambridge, UK: Cambridge University Press.
Kuhn, T. 2012. *The structure of scientific revolutions*. 4th ed. Chicago, IL: University of Chicago Press.
Küng, H & Kuschel, K-J. 1993. *A global ethic: The declaration of the parliament of the world's religions*. New York, NY: Continuum.
Küng, H. 1976. *The church*. New York, NY: Image Books.
Küng, H. 1991. *Global responsibility: In search of a new world ethic*. London, UK: SCM Press.
Liebert, E. 2008. 'Discernment for our times'. *Studies in Spirituality*, 18:333–355.
Lowney, C. 2003. *Heroic leadership: Best practices from a 450-year old company that changed the world*. Chicago, IL: Loyola Press.
Lowney, C. 2013. *Pope Francis: Why he leads the way he leads*. Chicago, IL: Loyola Press.
Loyola, St I. 1951 [1522–24/1548]. *The spiritual exercises*. Trans. LJ Puhl. Chicago, IL: Loyola University Press.
Lyotard, J-F. 1984. *The postmodern condition: A report on knowledge*. Minneapolis, MN: University of Minnesota Press.
Mannion, G & Mudge, LS. (eds). 2008. *The Routledge Companion to the Christian Church*. New York/London: Routledge.
Martin, J. 2010. *The Jesuit Guide to (Almost) Everything: A Spirituality for Real Life*. New York: HarperOne.
Miles, B. 2011. 'Ignatian Spirituality, Apostolic Creativity and Leadership in Times of Change'. *The Way* 50/4, 35–41.
O'Malley, JW. 1993. *The First Jesuits*. Cambridge MA: Harvard University Press.
Sheldrake, P. 2007. *A Brief History of Spirituality*. Oxford, UK: Blackwell.
Spohn, WC. 2005. 'Christian Spirituality and Theological Ethics'. *The Blackwell Companion to Christian Spirituality* ed. Arthur Holder. Malden/Oxford, UK: Blackwell), 269–285.
Sweet, L (ed). 2003. *The Church in Emerging Culture: Five Perspectives*. Grand Rapids, MI: Zondervan.
Taylor, C. 2007. *A Secular Age*. Cambridge, MA: Belknap Press/Harvard University Press.
Thompson, G., Frances, J., Levacic, R., & Mitchell, J. (eds.), 1991. *Markets, Hierarchies and Networks: The Coordination of Social Life*. London, UK/New Delhi: SAGE Press.
Toner, JJ. 1971. 'A method for communal discernment of God's will'. *Studies in the Spirituality of Jesuits*, 3,(4).
Tredget, D. 2002. '"The Rule of Benedict" and its relevance to the world of work'. *Journal of Managerial Psychology*, 17(3):219–229.
Wittgenstein, L. 1951. *Philosophical Investigations*. Oxford, UK: Basil Blackwell.
Woolfe, L. 2002. *The Bible on leadership: From Moses to Matthew – management lessons for contemporary leaders*. New York, NY: AMACOM.

Chapter 12

ECOLOGICALLY EMBEDDED LEADERSHIP
Jess Schulschenk

We in South Africa can be proud of our globally recognised leaders who have struggled for social justice and human rights, as well as those who have championed the cause of environmental conservation. The challenges society is facing today, however, require a new kind of leader who can understand, navigate, and take action with regard to the interconnected and interdependent challenges of business, society and environment. It is no longer possible to think about these leadership challenges in isolation. New leaders will have to engage with and address proactively the global megatrends of climate change, ecosystem collapse, and the resulting societal instability that are unfolding in South Africa today.

This presents not only a challenge, but also an opportunity to collaborate on new approaches that could lead to more resilient, and even more flourishing and abundant, futures for all.

The purpose of the chapter is to address how leaders of organisations come to make sense of the unfolding environmental (and connected social) challenges facing both their organisations and society at large. Topics covered include the unfolding megatrends, the limits of socio-ecological systems informing these challenges, and how these are changing the way we think about both managing organisations and the kinds of leadership competencies that are required in order for organisations to survive, and thrive, going forward.

Making Sense of Global Megatrends

Increasingly, individuals and organisations alike are trying to make sense of the large-scale environmental and societal changes under way. From extensive drought and rising food prices through to biodiversity loss and ecosystem collapse, these risks are increasingly being felt across the globe. The World Economic Forum (WEF) *Global Risks Report 2016*[1] identified these as global megatrends (which include climate change, environmental degradation, and rising income disparity) together with the most significant long-term risks worldwide resulting from these trends (including profound social instability, interstate conflict, and water crises), as shown in Figure 12.1.

The risks given in Figure 12.1 are interconnected, with cascading negative impacts of increasingly global reach. These risks are also real, unfolding and have tangible impacts on business and society at large. It is becoming increasingly challenging to argue otherwise that the large scale degradation of the earth's natural systems is directly related to collective human activity[i] Environmental and societal risks are not only informed by the other risks (economic, geopolitical and technological) but also reinforce them, resulting in large-scale societal decline and, potentially, collapse.

Environmental change has largely been presumed to be slow, predictable and reversible, but is more often experienced as abrupt, unexpected and irreversible.[3] Natural systems are "all complex adaptive systems, and the key characteristic about such systems is that they are self-organizing systems – but within limits."[4]

---

i See the work of the Intergovernmental Panel on Climate Change (IPCC) (*https://www2.ucar.edu/climate/faq/what-intergovernmental-panel-climate-change-ipcc*) and the Millennium Ecosystem Assessment (MEA) (*en.wikipedia.org/wiki/Millennium_Ecosystem_Assessment*) for further resources.

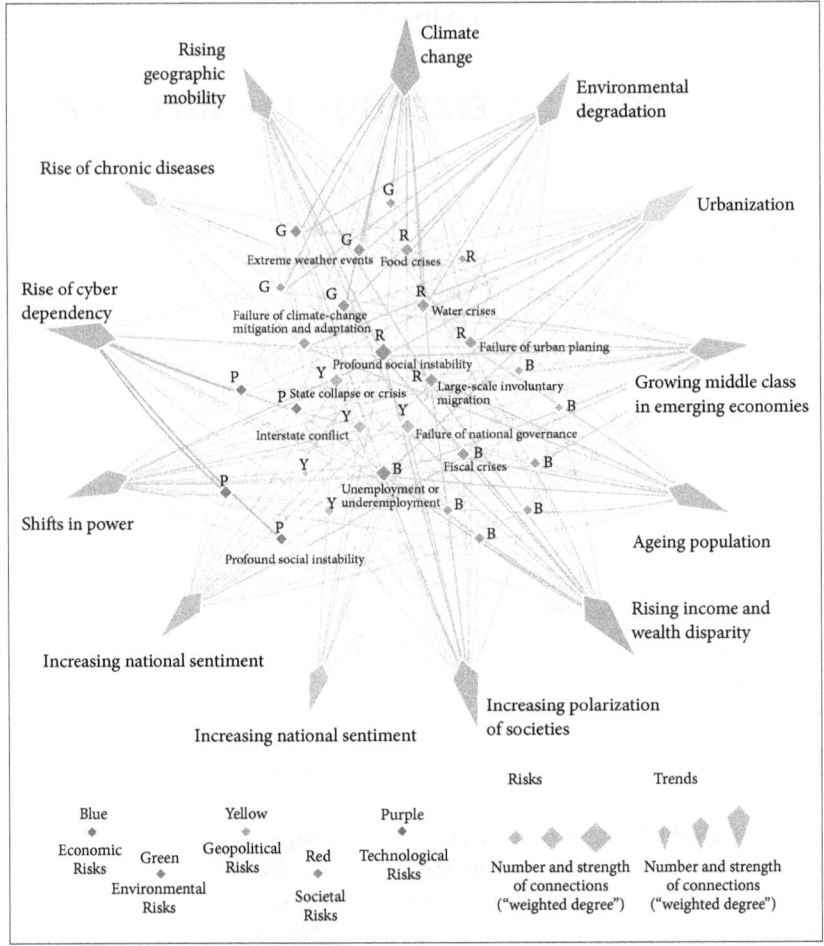

Figure 12.1: The Risks –Trends Interconnections Map 2016
Source: *WEF (2016)*[2]

Crossing Planetary Boundaries

The emerging megatrends we are experiencing today can be described as symptoms resulting from society collectively operating as though there were no social or ecological limits to human activity. The planet we live on is, however, limited in its ability to act as both a source and sink for indefinite human activities. The concept of planetary boundaries was established by Rockström et al.[5] It outlines nine critical ecological thresholds which, if crossed, fundamentally threaten the stability of the planet as a suitable habitat and provider of ecosystem services for humanity, as reflected in Figure 12.2.

Chapter 12: Ecologically embedded leadership

Planetary Boundaries
A safe operating space for humanity

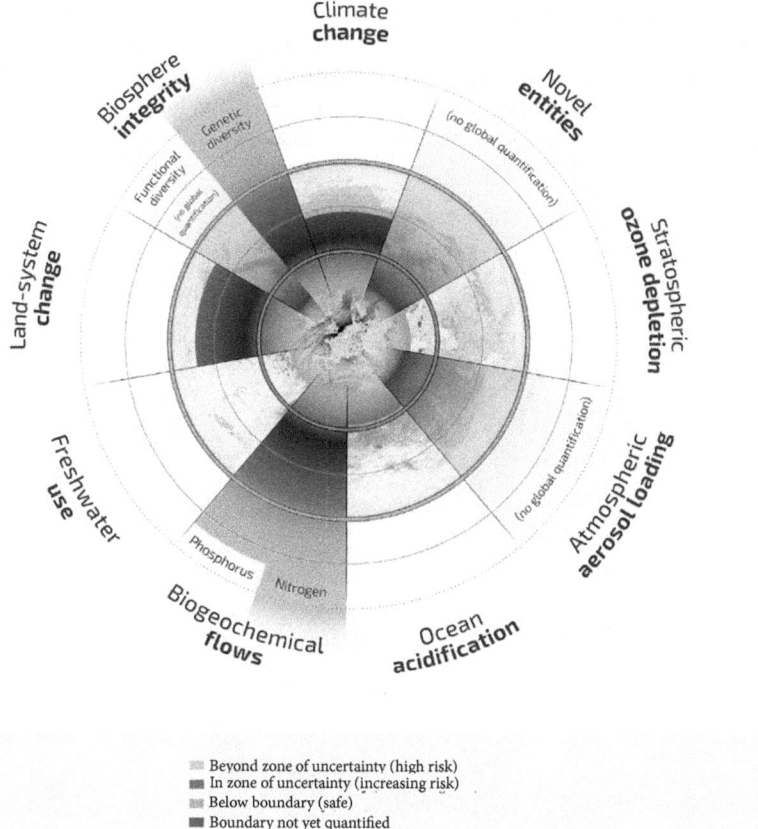

Figure 12.2: Current status of the control variables for seven of the planetary boundaries
Note: *For a clearer image, visit http://ec.europa.eu/epsc/publications/notes/sn18_en.htm*
Source: *Steffen et al. (2015)*[6]

Four of these thresholds – climate change, loss of biosphere integrity, land-system change, altered biogeochemical cycles (phosphorus and nitrogen) – have already been crossed, as indicated by the blue line in Figure 12.2. Others are fast approaching their tipping points, and three processes cannot yet be quantified (represented by the grey wedges). Boundary processes are impacted at different spatial scales (from local to regional in the case of biodiversity loss or chemical pollution) over varying periods of time, but aggregate to affect planetary resilience.

"Transgressing a boundary increases the risk that human activities could inadvertently drive the Earth System into a much less hospitable state, damaging efforts to reduce poverty and leading to a deterioration of human wellbeing in many parts of the world, including wealthy countries."[7] As a result, realising social equality and justice is inextricably linked with achieving ecological stability.

Social Justice and Ecological Stability

In 2012, Kate Raworth[8] presented a set of minimum social standards that would need to be realised within the limits of ecological foundations in order to ensure "a safe and just space for humanity." The social foundations are based on what will be required to ensure that humanity remains well (through food security, adequate income, water and sanitation, and healthcare), productive (through education, decent work, sustainable energy services, and resilience) and empowered (through gender equality, social equity, and political voice). These are recognised for their role in realising quality of life for both individuals and for society as a whole, which is dependent on collectively realising these social foundations.

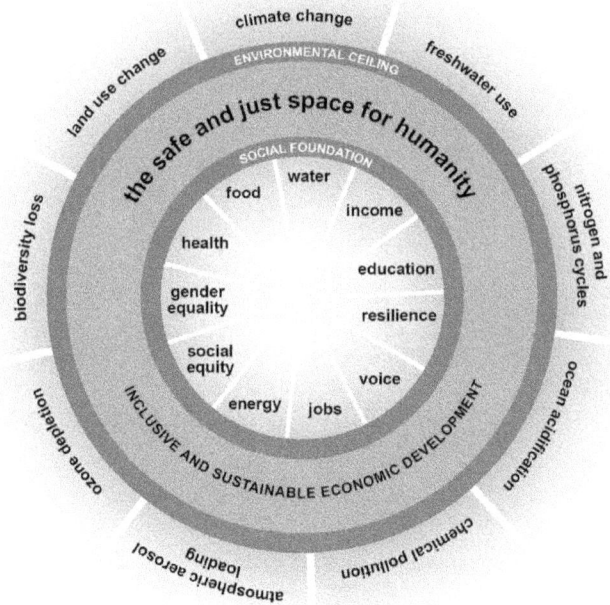

Figure 12.3: *The safe and just space for humanity*
Source: *Raworth (2012)*[9]

Sustainability as Nested Dependencies

The term "sustainable development" can be defined as improvement in the quality of life for all humans equitably, both intra- and inter-generationally, within the context of minimum societal foundations and the earth's limited carrying capacity. Business sustainability is understood to be inextricably linked to societal sustainability, given the direct dependence of business on the existence of society and the supporting natural environment.

In the context of limited resources, ecological thresholds and changing socio-economic landscapes, a transition towards sustainability is both desirable and, arguably, inevitable. Societal change at this scale will require "major, system-wide changes that are likely to involve breakthrough technologies and possibly fundamental changes in social aims, institutions, industrial structure and demand."[10] This will require bold leadership if we are to make the transition towards an ecologically resilient and equitable future.

Shifting Perceptions in Management Theory and Practice

Management theory and practice has tended to reinforce the perception that organisations can exist independently of the natural environment.

> "Since the Enlightenment, thinkers have progressively differentiated humanity from the rest of nature and have separated objective truth from subjective morality. The greatest challenge of postmodern society may reside in their reintegration.[11] A similar challenge may exist for management theorists. Organisational science has evolved within a constricted or fractured epistemology, such that it embraces only a portion of reality." – Gladwin et al.[12]

Traditional views of the environment have represented it as separate from – or merely interacting with – business and societal systems. An embedded view of business within society explicitly identifies limits to economic and social growth in a finite world. In this way, an embedded view subjugates economic entities and outcomes because of their dependency on the stability of this nested system in which they operate.[13]

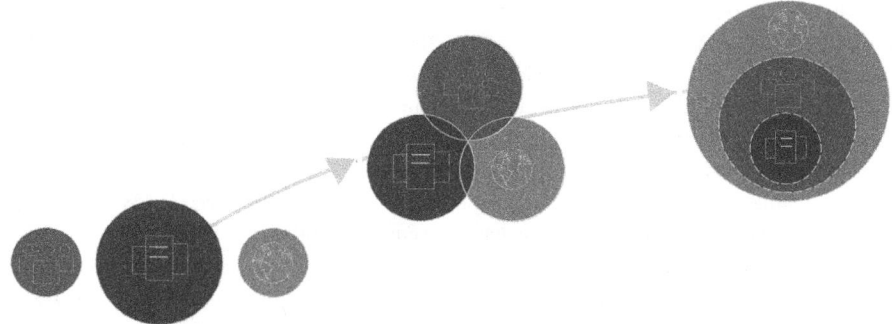

Figure 12.4: From separate to embedded views of organisations, in society and ecological systems
Source: NBS (2015)[14]

An embedded view of business in society (in nature) also recognises that business interests should not come before societal interests and that by undermining societal well-being, any economic development is fundamentally unstable. The following guiding principles can help inform decision making if leaders wish to shift their organisations towards operating sustainably, for both their organisation and the systems on which they depend:

i. Organisations are embedded in social systems and are critically dependent on societal wellbeing.
ii. Both organisations and societies at large are embedded in natural systems and are critically dependent on ecological resilience, which relies on biodiversity, adequate stocks and adaptive capacities for ecosystem health.
iii. Natural, human, social, intellectual and financial capitals are irreplaceable and cannot be transferred among each other.
iv. There are real limits to growth, recognised by planetary boundaries and social foundations.

Sustainability in this way becomes a lens through which to acknowledge the real and emergent complexity of the systems in which organisations are embedded and to recognise the inherent potential for these systems to collectively fail, or flourish.

Responsible Leadership in Uncertain Times

In the context of these challenges, responsible leadership has been defined as:

> "the art and ability involved in building, cultivating and sustaining trustful relationships to different stakeholders, both inside and outside the organization, and in coordinating responsible action to achieve a meaningful, commonly shared business vision. Arguably, in a stakeholder society an agreeable vision would need to include the aspiration to be(come) an inclusive, responsible, and active business in society; one that aspires to be part of a sustainable future and thus of the solution to and not part of the world's problems." – Thomas Maak[15]

Responsible leadership is essential to enacting a vision for a sustainable future through co-creating these futures with key stakeholders. The type of leadership required to navigate such change is both relational and ethical, in that it occurs through social interactions that give both purpose and direction to such leadership.

There are many examples of leaders responding to the real and pressing ecological limits against which we are collectively pushing. Often-cited examples include the commitments being made by leaders of companies such as Unilever and IKEA to sustainable sourcing, renewable energy, and carbon neutrality. In South Africa, the National Development Plan 2030 (NDP), developed by the National Planning Commission's Department of the Presidency,[16] explicitly recognises the critical dependency of the country on the supporting natural environment, that our economy is unsustainably resource intensive and calls for strategic investments that would ensure the long-term resilience of the natural environment that supports life.

Companies such as Nedbank have long been identified for their 'green' credentials, but in response to the ecological and societal megatrends currently unfolding, Nedbank has responded with strategic commitments to building the South Africa of the future in which they wish to operate. Four of Nedbank's eight long-term strategic goals within their *FairShare 2030 Plan*[17] relate specifically to ecological resilience and the security of ecosystem service provision.

At an individual level, leaders such as the late Wangari Maathai have been instrumental in initiating and leading large scale change for environmental restoration. Maathai was a politician, activist, Nobel Peace Prize-recipient, and founder of the Green Belt Movement in Kenya, responsible today for planting over 51 million trees, activity that has led to the restoration of ecosystems and the security of livelihoods for thousands of women in East Africa.

> "Today we are faced with a challenge that calls for a shift in our thinking, so that humanity stops threatening its life-support system. We are called to assist the Earth to heal her wounds and in the process heal our own – indeed to embrace the whole of creation in all its diversity, beauty and wonder. Recognizing that sustainable development, democracy and peace are indivisible is an idea whose time has come."
> – Wangari Maathai[18]

Leadership Competencies for Ecological Embeddedness

The task ahead for leaders of today, and tomorrow, is unprecedented. Ultimately, this will require leaders with the ability to navigate complexity, and translate risk into opportunity. The Embedding Project[19] is a public-benefit research project that relies on strong social science research methods to bring together thoughtful sustainability intrapreneurs from across industries and around the world, and harnesses their collective knowledge in order to develop rigorous and practical guidance that benefits everyone.

A forthcoming guideline[20] by the Embedding Project on developing competencies for sustainable business practice identifies three critical competencies for sustainability leadership – systems thinking, anticipatory thinking and the ability to influence. This guideline outlines both the importance of these competencies, and how they can be further developed.

Systems thinking

Systems thinking is the ability to see systems both in terms of their parts, and also how they relate and connect to each other as part of a greater whole. It is critical for shifting thinking to recognise the impact of individual decisions, and the role of broader system dynamics in affecting individuals and organisations alike. Ultimately, systems thinking enables better strategies to be developed that can both reduce risk and increase opportunities.

Anticipatory thinking

It is the capacity of individuals to identify and consider possibilities and probabilities, allowing for potential challenges to be explored and planned for.

The ability to influence

The ability to influence is indicative of the manner in which successful leaders are able to enlist the support of others in advancing an agenda for sustainability in their organisations, and beyond. The ability to motivate, enable and facilitate collaboration requires skills such as listening and dialogue, negotiating and other qualities, all required by leaders who seek to navigate complex challenges and competing agendas.

Approaches for developing these competencies at an organisational and leadership level are included in the guideline and provide valuable insights through practical approaches that have been taken by leading companies to foster and develop these competencies. The value of lived experience, leadership commitment and ongoing organisational development can also not be underestimated in the building of these competencies.

In a recent study interviewing a broad range of CEOs and change agents in South Africa and abroad, we found that many factors influenced a leader's perspective and commitment to sustainability.[21] Many of these factors were formed by their upbringing, education and early career. Competencies for sustainability can and should be developed in leaders through professional development and leadership programmes, as well as through informal mentoring and experiences. We concomitantly need to be introducing these competencies in foundational education programmes, from primary through to tertiary education, across the board.

A Future Perspective

Looking ahead, the need for leadership on ecological issues is only going to intensify. As we continue to push against, and overstep, planetary boundaries, the risks and threats experienced by organisations and society at large will reinforce each other. We are going to require a generation of leaders with greater ecological literacy than we have previously had, sought or educated for. As such, we can expect to see:

- Increasing resource shortages, especially of energy, water and critical minerals.
- Decreasing health and resilience of critical ecosystems and their provisioning, regulating, supporting and cultural services.
- Increasing social and political disruption, deepening poverty, inequality and social upheaval.

Responding to the reality of ecological disruptions, we would anticipate seeing:

- Growing expectations from society requiring organisations and governments to respond to ecological threats.
- Greater emphasis on and true incorporation of ecological literacy and systems thinking across our education systems, from early childhood development through to MBAs and PhDs.
- The economy will shift to recognise the critical dependencies on ecological systems, leading to new product, service, and whole industry-level innovations.
- Organisations actively looking for, hiring and promoting individuals with strong ecological literacy, the ability to think and act in systems, and a value system that recognises the intrinsic value of ecological systems.
- Leaders moving beyond conservation initiatives to make real and tangible commitments to operating within planetary boundaries.

Conclusion

The scale of the challenges unfolding in society today calls for unprecedented leadership – across all facets of society. Ultimately, we require not only new ways of thinking about our individual and collective roles in society (such as systems thinking), but we also need to be able to see how these connect to the potential futures which we all share in creating, and factor these into our decision making today (anticipatory thinking). New leaders who will be able to navigate and still flourish in these uncertain times will be those with the ability to influence, which rests on the ability to listen, to relate, and to understand.

Improving ecological leadership perhaps truly begins with taking the time to make sense of the many warning signs with which we are being presented. It may also require slowing down and appreciating the tremendous living world that we are fortunate to be a part of, and revisiting the true value of things we consider to be good and right.

Given the scale and impact of the global megatrends and risks being experienced today, we stand at a great impasse whereby the future of our collective wellbeing will be determined by the individual and collective leadership shown to 'do the right thing'.

"When the history of our times is written, will we be remembered as the generation that turned our backs in a moment of global crisis, or will it be recorded that we did the right thing?" – Nelson Mandela (2005)

Endnotes

1. WEF, 2016.
2. Ibid.
3. King, 1995.
4. Whiteman, Walker & Perego, 2013.
5. Rockström, Steffen & Noone, 2009.
6. Steffen et al., 2015.
7. Ibid.
8. Raworth, 2012.

9   Ibid.
10 Van den Bergh, Truffer & Kallis, 2011, p7.
11 Van den Bergh, Truffer & Kallis, 2011.
12 Gladwin, Kennelly & Krause, 1995.
13 Marcus, Kurucz & Colbert, 2010.
14 Network for Business Sustainability (NBS), 2015.
15 Maak, 2007.
16 NPC, 2012.
17 Nedbank, 2014.
18 Maathai, 2004.
19 See endnote 14.
20 Ibid.
21 Ibid. Report forthcoming.

References

Gladwin, TN, Kennelly, JJ & Krause, T-S. (1995). 'Shifting paradigms for sustainable development: Implications for management theory and research'. *Academy of Management Review*, 20(4):874–907.
Intergovernmental Panel on Climate Change (IPCC). [Online]. Available: https://www2.ucar.edu/climate/faq/what-intergovernmental-panel-climate-change-ipcc. *[Accessed 20 June 2016].*
King, A. 1995. 'Avoiding ecological surprise: Lessons from long-standing communities'. *Academy of Management Review*, 20(4):961–985.
Maak, T. 2007. Responsible leadership, stakeholder engagement, and the emergence of social capital. *Journal of Business Ethics*, 74(4):329–343.
Maathai, W. 2004. 'Nobel Lecture, Oslo, December 10, 2004'. [Online] Available: http://www.nobelprize.org/nobel_prizes/peace/laureates/2004/maathai-lecture-text.html [Accessed 5 July 2016].
Marcus, J, Kurucz, EC & Colbert, B. 2010. 'Conceptions of the business-society-nature interface: Implications for management scholarship. *Business & Society*, 49).
Millennium Ecosystem Assessment (MEA). [Online]. Available: *en.wikipedia.org/wiki/Millennium_Ecosystem_Assessment*. [Accessed 20 June 2016].
National Planning Commission (NPC). 2012. *Our future – make it work: Executive summary. National development plan 2030 (NDP)*. National Planning Commission & Department of The Presidency.
Nedbank. 2014. *FairShare 2030 plan*.
Network for Business Sustainability (NBS). 2015. *Embedding project: Resources for embedding sustainability*. [Online]. Available: https://embeddingproject.org/resources/pathway/manage-talent/practice/develop. [Accessed 27 June 2016].
Raworth, K. 2012. 'A safe and just space for humanity'. *Oxfam Discussion Papers*. [Online] Available: https://www.oxfam.org/sites/www.oxfam.org/files/dp-a-safe-and-just-space-for-humanity-130212-en.pdf [Access 5 July 2016].
Rockström, J, Steffen, W & Noone, K. 2009. 'A safe operating space for humanity'. *Nature*, 461:472 – 475, September.
Steffen, W, Richardson, K, Rockström, J, Cornell, SE et al. 2015. 'Planetary boundaries: Guiding human development on a changing planet'. *Science*, 1259855.
Van den Bergh, JCJM, Truffer, B & Kallis, G. 2011 'Environmental innovation and societal transitions: Introduction and overviews. *Environmental Innovation and Societal Transitions*, 1:1–23.
Whiteman, G, Walker, B & Perego, P. 2013. 'Planetary boundaries: Ecological foundations for corporate sustainability'. *Journal of Management Studies*, 50(2):307–336.
World Economic Forum (WEF). 2016. *The global risks report 2016*. 11th ed. Geneva, CHE: World Economic Forum.

SECTION 4

LEADERSHIP CONTEXTUAL ENGAGEMENT

Chapter 13

LEADERSHIP ENGAGEMENT WITH THE CONTEXT
Theo H Veldsman

In engaging with its Context, as delineated in the selected Operating Arena of the organisation, leadership have to decide on the appropriate engagement mode to make sense of, interpret and act upon the Context: "Which is the right set of glasses to wear?" The set of glasses used by leadership must enable and empower him/her to see the Context with 20/20 sight, and effectively engage with the Context, in the present and going into the future.[1] Putting on the right set of glasses is the ultimate action in achieving Best Leadership-Context fit. Figure 13.1 shows graphically the positioning of the leadership engagement mode within the Context.

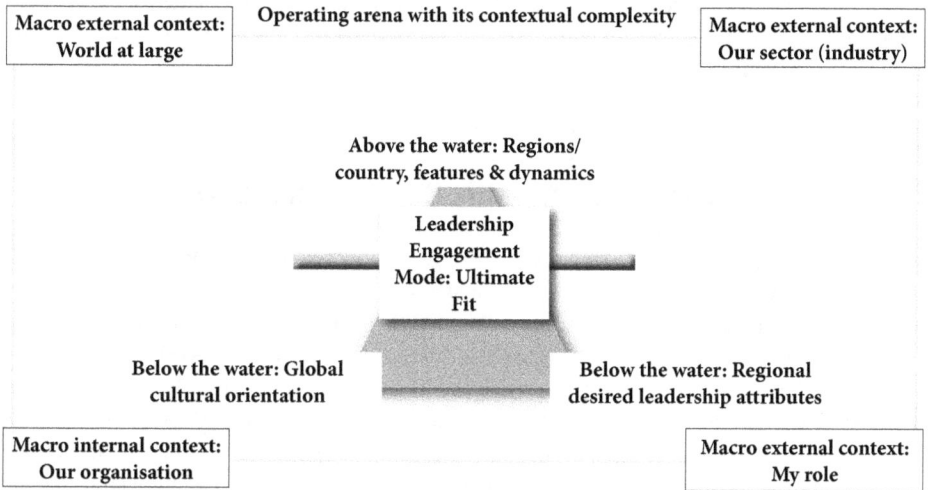

Figure 13.1: Engagement mode as set of glasses to look at context

The set of glasses that leadership puts on can "liberate" his/her thinking about, understanding of and acting upon the Context – Leadership Fit – by not only allowing him/her to see the Context "right", but also by opening up potential new perspectives regarding the Context: "I/We see well, and see what no one-else has seen, even when we look at the same things." In other words, a good Fit. Leadership's set of glasses, however, may blind them to seeing the Context poorly or incorrectly, or to not seeing some contextual features and dynamics at all – a poor Fit. A set of glasses may therefore also "imprison" leadership by creating blind spots about and/or by setting constraints with regard to their thinking about, understanding of, and acting upon the World.[2] Metaphorically, it is the difference in thinking, decisions and actions between a person who believes the world is flat and a person who believes the world is round.

Leadership's set of glasses – engagement mode – is made up of at least three interdependent components: a Worldview, a Decision-making Framework, and a Value Orientation, as shown in Figure 13.2.[3] These components are critical inputs to the Contextual Intelligence of leadership, that is, acting with wise insight regarding the Context. A Worldview enables leadership to see the world correctly; a Decision-making Framework allows leadership to make well-founded decisions about the seen world; and a Value Orientation guides leadership to make ethical (or right) decisions about the seen world.

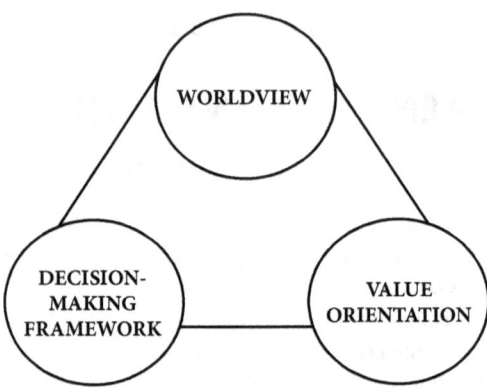

Figure 13.2: The make-up of leadership's set of glasses: the engagement mode with the Context

The purpose of this chapter is to elucidate the three components of the contextual engagement mode as depicted in Figure 13.2, proceeding from Worldview, through the Decision-Making Framework, to Value Orientation. With regard to each, the component will firstly be described; options with regard to the component will be reviewed; and arguments will be offered for a preferred desirable option, given the emerging world order.

Worldview: What is Reality All About?

The first component of the leadership's set of glasses is a Worldview. A Worldview provides leadership with an understanding about the make-up, functioning and evolution of reality, its ontology.[4] In terms of this understanding, leadership then engages in a certain way with reality. The implicit or explicit choice of a Worldview is an "Either-Or" choice: the world is either flat or round. One "converts" to a Worldview though an "Aha!" experience: "This is how it is. It cannot be otherwise." Such a conversion may be triggered by anomalies: "Things do not seem to make sense or work. There must be a better way of making sense of reality." No empirical facts can be offered to prove it is better because the acceptance of a worldview is based in the faith that the chosen Worldview offers the best understanding of reality and "works better".

Eight dominant major Worldviews can be distinguished: Newtonian (or Mechanistic); Cybernetic (or Systems); Chaos/Complexity (or Systemic/Organic); Social Constructivist (or Symbolic interpretative); Relativistic (or Postmodern); Mythical; Fatalistic and Nihilistic.[5] The essence of each in shorthand fashion is as follows:

- **Newtonian (or Mechanistic):** Reality works like a machine with interlocking, turning cogs, and gears.
- **Cybernetic (or Systems):** Reality is made up of systems, one embedded in the other from micro-, through meso-, to macro systems. A system is located in an environment and made up of inputs-throughput-outputs-feedback loops.
- **Chaos/Complexity (or Systemic/Organic):** Reality forms a systemic, integrated, holistic whole of interacting variables, manifested in dynamic self-designing patterns, virtuous or vicious.
- **Social Constructivist (or Symbolic interpretative):** Reality is co-created and enacted by people through shared, contacted meanings, expressed *inter alia* in language, artefacts and symbols.

- **Relativistic (or Postmodern):** Each person creates his/her own personalised reality with its own truth. Everyone's truth is equally valid. No universal, single truth exists. Thus many personal worlds exist with their own truths.
- **Mythical:** Other (invisible) realities beyond this visible reality exist with their own forces/entities, affecting this reality to a greater or lesser extent.
- **Fatalistic:** Events in reality are completely pre-determined, and cannot in any way be influenced. What will happen, will happen.
- **Nihilistic:** Reality has no meaning at all. It is and has no-sense. One has to make the best of a "bad" job.

Table 13.1 provides more detailed descriptions of the eight Worldviews.[6] Many versions exist with regard to each Worldview. For the purpose of this chapter, the intention is to give only the core essence of each.

Table 13.1: Overview of eight dominant Worldviews

NEWTONIAN (or Mechanistic)	CYBERNETIC (or Systems)	CHAOS/COMPLEXITY (or Systemic/Organic)	SOCIAL CONSTRUCTIVIST (Symbolic interpretative)	RELATIVISTIC (or Postmodern)	MYTHICAL	FATALISTIC	NIHILISTIC
• Reality is made up of fixed, interchangeable and stand-alone objects • These objects exist independently, like separate cogs in a machine • The objects relate to each other through linear cause-and-effect relationships • The causal relationships are governed by given immutable laws	• Reality consists of various systems, hierarchically arranged from more to less complex: micro, meso, macro • Each system takes inputs from its environment, and converts them – the throughput – into outputs • Outputs in turn are linked to the inputs via feedback loops • The goal is to reach and maintain homeostasis – balance – and avoid negative entropy – the running down of the system – by ensuring a constant feedback (= information)	• Reality forms an interconnected whole of reciprocally influencing, interacting variables • The interactions between variables are characterised by the ongoing resolution of dynamic, opposing tensions • Through self-organising, tensions are resolved, which manifests itself in dynamic patterns of interaction • A pattern is governed by a limited number of underlying organising rules • A pattern forms either a virtuous or vicious cycle of interaction • Reality as an interconnected whole moves through successive states of chaos – the breakdown of a pattern – and order – the emergence of a pattern	• Reality is co-created through interactions – in the form of dialogue – among persons forming part of a group, community and/or society • Through their interactions, persons ascribe shared meaning and purpose to reality • The shared meaning and purpose are expressed in beliefs, norms, values, language, symbols, and artefacts • The co-created beliefs, norms, values, language, and symbols are internalised by a person and then externally enacted	• Everyone has his/her own unique understanding of reality, carrying equal weight • No single, shared, general truth of reality exists. Hence multiple personal realities and truths exist • Often, however, those who have power or are in power impose on the "powerless" their understanding of reality – their truth in the form of an ideology – to which the powerless must subscribe or face sanctions • The power enforced externally-imposed reality – ideology – must be deconstructed in order to enable each individual to find his/her own truth	• At least two distinct realities exist: one physical and another metaphysical • The metaphysical reality is populated by positive and/or negative forces or a divine being(s) • These forces/divine being(s) affect to a greater or lesser extent what has happened, happens and will happen in the physical reality • Persons may have a personal relationship with such forces/divine being(s) which/whom they may attempt to influence with lesser or greater success • The metaphysical reality may be revealed through sacred text(s) (e.g. Bible, Koran), which has a divine source, and have been conveyed by a prophet(s) and/or holy person acting on behalf of the divine being(s). The believer accepts the revelation as encoded in the text in faith	• Every (future) event in reality is already pre-determined (by a (super) natural force) and is inevitable • Reality is unchangeable and hence unmanageable because events are pre-set • What will happen, will happen regardless of what one knows and does • One is totally at the mercy of the luck of the draw	• Reality has no meaning and purpose at all • Reality is and has no-sense • One is thrown into the world and has to make the best of a "bad" job • One seeks instant gratification and pleasure in the here-and-now because tomorrow may never come or one may be dead

Chapter 13: Leadership engagement with the context

A demonstration of the application of the worldviews to our conceptualisation of organisation

To illustrate practically the application of the different worldviews described in Table 13.1, four different graphic conceptualisations are given of the organisation based respectively on a: Newtonian (or Mechanistic) (see Figure 13.3); Cybernetic (or Systems) (see Figure 13.4); Chaos/Complexity (or Systemic/Organic) (see Figure 13.5); or Social Constructivist (or Symbolic Interpretative) (see Figure 13.6) Worldview.

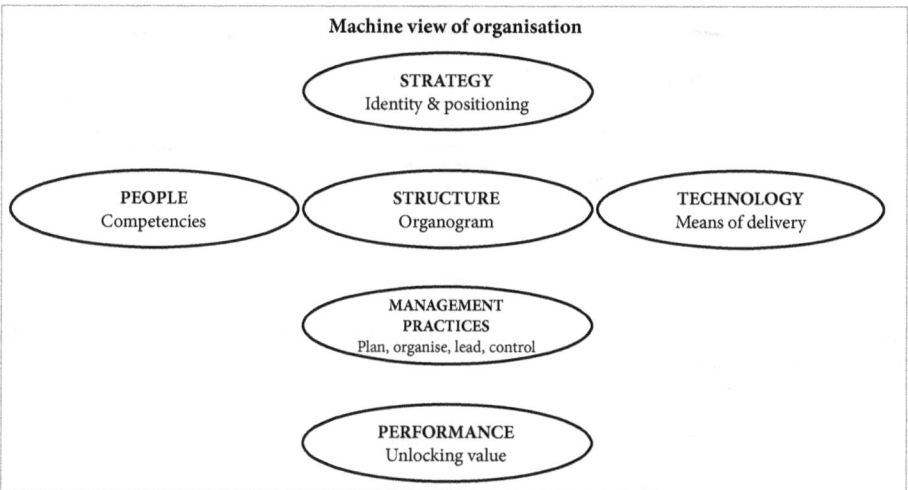

Figure 13.3: The organisation as seen through a Newtonian (or Mechanistic) Worldview: The organisation made up of separate elements, like cogs in a machine

Source: *Constructed by author*

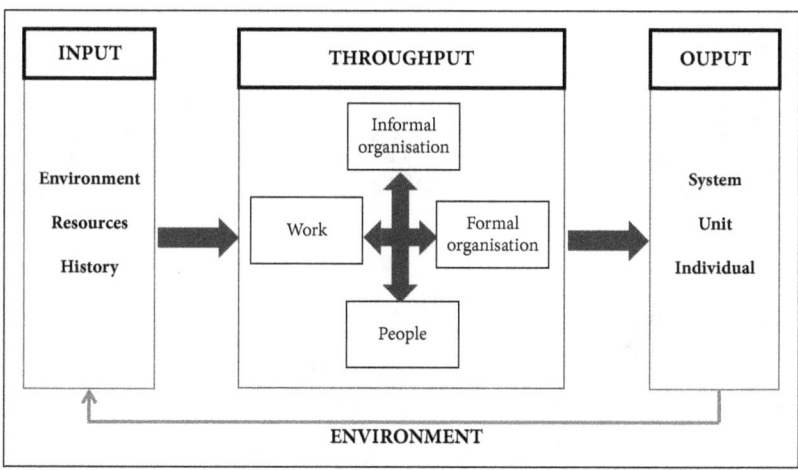

Figure 13.4: The organisation as seen through a Cybernetic (or Systems) Worldview: The organisation as an input-conversion-output-feedback system

Source: *The congruence model of David Nadler & Michelle Tushman*[7]

173

Leadership in Context

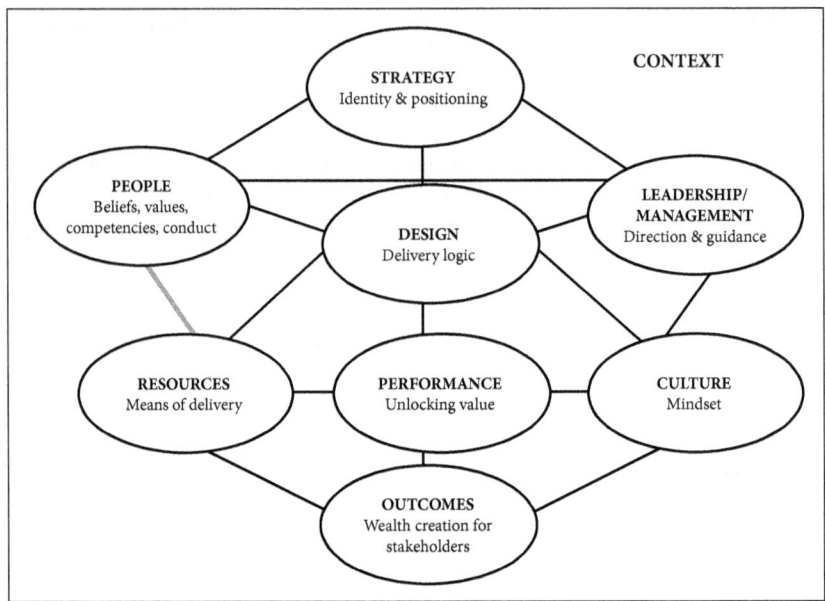

Figure 13.5: The organisation as seen through a Chaos/Complexity (or Systemic/Organic) Worldview: The organisation as a holistic, integrated, dynamic whole
Source: *Author in conjunction with Wynand Geldenhuys*

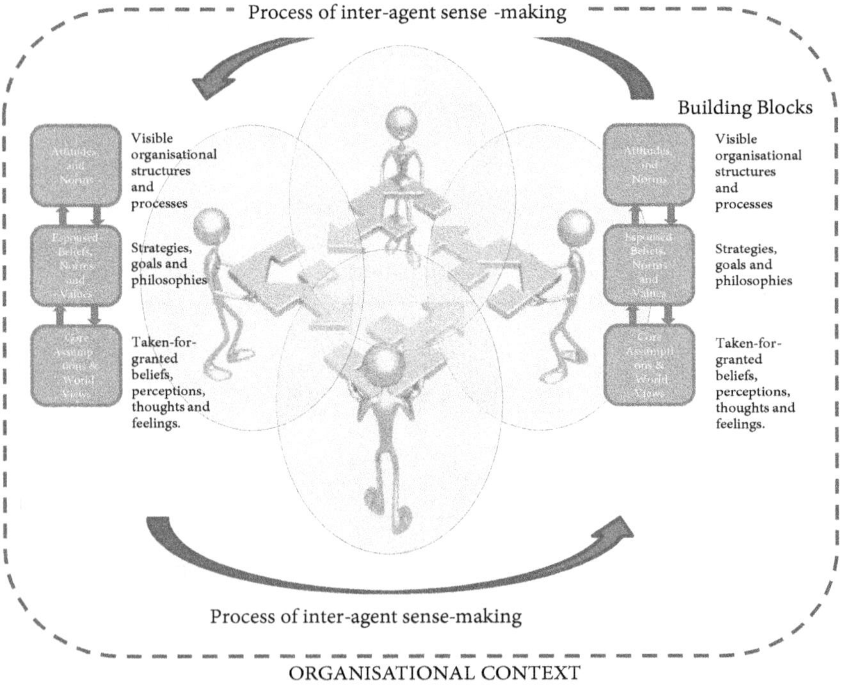

Figure 13.6: The organisation as seen through a Social Constructivist (or Symbolic Interpretative) Worldview: The organisation as co-constructed by organisational members as a sense-making and meaning-giving entity
Source: *Johann Kritzinger*

In search of a best-fit Worldview: A combination of the chaos/complexity and social constructivism Worldviews

It can be postulated that at present the Worldview appearing to provide the best understanding of reality in general is based on a combination of the Chaos/Complexity and Social Constructivism Worldviews. According to this combined Worldview, reality has to be understood in terms of the following principles:[8]

- **Holism:** Reality forms an *integrated whole* of reciprocal, interacting variables, with the whole being larger than the sum of its parts.
- **Interconnectivity:** The variables making up reality are *connected in multiple ways* and affect each other in many and diverse ways. These interactions are non-linear. Minor changes can cause proportionately large, knock-on consequences. *Effects and counter-effects* therefore exist, resulting from the multiple ways in which the integrated whole of variables is interconnected, and hence interacts. The determination of one-on-one cause-and-effect relationships is virtually impossible because of interconnectivity.
- **Dynamic tensions:** Frequently the interconnected variables have *opposing requirements*, which create dilemmas and paradoxes. "Both/And" instead of "Either-Or" resolutions have to be sought for these tensions. Opposites have to be fused in a balanced fashion. At most, dynamic stability can be created – in other words, order for a transitory period of time. One-sided resolutions of dilemmas and paradoxes are unstable and over time result in ever stronger counter-effects.
- **Convergence:** The interconnected, integrated variables over time configure (or self-organise) themselves into a set *pattern of interaction emerging over time*. A pattern expresses itself in vicious and/or virtuous interaction cycles, which resolve in one way or another, at a given point in time/space, the dynamic tensions within and between variables. The interaction pattern is based on a *limited set of underlying rules* that govern the dynamic functioning of the pattern. A pattern orders reality at a given point in time and space.
- **Divergence:** A *pattern over time spontaneously disintegrates* because of the one-sided resolutions of dilemmas and paradoxes. The difficulty of maintaining a balanced fusion of the dynamic opposites over time progressively undermines the continued existence of a pattern; and/or the strengths of a pattern over time invert to become weaknesses because the overemphasis of a strength creates blind spots that limit the detection of new trends. Under conditions of pattern dismantling and destruction, chaos reigns until a new pattern commences emerging, which will again create order at that point in time/space. The new pattern may be based on a different underlying set of governing rules.
- **Potentiality:** Any pattern reflects merely *one possible actualisation* out of a wide range of potential patterns. The reality contains infinite possibilities. There is no indefinite "best way only".
- **Immersion:** Everyone is embedded in reality with a *parochial view of the pattern* in existence at that time and place, depending on one's location in time and space within that pattern. One's perspective on reality, as derived from one's view of the pattern in force at that point in time and space, is only *one* perspective on that reality as constituted by oneself for oneself or by the action of the community in which one is embedded. The perspective one has enables one to have or gain insight, but concurrently also locks one into a certain view of reality, which creates tunnel vision.
- **Shared and enacted meaning:** The *triangulation of the parochial reality perspectives* of the various stakeholders of the organisation immersed through the internalised, co-created meaning and externalised shared beliefs, norms, values, language, symbols, and artefacts

which they enact, is therefore critical in order to arrive at a truer approximation of the overall pattern in force or which needs to be in force at a given time and place, and how to enact the shared understanding collectively.

Decision-Making Framework: How Do We Judge What Action Has to be Taken?

Making effective decisions (or rendering judgements) regarding the appropriate action to take in order to attain desired end states is central to leadership. It is perhaps the very essence of everyday leadership.[9] The second component of the leadership's set of glasses is therefore a Decision-making Framework. A Decision-making Framework specifies in a systemic fashion what aspects need consideration in guiding and enabling leadership to render good judgements and act effectively upon the World as "seen" through leadership's adopted Worldview. The crafted Framework does not represent the daily decision-making process itself – the choice of means to accomplish ends[10] – but provides guidelines for the "bases" to be covered, and the alternatives to consider with regard to each base.

A comprehensive, systemic and multidimensional Decision-Making Framework is proposed, consisting of seven interdependent, interactive, decision-making domains.[11] The Domains with their respective decision-making options are depicted in Figure 13.7. The suggested Framework requires coherence in making aligned choices regarding options across the different Domains. The attributes of the individual decision maker are not included as part of the Framework, though they would most certainly affect the manner in which the Framework is used and applied, for example, his/her information capacity, creative ability, risk-taking propensity, leadership style and aspiration level.[12]

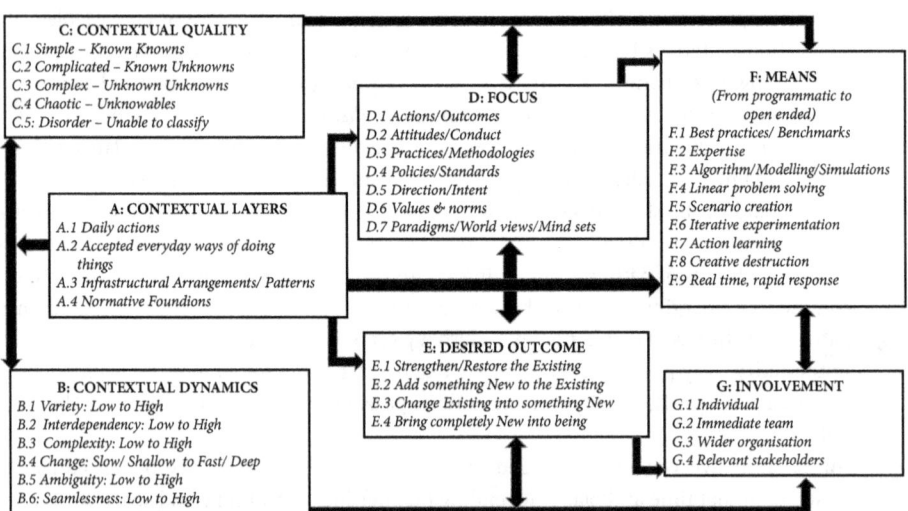

Figure 13.7: A comprehensive decision-making framework

As can be seen from Figure 13.7, the proposed Decision-Making Framework – believed to be fit for the world of tomorrow – consists of the following Decision-Making Domains with their commensurate options:

- **A: Contextual Layers:** This Domain pertains to the different, interdependent layers making up the Context where a deeper layer forms the foundation and sets the parameters for a

shallower layer: from A.1 Daily Actions to A.4 Normative Foundations. Leadership has to consider at which layer they wish/need to intervene, with the implication that a decision to engage at a deeper layer implies that there is/are a shallower layer(s).[13]
- **B: Contextual Dynamics:** This Domain encompasses the dynamics informing the layer(s) to be engaged in the emerging world, expressed in the acronym VICCAS : Variety, Interdependency (that is, connectivity), Complexity, Change, Ambiguity, and Seamlessness. Leadership has to assess what the state of the respective contextual variables is – low to high – affecting the Contextual Dynamics with regard to the Contextual Layer(s) they wish to engage with. The higher these variables, the more the Contextual Dynamics resemble the VICCAS world order. Drucial to the Contextual Dynamics is the Contextual Vantage Point (also discussed in that chapter) which leadership decides to adopt: either to adapt/enhance, or to transform/recreate the Context. If the latter Vantage Point is adopted, the chances are high that all of the contextual variables making up VICCAS will be high.[14]
- **C: Contextual Quality:** This Domain relates to the assessment by leadership of the "Knowness" of the variables – for example, persons, things, events, outcomes – making up the selected Contextual Layer(s) and Dynamics: the Quality of the Context they have to deal with. From Known Knowns – a Simple Context to Unknowables – to Chaotic Context (excluding the Context of pure Disorder where one is unable to do any classification). Through information gathering leadership typically attempts to move Contexts from Chaotic to Simple in order to increase its knowability, inter alia by lowering VICCAS.
- **D: Focus:** This Domain entails what Leadership wants to make decisions about, the focus of its decision-making: from D.1 Actions/Outcomes to D.7 Paradigms/Worldviews/Mindsets. The options regarding the Contextual Layer will be engaged in and the intended Focus will correspond approximately. Table 13.2 depicts this correspondence.

Table 13.2 Approximate correspondences between A: Contextual Layer and D: Focus Decision-Making options

A: CONTEXTUAL LAYERS	D: FOCUS
A.1 Daily actions	D.1 Actions/Outcomes
A.2 Accepted everyday ways of doing things	D.2 Attitudes/Conduct D.3 Practices/Methodologies
A.3 Infrastructural Arrangements/Patterns	D.4 Policies/Standards D.5 Direction/Intent
A.4 Normative Foundations	D.6 Values and norms D.7 Paradigms/Worldviews/Mindsets

- **E: Desired Outcome:** This Domain refers to what type of change leadership intends to bring about: from E.1 Strengthen/Restore the Existing to E.4 Bring the completely New into Being. As one moves from E.1 to E.4, it may move B: Context Dynamics and C: Contextual Quality to more Unknowns and higher VICCAS decision-making options respectively.
- **F: Means:** This Domain pertains to the way in which leadership wants to affect the change aligned to and in support of the options exercised with regard to the preceding Domains. Generally speaking, the more the movement is from lower to higher numbered options in these Domains, for example, A: Contextual Layers (from A.1 Daily actions to A.4 Normative foundations); B: Contextual Dynamics (from low to high on VICCAS), and so on, the more the choice of Means moves from F.1 Best practices/Benchmarks to F.9 Real time, rapid response.

- **G: Involvement:** This Domain relates to whom to involve in the decision-making: from the G.1 Individual to G.4 Relevant Stakeholders. Similar to F: Means, the more the movement is from lowered to higher numbered options in the preceding Domains, the more the choice of Involvement moves from G.1 Individual to G.4 Relevant Stakeholders because the need for widespread, creative and diverse input into, buy-in and ownership of decisions by more parties increase.

Table 13.3 indicates typical Decision-Making Domain option choices for different Decision-Making Approaches relative to different Contexts, as derived from the Decision-Making Framework given in Figure 13.2.[i]

Table 13.3: Decision-making domain option choices for different decision-making approaches relative to different contexts

DECISION-MAKING DOMAIN	STABLE, PREDICTABLE CONTEXT	INCREMENTALLY, RELATIVELY PREDICTABLE CHANGING CONTEXT	REVOLUTIONARY, UNPREDICTABLY, RAPIDLY CHANGING CONTEXT
A: CONTEXTUAL LAYERS	A.1 Daily actions	A.2 Accepted everyday ways of doing things	A.3 Infrastructural Arrangements/Patterns A.4 Normative Foundations
B: CONTEXTUAL DYNAMICS B.1 Variety; B.2 Interdependency; B.3 Complexity; B.4 Change; B.5 Ambiguity; B.6: Seamlessness	Low	Medium	High
C: CONTEXTUAL QUALITY	C.1 Simple – Known Knowns	C.2 Complicated – Known Unknowns	C.3 Complex – Unknown Unknowns C.4 Chaotic – Unknowables
D: FOCUS	D.1 Actions/Outcomes	D.2 Attitudes/Conduct D.3 Practices/Methodologies	D.4 Policies/Standards D.5 Direction/Intent D.6 Values & norms D.7 Paradigms/Worldviews/Mindsets
E: DESIRED OUTCOME	E.1 Strengthen/Restore the Existing E.2 Add something New to the Existing	E.3 Change Existing into something New	E.4 Bring completely New into Being

➡

---

i Osborn, Hunt & Jauch (2002) distinguish four types of Context: Stability, Crisis, Dynamic equilibrium, and Edge of chaos.

DECISION-MAKING DOMAIN	STABLE, PREDICTABLE CONTEXT	INCREMENTALLY, RELATIVELY PREDICTABLE CHANGING CONTEXT	REVOLUTIONARY, UNPREDICTABLY, RAPIDLY CHANGING CONTEXT
F: MEANS	F.1 Best practices/ Benchmarks F.2 Expertise	F.3 Algorithm/ Modelling / Simulations F.4 Linear problem solving F.5 Scenario creation	F.6 Iterative experimentation F.7 Action learning F.8 Creative destruction F.9 Real time, rapid response
G: INVOLVEMENT	G.1 Individual G.2 Immediate team	G.2 Immediate team G.3 Wider organisation	G.3 Wider organisation G.4 Relevant stakeholders

Although a single, given Decision-Making Framework has to be agreed on by leadership in order to engage appropriately with the Context like the one suggested in Figure 13.2, Table 13.3 shows that a fit-for-purpose Decision-Making Approach(es) – as derived from the agreed upon Decision-Making Framework – has to be constructed specifically to the Context concerned in order to make good decisions. This is in contrast to the conversion and attachment to a single Worldview.

Metaphorically, a Decision-Making Framework maps the rules for the playing field whereas a fit-for-purpose Decision-Making Approach outlines the game plan for a specific playing field. Thus an open mind, agility, responsiveness, and a decision on who to involve are critical success factors in arriving at a fit-for-purpose Decision-Making Approach suitable to a specific Context(s) as they emerge or are changed.

Value Orientation: What is the Relative Worth of Persons, Things, Events and Outcomes?

As was elucidated above, a Worldview enables leadership to see the world correctly. A Decision-making Framework allows leadership to render good judgements regarding action in respect of the seen world. The third component of the leadership's set of glasses is a Value Orientation. Leadership needs to render *value judgements* when engaging with their Context through the use of their adopted Decision-making Framework, as operationalised in a Decision-Making Approach relevant to a specific Context.

These value judgements are derived from and based on a certain **Value Orientation** explicitly adopted by leadership, and/or having been implicitly socialised into. A Value Orientation enables leadership to make moral and ethical judgements with regard to the relative worth of persons, things, events, outcomes by providing them with the criteria to judge their Importance, Rightfulness, Desirability and/or Beauty.

A Value Orientation translates into a certain value-informed mode of seeing, thinking, interpreting and acting by leadership. Leadership Excellence requires not only knowing what one's Value Orientation is, but also being sure that it is credible, sound, robust and ethically justifiable. A Value Orientation is not to be confused with the more visible and concrete values of organisation – for example, integrity, client centricity, and professionalism. A Value Orientation forms the ultimate fountain head and source of such organisational values.

A bewildering array of Value Orientations exists. In order to make sense of this most confusing state of affairs, the intention here, for the purpose of this chapter, is to arrive at integrated meta-conceptual schemata within which different Value Orientations can be crafted by: (1) demarcating the essential Value Categories to consider; and (2) identifying the more critical Value Judgements associated with each category. Figure 13.8 depicts the proposed Value Orientation Schemata.[15] What is not incorporated into the Schemata is how the Value Categories and Judgments may vary across different cultural contexts and orientations.

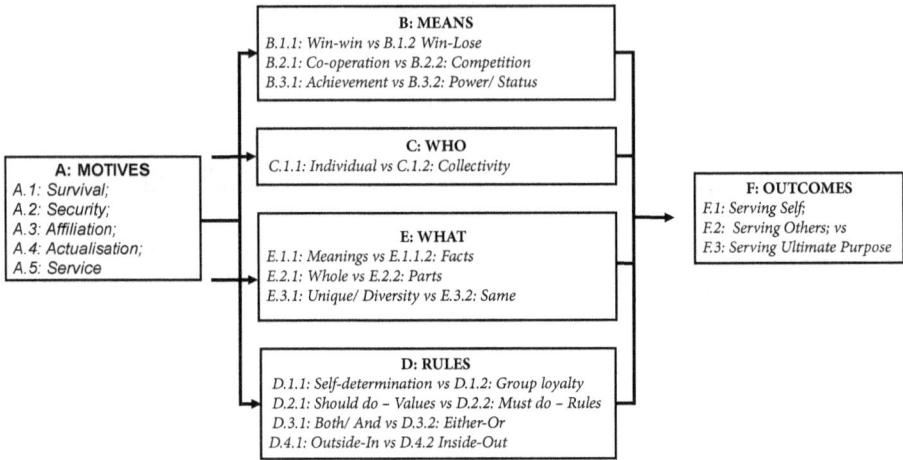

Figure 13.8: Proposed value orientation schemata

According to Figure 13.8, the suggested Value Orientation Schemata are made up of the following seven Value Categories with their respective value judgements that indicate what may be chosen to be ethically acceptable:

- **A: Motives:** The *why* of (or rationale for) action, for example, survival or service
- **B: Means:** The *how* of action, for example, win-win or win-loose
- **C: Who:** The *party* involved in the action, for example, individual or collectivity
- **D: What:** The *aspect* to consider during action taking, for example, meanings or facts
- **E: Rules:** The applicable *action guideline* to follow, for example, self-determination or group loyalty
- **F: Outcomes:** The intended *effect* of the action, for example, serving Self or Others

Based on the Value Orientation Schemata given in Figure 13.8, a multitude of Value Orientations are possible. Four archetypical Value Orientations are given in Table 13.4 (below), in hierarchical order from a Lower to the Highest Value order: from Predator – self-survival; Clan – loyal group membership; Egocentric – personal-need actualisation; to Steward – service to greater humanity.[ii]

---

ii   Spiral Dynamics is made up of eight levels of evolving, layered, Value Orientations (= Human Niches): from a primitive Niche – Survival: egocentric and individualistic – through to an advanced Niche – Holistic: ultimate purposes/meanings and spirituality. The four Value Orientations proposed in the accompanying box correspond roughly to two Niches combined at a time from the bottom up to the highest two Niches of Spiral Dynamics.

Table 13.4: Archetypical value orientations

VALUE ORIENTATION	A: MOTIVES	B: MEANS	C: WHO	D: WHAT	E: RULES	F: OUTCOMES
Lowest order: *Predator*	A.1: Survival A.2: Security	B.1.2 Win-Lose B.2.2: Competition B.3.2: Power/Status	C.1.1: Individual	D.1.1: Self-determination D.2.2: Must do – Rules D.3.2: Either-Or D.4.2 Inside-Out	E.1.1.2: Facts E.2.2: Parts E.3.2: Same	F.1: Serving Self
Middle order: *Clan*	A.3: Affiliation	B.1.1: Win-win B.2.1: Co-operation B.3.2: Power/Status	C.1.2: Collectivity	D.1.2: Group loyalty D.2.2: Must do – Rules D.3.2: Either-Or D.4.1: Outside-In	E.1.1.1: Meanings E.2.1: Whole E.3.2: Same	F.2: Serving Others
High order: *Egocentric*	A.4: Actualisation	B.1.1: Win-win B.2.2: Competition B.3.1: Achievement	C.1.1: Individual	D.1.1: Self-determination D.2.1: Should do – Values D.3.1: Both/And D.4.2 Inside-Out	E.1.1: Meanings E.2.1: Whole E.3.1: Unique/ Diversity	F.1: Serving Self
Highest order: *Steward*	A.5: Service	B.1.1: Win-win B.2.1: Co-operation B.3.1: Achievement	C.1.2: Collectivity	D.1.1: Self-determination D.2.1: Should do – Values D.3.1: Both/And D.4.1: Outside-In	E.1.1: Meanings E.2.1: Whole E.3.1: Unique/ Diversity	F.3: Serving Ultimate Purpose

The proposed hierarchical order given in the accompanying box has at least three implications: (1) a higher order Orientation is more ethically, moral, humane, and hence more desirable; (2) evolution from a lower to a higher Value Orientation level is possible, and is to be aspired to. Inversely, regress to a lower level can also occur; and (3) a higher order Value Orientation does not mean that a lower order Orientation(s) becomes inactive, but it reframes a lower order(s) to take on the higher order qualities. For example, survival – obtaining food – at the lowest order is transformed in order to be placed in the service of humanity at the highest order – food security for a nation. At present the most desirable Value Orientation punted is that of Steward.

In terms of Value Orientation Schemata (refer to Figure 13.8), leadership can identify its current Value Orientation, and consider its "value-add" in terms of rendering credible, sound, robust and ethically justifiable value judgements relative to the Context with which it is engaging. Leadership may decide to shift its existing Value Orientation to one more justifiable, which is in its own right a value judgement.

Conclusion

The premise of this chapter has been that putting on the right set of glasses to provide 20/20 vision is the ultimate action by leadership in achieving Best Leadership-Context fit. Either one can see distinctly and clearly, or one is impaired in seeing what is out there. As was discussed, the set of glasses is made up of at least three interdependent components: a Worldview, a Decision-making Framework, and Value Orientation.

The choice of a Worldview is an "Aha!" experience or an "Either-Or" conversion choice. At present it appears as if the best understanding of reality in general is provided by a combination of Chaos/Complexity and Social Constructivism. The imperative for a Decision-making Framework is having a complete, comprehensive Framework enabling one to construct context-specific, fit-for-purpose Decision-making Approaches, and switching Approaches as Contexts change. Such a Framework was presented, and three context-specific Decision-making Approaches outlined: Stable, predictable; Incrementally, relatively predictably changing; and Revolutionary, unpredictably, rapidly changing. And, finally, having a well-developed, all-embracing Value Orientation Schemata allows one to assess and take action in terms of one's current and desired Value Orientation order level. Four value order levels were suggested: Predator, Clan, Egocentric and Steward. Currently, the last-mentioned is being promoted as the aspirational order.

The appropriate engagement mode needs to form the basis of the Organisational Landscape (including its strategic intent, culture and climate), and inform the identification, selection, growth and development of the organisation's leadership and members.

Endnotes

1. Bawden, 2010.
2. Ibid.
3. Ibid.
4. Bawden, 2010; Koltko-Rivera, 2004; Moghalu, 2014.
5. Cf. Alvesson, 2002; Boal, Hunt & Jaros, 2003; Boje, Gephart & Thatchenkery, 1996; Cromby & Nightingale, 2002; Boulding, 1976; Cromby & Nightingale, 2002; Drack, 2009; Dubtovsky, 2004; Fairhurst, 2009; Fitzgerald, 2001; Gephart, Boje & Thatchenkery, 1996; Gharajedaghi, 2011; Guastello Koopmans & Pincus, 2009; Guba & Lincoln, 1994; Hatch, 2006; Hassard, 1993; Hazy, Goldstein & Lichtenstein, 2007; Kurtz & Snowden, 2003; Nightingale & Cromby, 2002; Obolensky, 2010; Peery, 1975; Stacey, Griffin & Shaw, 2000; Weick, 1969; Westwood, R & Clegg, S., 2003; Wheatley, 2010.
6. Cf. Alvesson, 2002; Boal, Hunt & Jaros, 2003; Boje, Gephart & Thatchenkery, 1996; Cromby & Nightingale, 2002; Boulding, 1976; Cromby & Nightingale, 2002; Drack, 2009; Dubtovsky, 2004; Fairhurst, 2009; Fitzgerald, 2001; Gephart, Boje & Thatchenkery, 1996; Gharajedaghi, 2011; Guastello Koopmans & Pincus, 2009; Guba & Lincoln, 1994; Hatch, 2006; Hassard, 1993; Hazy, Goldstein & Lichtenstein, 2007; Kurtz & Snowden, 2003; Nightingale & Cromby, 2002; Obolensky, 2010; Peery, 1975; Stacey, Griffin & Shaw, 2000; Weick, 1969; Westwood, R & Clegg, S., 2003; Wheatley, 2010.
7. Nadler & Tushman, 1999.
8. Adapted and expanded from Veldsman, 2002. See also Bawden, 2010.
9. MacCrimmon & Taylor, 1976; Useem, 2010.
10. Chester Barnard, cited by Useem, 2010.
11. Cf., for example, Kurtz & Snowden, 2003; MacCrimmon & Taylor, 1976; Snowden & Boone, 2007;
12. MacCrinnon & Talylor (1976)

13   Veldsman, 2015.
14   Cf., for example, Kurtz & Snowden, 2003; MacCrimmon & Taylor, 1976; Snowden & Boone, 2007; Useem, 2010.
15   The Value Categories with their respective value judgements were extracted by a 'conceptual factor analysis' of the ethical and leadership literature in general, and a comprehensive Value Orientation, called Spiral Dynamics. It is based on a bio-psychosocial theory of evolving human development (Beck & Cowan, 2006). See also Hernandez, (2012); Mirvis, P. & Gunning, L.T. (2006) on stewardship.

References

Alvesson, M. 2002. *Postmodernism and social research*. Philadelphia, PA: Open University.
Bawden, R. 2010. 'Messy issues, worldviews and systemic competencies'. In C Blackmore (ed). *Social learning systems and communities of practice*. London, UK: Springer. 89–101.
Beck, DE & Cowan, CC. 2006. *Spiral dynamics. Mastering values, leadership and change*. Malden, MA: Blackwell Publishing.
Berrien, FK. 1976. 'A general systems approach to organisations. In MD Dunnette (ed). *Handbook of industrial and organisational psychology*. Chicago, IL: Rand McNally College Publishing. 41–62.
Boal, KB, Hunt, JG & Jaros, SJ. 2003. Ontology. In R Westwood & S Clegg (eds). *Debating organisations*. Malden, MA: Blackwell. 83–98.
Boje, DM, Gephart, RP & Thatchenkery, TJ (eds). 1996. 'Management, social issues, and the postmodern era' & 'Exploring the terrain of modernism and postmodernism in organization theory' (Chs 2 & 3). In DM Boje, RP Gephart & TJ Thatchenkery (eds). *Postmodern management and organisation theory*. Thousand Oaks, CA: Sage.
Cromby, J & Nightingale, DJ. 2002. 'Social constructionism as ontology'. *Theory and Psychology*, 12(5):701–713.
Drack, M. 2009. 'Ludwig von Bertalanffy's early systems approach'. *Systems Research and Behavioural Sciences*, 26:536–572.
Dubtovsky, V. 2004. 'Towards systems principles: General systems theory and the alternative approach'. *Systems Research and Behavioural Sciences*, 21(2):109–122.
Fairhurst, GT. 2009. 'Considering context in discursive leadership research'. *Human Relations*, 62:1607–1633.
Fitzgerald, LA. 2001. 'Chaos: The lens that transcends'. *Journal of Organisational Change Management*, 15(4):339–358.
Gephart, RP, Boje, DM. & Thatchenkery, TJ. 1996. 'Postmodern management and the coming crises of organisational analysis'. In DM Boje, RP Gephart & TJ Thatchenkery (eds). *Postmodern management and organisation theory*. Sage. 1–18.
Gharajedaghi, J. 2011. *Systems thinking. Managing chaos and complexity*, Amsterdam, NL: Elsevier.
Guastello, S, Koopmans, M & Pincus, D (eds). 2009. *Chaos and complexity in psychology*. Cambridge, UK: Cambridge University Press.
Guba, NK. & Lincoln, YS. 1994. 'Competing paradigms'. In D Lincoln (ed). *Handbook of qualitative research*. Thousand Oaks, CA: Sage.
Hatch, MJ. 2006. *Organisation theory*. Oxford, UK: Oxford University Press.
Hassard, J. 1993. 'Postmodernism and organisational analysis: An overview'. In J Hassard & M Parker (eds). *Postmodernism and organisations*. London, UK: Sage.
Hazy, JM, Goldstein, JA. & Lichtenstein, BB (eds). 2007. *Complex systems leadership theory*. Mansfield, MA: ISCE Publishing.
Hernandez, M. 2012. 'Toward an understanding of the psychology of stewardship'. *Academy of Management Review*, 37(2):172–193. [Online]. Available: http://dx.doi.org/10.5465/amr.2010.0363.
Koltko-Rivera, ME. 2004. 'The psychology of worldviews'. *Review of General Psychology*, 8(1):3–58.
Kurtz, C & Snowden, DJ. 2003. 'The new dynamics of strategy: Sense-making in a complex and complicated world'. *IBM Systems Journal*, 42:462–483.
MacCrimmon, KR. & Taylor, RN. 1976. 'Decision making and problem solving'. In MD Dunnette (ed). *Handbook of industrial and organisational psychology*, 1397–1453. Chicago, IL: Rand McNally.
Mirvis, P & Gunning, LT. 2006. 'Creating a community of leaders'. *Organizational Dynamics*, 35(1):69–82.
Moghalu, KC. 2014. *Emerging Africa*. Strand, ZA: Penguin Books.
Nadler, D & Tushman, M. 1999. 'The organisation of the future: Strategic imperatives and core competencies

for the 21st century'. *Organisational Dynamics*, 28(1):45–60.

Obolensky, N. 2010. *Complex adaptive leadership*. Farnham, UK: Ashgate Publishing.

Osborn, RN, Hunt, JG & Jauch, LR. 2002. 'Toward a contextual theory of leadership'. *The Leadership Quarterly*, 13:797–837.

Nightingale, DJ & Cromby, J. 2002. 'Social constructionism as ontology: Exposition and example'. *Theory and Psychology*, 12(5):701–712.

Peery, NS. 1975. 'General systems approaches to organisations: Some problems in applications'. *The Journal of Management Studies*, 12(3):266–275.

Snowden, DJ. & Boone, ME. 2007. 'A leaders' framework for decision making'. *Harvard Business Review*, 1–8, November.

Stacey, R 2015. 'Understanding organisations as complex responsive processes of relating'. In GR Bushe & RJ Marshak (eds). *Dialogic organisation development. The theory and practice of transformational change*. Oakland, CA: Berrett-Koehler. 151–176.

Stacey, RD, Griffin, D & Shaw, P. 2000. *Complexity and management. Fad or radical challenge to systems thinking?* London, UK: Routledge.

Useem, M. 2010. 'Decision making as leadership foundation'. In N Nohria & R Khurana (eds.) *Handbook of leadership theory and practice*. Boston, MA: Harvard University Press. 507–525.

Veldsman, TH. 2002. 'Perspective 3: Navigating galaxies of leadership stars: Aligning context, roles and competencies for leadership effectiveness'. In TH Veldsman. *Into the people effectiveness arena. Navigating between chaos and order*. Johannesburg, ZA: Knowledge Resources. 72–98.

Veldsman, TH. 2015. 'The power of the fish is in the water'. *African Journal of Business Ethics*, 9(1):63–83.

Weick, K. 1969. *The social psychology of organising*. Reading, MA: Addison-Wesley.

Westwood, R & Clegg, S. 2003. *Debating organisation. Point-counterpoint in organisation studies*. Malden, MA: Blackwell.

Wheatley, MJ. 2010. *Leadership and the new science*. San Francisco, CA: Berrett-Koehler.

SECTION 5
LEADERSHIP STORIES

Chapter 14

LEADERSHIP STORIES

Introduction

In its very essence, the organisation is a dialogical network of interpersonal interconnections based on conversations, expressed in the form of stories. Stories are naturally-occurring phenomena in organisations through which information, shared experiences, expectations, culture, and identity are passed on. Stories are the very fabric of organisational life. They add a psychological dimension to organisational life through its feeling and experiencing dimension in the form of sense-making, meaning-giving, as well as emotional attachment and involvement which rational, empirical information and lack of knowledge cannot provide.

Storytelling infuses the whole Strategic Leadership Value Chain. It is persuasive leadership-in-action. A story as a form of conversation is capable of representing and transferring complex, multidimensional organisational realities to listeners in a simple and effortless way in order to make sense of, and give meaning and purpose to, organisational reality.

At its most basic level, storytelling as a conversation (or dialogue) refers to what is being said and listened to between people. The word 'dialogue' stems from two Greek roots, "*dia*" and "*logos*", jointly suggesting the sense of "meaning flowing through". Stories help organisational members to make sense of who they are, where they come from and fit in, and what they want to be. They help reduce organisational uncertainty, complexity and ambiguity by quickly and coherently disseminating information; they frame organisational events through their value-laden features; and they promote organisational culture and identification by establishing a context for organisational members.

Using stories is one of the best ways to:

- make abstract concepts meaningful;
- help connect people and ideas;
- inspire imagination and motivate action;
- give "breathing space" in the frenetic and merciless task-driven nature of the organisation;
- allow different perspectives to emerge;
- create sense, coherence, and meaning;
- develop value-centric descriptions of situations, allowing knowledge to be applied and solutions to be found;
- convey organisational values and culture;
- communicate complex messages simply;
- connect people into a shared frame of reference; and
- inspire change.

In the *first instance* leaders are, and have to be, storytellers about themselves: from where they have come; who they are; what they stand for; what they believe in; what they want to achieve and how; and what they want to leave behind as a legacy. The character, competence, connectedness, caring and commitment of leaders are manifested *inter alia* in how well they understand, and are able and willing to share, their personal journeys as leaders: from the past, through the present, into the future. It is a most powerful way in which to connect with others.

In the *second instance*, leaders have to be able to tell the story of the organisation they are currently involved in: the identity and ideology of the organisation; where the organisation has come from; its desired future destination and legacy; the journey travelled to date by the organisation; the journey still to be travelled; and how things are done and not done in the organisation.

This Section provides examples of the first kind of leadership stories: leaders' stories about themselves as leaders.

The accompanying box gives a list of the leaders whose stories follow – with their respective core themes – are included in this Section.

LEADER'S STORY	THEME OF STORY
Bridgette Gasa	*Good leaders unite people*
Cheryl Carolus	*Leaders must lead by example*
Ali Bacher	*Captaining on and off the field*
Shameel Joosub	*Creating movement as a leader in a constantly evolving and changing environment*
Herman Mashaba	*Good leaders are guided by reality, not wishful thinking*
Pfungwa Serima	*Head in the Clouds and feet on the ground*

References

Boje, D. 2008. *Storytelling organizations*. Thousand Oaks, CA: Sage.

Boyce, M.E. 1996. 'Organisational story and storytelling: A critical review.' *Journal of Organisational Change Management*, 9(5):5-26.

Christie, P. 2009. *Every leader a story teller – storytelling skills for personal leadership*. Johannesburg, ZA: Knowres.

Denning, S. 2011. *The leader's guide to storytelling*, San Francisco, CA: Jossey-Bass

Gabriel, Y. 2000). *Storytelling in organisations: Facts, fictions and fantasies*. New York, NY: Oxford University Press.

Ibarra, H & Lineback, K. 2005. 'What's your story?' *Harvard Business Review*, 1–7, January.

Veldsman, D & May, M. S. 2012. 'The stories that leaders tell during organisational change: The search for meaning during organisational transformation'. Unpublished Masters thesis, University of South Africa, Pretoria, South Africa.

Good leaders unite people

Bridgette Gasa

Article published in Sake Beeld on 24 September 2015.
Translated from Afrikaans. Used with permission

It is becoming increasingly difficult in South Africa's economic and political climate to structure consensus on how best to define leadership that is required in all of society. Across dinner tables and in social settings there is a discussion around the lack of leadership and the accompanying anecdotes are around an increasing depletion of leaders of exemplary and unquestionable character and disposition. This discourse is usually accompanied by an incomplete analysis of the state of collapse in public entities, and the questionable behaviour of those in leadership in private entities/society at large and, of course, in the political sphere.

How we define leadership has in itself transformed from a phase of one to two or more distinct stages or a whole new meaning in and of itself. One would ask: are we fast becoming a country whose leadership and moral compass is consistently being rigorously reviewed? There are all sorts of arbiters who use a litmus test – known only to themselves – to weigh in on this leadership discourse. I have often found myself battling to understand what it is that we should know and appreciate today regarding leadership. In this quest I reflected back on inspirational leaders who have inspired me – living or dead – to gauge what it is that was or is commendable that we could learn from them. I also reflected on the definition of leadership itself.

To respond to the first point of reflection: I have been greatly inspired by people who are not only visionaries but have consistently been resolute in the execution of their vision. I have drawn inspiration from people who were bold enough to take decisions that may not necessarily have made them popular but were imbued with the requisite emotional intelligence to be able to carry through those tough decisions. I have learnt from individuals who were not only self-aware of their strengths and weaknesses, but were also astute self-masters.

To respond to the latter point of reflection: Leadership in my view is, firstly, about possessing an innate ability to rally stakeholders around a set of common objectives. Secondly, it involves efforts beyond the rallying, which often require one to take full accountability in ensuring that the followers of that common vision are active participants in the functional application of all aspects necessary for the attainment of that vision. Thirdly, leadership is about arriving at an end and having the requisite humility to accept the outcomes. If the end has yielded desired outcomes, one celebrates with the collective. If the end has an adverse outcome, inspirational leaders draw key learnings and refine the approach for yet another attempt.

If the above definition in three parts finds resonance with most readers, the questions to ask ourselves about leadership therefore are: Does this innate ability to rally exist in South Africa in healthy doses across all sectors of society? Does its existence further the aims of a positive set of outcomes? Are our leaders accountable and present right throughout whatever process they may have initiated?

It is true however that identifying individuals with the 'right stuff' to be leaders is more art than science. After all, the personal styles of superb leaders vary and, just as important, different situations call for different types of leadership.

One of the greatest leadership mistakes I personally have made in the past was to be too trusting of results that get tabled before me. As a result I ended up having someone within our organisation who caused us a tremendous amount of reputational damage. Had I enquired thoroughly enough, had I 'peeled' to yet another layer, the facts about the person's character flaws would have been starkly before me – preventing me from making that appointment.

I learnt through that experience that empathy is sometime misconstrued or abused by those whose aim is to take you for granted in the first place. One may argue that during certain pressured times I had lost that enquiring edge whilst trying to balance too many responsibilities at the same time. I am not suggesting that leaders ought to now acquire paranoia and dig in unnecessary trenches. However, taking things and people at face value, and as they present themselves to one, can prove quite costly at times.

Looking at the demands that lie ahead, our country will require leaders who are able to self-govern; leaders with that innate ability to rally others around a set of common objectives; leaders who are not absent in the application process of those set of objectives and are accountable throughout the process. These leaders must emerge from all sectors of society if our country is to realise the imagined future well-articulated in the national vision.

Bridgette Gasa holds a PhD in Construction Management. She is the Founder and Managing Director of The Elilox Group, a consulting firm active in infrastructure development and agricultural enterprises. Prior to that she was Executive Head of the Khukhulela Consortium, an infrastructure Group. She was a member of the National Planning Commission. In 2008 she received the Department of Science and Technology's award for the leading woman scientist in industry. In 2013 she was crowned as Africa's most influential businesswoman in the category: basic industries.

Leaders Must Lead by Example

Cheryl Carolus

*Article published in Sake Beeld on 26 November 2015.
Translated from Afrikaans. Used with permission*

Leadership is a rare privilege – by definition, only a few can lead the many – and a wonderful opportunity to shape the future you desire. Needless to say, this comes with a huge burden of responsibility which calls for wisdom, but holds the threat of incarceration if you exercise this duty in an irresponsible manner.

The world is in a sorry state. Economies are under pressure, and previously rare events which have now become commonplace, like suicide bombings, increasingly define our understanding of what it means to be safe. Conflict has become an intra-national phenomenon with international consequences. The issues which cause conflict today are markedly different from those which once unleashed two world wars.

Our understanding of power has changed. Nowadays, those in power are more interested in 'controlling' than 'ruling' the masses. Governments are but one link in the chain of governance which ensures that societies function optimally.

A great deal of time and serious introspection is needed before we can develop social theories which fully encompass and institutionalise this knowledge. So great is the need, South Africa is compelled to adopt a 'fast forward' mode in everything it does. Here, the opportunities and the risks are much greater than one would find in a boring, run-of-the-mill democracy.

In this value chain, elected leaders play a vital role. They must strike a balance where conflicting needs arise, while serving the interests of the majority. I was furious, to say the least, that our elected leaders wasted so much time on ridiculous semantics as regards the private residence of an empowered citizen (the president) and the dress code of those in power who like a touch of 'bling'. I am livid that our parliament allowed the president to be subjected to political mud-slinging and uncouth behaviour. In my view, that is not leadership.

Even more lamentable are the actions of the various party leaders that overshadow the unbelievable achievements of many in those institutions. Achievements which even more established democracies cannot lay claim to, such as the wide-spread roll-out of antiretroviral medication; women in public leadership positions; the inclusion of people with disabilities; scientific innovations such as the Square Kilometre Array project; and world-renowned achievements in the arts.

Time is running out – we have to defuse the ticking time bombs of inequality and poverty. We cannot waste another 20 per cent of a democratic term in office. What will cure these ailments? Inclusivity and accountability.

The benefits of women's participation are evident on a global scale. We would be extremely short-sighted not to utilise our capabilities. Worldwide, women now make up more than 50 per cent of all graduates. The same goes for people with disabilities, who are fully capable of helping us tackle these significant challenges. To those whom history has marginalised, I say: Our constitution is a gift, if you choose to use it. Going it alone is one option, but working with others in an organised way is better. That way you can help to build a strong society. This not only applies to the public sector – truth be told, when it comes to inclusivity, the private sector is lagging behind.

How many of us use the mechanisms which are in place to ensure accountability, also as regards promulgating laws in this country? Do you participate in public hearings at provincial or national government level? Or in sectoral committee meetings? Do you serve on a school governing body? Those who wish to hamper progress in this country frequently make use of these mechanisms.

As a country, we can do so much better. We must compel our leaders to do a better job – in both the private and the public sector, as well as in the political arena. Accountability is plagued by two issues: corruption and the fact that the lives of the poor seemingly do not matter. Perhaps the time has come to consider mobilising public opinion as well as resources to prosecute any leader who benefits from corruption in the private or public sector. Perhaps we should use the full might of the law to prosecute an executive director if an employee is killed in the workplace. It may be time to launch a more thorough investigation into the impact of certain non-governmental organisations (NGOs), while simultaneously aligning their salaries with those of their counterparts in the private sector.

Let those of us who bear the title of leader, lead the way by example.

Cheryl Carolus is the Executive Chairperson of the investment management firm, Peotona, and non-Executive Chairperson of the mining company, Gold Fields. She is a former Executive Head of SA Tourism and also served as South African High Commissioner in London. Until 2012, she was the Chairperson of South African Airways.

Captaining On and Off the Field

Ali Bacher

Interview conducted by Wilhelm Crous of Knowledge Resources during April 2016.

Leading on the field

In my book top leaders and captains of sports teams have a lot in common. They are born with the gene to motivate people. I do not believe this is a skill that can be taught. I have worked with magnificent cricketers such as Jacques Kallis, one of South Africa's greatest all-rounders, who never wanted to be a captain, a leader. It just was not part of who he was. Whereas Hansie Cronje was someone who I considered a born leader throughout his entire career. He had the ability to motivate and stimulate a team.

It was the same for me. I was always able to captain teams. From primary school, where I captained soccer, cricket and tennis teams right through to captaining South Africa's Under 21s and then the Springboks. I really enjoyed every moment, doing my best to motivate players to improve their performances. That is what real leadership is about.

Whenever a cricket team is selected, there are probably about nine guys who are guaranteed places. They are doing well and you do not have to worry about them. But at every level there are always two or three who are a bit nervous. They might have had a few bad games and are feeling the pressure that if they fail again they could be dropped from the team. Those were the guys I used to focus on, without them being overtly aware of it. I would be there encouraging them at net practices and on the field, subtly lifting their performance. I not only enjoyed doing this, but I really wanted to do it.

It is all about the strategy

Being a captain also meant working out strategies which I loved doing. I would call a player or two before a game, trying to get their input or lift their performance, whatever it took.

I particularly remember one of the most extraordinary games I ever played in. I was captaining our school team and we were playing another school, our big local rival in a two-day game over a Wednesday and a Saturday. The Saturday game was a disaster for us as we found ourselves 29, all out and we had to follow on. Their captain came up to me after the game and said, 'perhaps we should call it a day and forget about next Wednesday?' I said absolutely not. It's part of the programme and you must arrive on Wednesday. The following Monday I rounded up a couple of my teammates and we went to the back of the science laboratory where we put together a strategy on how to beat these guys. I was always strategising. Wednesday arrived. They showed up 22 minutes late. By 4 pm I had worked out we needed about 170 runs to put us in a good position to win. I declared leaving them 105 minutes to get 70 runs. We bowled them out …

A born leader

There was a famous English captain, Mike Brearley (1977-1980) who although his test batting average was only about 24 – poor for a recognised test batsman – successfully captained England 31 times out of 39 matches. He was known as a great leader. He had the ability to bring out the best in his players, such as Ian Botham, who eventually took over the captaincy from him. When he finished his test career he became a psychologist, which was a perfect transition for him. Again a born leader.

Leading through people

You also have those captains who lead from the front by example, such as Eddie Barlow and AB de Villiers. Eddie Barlow was always up there at the front, getting runs, taking wickets – that was part of his personality. I was not like that. I was more of a quiet behind-the-scenes kind of guy – trying to get the best out of people by my own methods. I led through people. Leading through people is perhaps more sustainable. Morné du Plessis was a great example of leading through people.

Pressing the right buttons

Motivating people is not one size fits all. Take a player such as Graeme Pollock. There was a player you had to constantly assure he was the greatest batsman the world had ever seen. He liked hearing that. It motivated him and made him feel good about himself.

When I was captain of Transvaal, now the Highveld Lions, I had a fantastic medium fast bowler, Don Mackay-Coghill, who remains my best friend and now lives in Perth, Australia. We had a very ordinary attack in that team but he was our kingpin. I had to make sure I got the best out of him. There was only one way and that was to make him really angry. What I did was to get other players to subtly say to him: "You know what Barlow said about you the other day…" and he used to fall for it. He would get provoked, a bit cross, and he would go firing away. It was all about pressing the right buttons.

Before a match I would quietly phone some members of my team enquiring how they were feeling, how things were going: "Could I help?" This gave me a great insight as to their mindset before a game.

Although AB de Villiers leads from the front, he also falls into the category of a great leader. He is a very special person. In all my interactions with him I have come to know him as one of the most sincere, down to earth players I have ever dealt with. People like this and others, such as Morné du Plessis and Francois Pienaar, are meant to be leaders. People and players look up to them and respect them.

Great leaders on the field

There is far more to being a great leader than just ball skills. Mark Taylor, captain of Australia from 1994 to 1999 was not only a great tactical player and captain, but had a very warm disposition. A great mix for a captain. And then there is Steve Waugh, who took over the captaincy from Taylor in 1999, whose cricket thinking was unique. There is no other cricketer who has thought more about the game than him. He would look closely at his opposition and then work on how to get them out. He would know which batsman would work best against a particular left arm swing bowler or which bowler would lose their cool if you went after them quickly. This is what goes into making a great captain and leader: great thought processes.

Keeping up the motivation

This is sometimes the hardest part of being a leader. When we played Australia in the 1970 series there were some really brilliant performances. My problem was even though we were winning and giving the Aussies a thumping, how could we keep playing at the same level?

The Aussies had given us a battering in 1935 with the great Donald Bradman and again when they visited in 1949. We should have beaten them in the 1957/58 tour but again they won the series hands down. When they were coming here for the 1969/70 tour we were a young team, but we knew we were good and were very excited to be playing test cricket. We had players such as Barry Richards, Graeme Pollock and Mike Procter. I called them together and said to the team that they knew we had got pummelled by these guys in the past so we must make sure we give them a hiding like they have never had before. At the back of my mind was to try and get some comfort for those guys who had been so horribly beaten in all those previous tests.

We did just that, and if there had been a fifth test match we would have done the same again. South Africa won the series 4-1. We really went after them quietly. We did not shout the odds. It was not just because we had a great team. Sometimes you can have great players and something can go wrong and the aggro can start. There have been great teams with great players who should have won and they did not.

The challenges today

Today's teams face very different challenges. Mainly because of the huge press corps that goes wherever they go these days on and often off the pitch. When I think back for instance to our tour of England in 1965 we had the inimitable Charles Fortune, Gerhard Viviers (Spiekeries), a reporter from SAPA (South African Press Association) and George Scott from the Argus Group. That was it. This meant when we misbehaved – and we did – no one would know about it.

In today's world with social media and mobile phones, pressures on the captain and coach are far more formidable. Wherever you have countries with diversity you will be faced by political correctness. And being a sports leader, a captain, chairman of a union or a coach in these circumstances can be difficult.

My first piece of advice here is learn how to handle the media. I always had good interaction with the media, especially when I was in the administrative side of cricket. I used the media to promote the game. If I had a good idea of something new I thought would promote cricket I would give it to the media. They did not have to call me. Sometimes I would call them at 7am with a story because I knew it was newsworthy and they would publish it. I was proactive. Today very few people in cricket or even other sports know how to handle the media.

From the field to the boardroom, and making risky decisions

In 1981 I became the first CEO of SA Cricket until I left in 2003 after 23 years at the helm. And when I think back to some of the major decisions I made in the eighties I shudder. I remember going for early morning walks and saying out loud to myself: "Are you mad? If this goes south, you're gone!" Fortunately it did not happen.

Today working alongside CEOs making the same mistakes I did, I jump in and quickly tell them that before they make a move, to get approval from the financial guys. Do not wait until the Board meeting and spring your idea on them. Rather go and see the chairman and get him on your side first. I learnt you have to cover yourself. You cannot make huge decisions on your own. Be more democratic, participative in reaching decisions.

Compassion and kindness play a role

There have been many times when I have stepped in outside of my mandate as captain or CEO to help someone out. With Makhaya Ntini in particular, when I heard he had been accused of rape I really found it hard to believe. I went to Advocate Jeremy Gauntlett and asked him to step in and act for Makhaya. Gauntlett told me if he had believed he was guilty he would never have taken the case. He was convicted but it went to appeal, which eventually saw the case thrown out. A great relief.

Transformation in the future – it is all about opportunities

Right now cricket and rugby in South Africa are still producing good players. We have around 30 high schools renowned for continually producing Springbok rugby players alone. These are schools with a culture of these games. They have good coaches, players, headmasters, support staff and parents who attend the games. Grey College is a great example. The question that is being asked is how do we reach young black players. Do we go into the townships? Yes, to initially get their interest in the sports. But will we get players directly from there? No. Unless an African schoolboy has Brian Lara's genes he is not going to make it to a national side without resources, a great coach and support.

All our top young black players today have gone to the right schools. Take the current Proteas: Kagiso Rabada, the dynamic young bowler went to St Stithians; batsman Temba Bavuma to St Davids; Hashim Amla Durban Boys High and Makhaya Ntini, who we sent to Dale College. It is only by spotting talent and then directing them to these kinds of schools that we will get top black players right now. It is just a fact. Even if you are a young white rugby player at an obscure school in a small town. Unless you go to Affies, your chances of becoming a Springbok are small.

Makhaya Ntini is a perfect example of the current status of black players in South Africa. He was spotted by a black coach at the age of 14 at a mini-cricket clinic in a rural area of the Eastern Cape. He had one look at him and contacted one of our top coaches. If Makhaya had not gone to Dale College on a bursary he would still be there: in the townships. Cricket can change lives. We need sporting leaders to make this happen.

Rubbing shoulders with the mighty – what rubbed off

Perhaps the highlight of my career and the greatest lessons in leadership I have gained have come through having the privilege of interacting with people such as Nelson Mandela. The first thing that struck me when I met him was here was this man, imprisoned for 27 years, who has absolutely no malice.

In 1995 when we were hosting the Rugby World Cup he went public on a Friday morning with the decision that he would back the use of the Springbok emblem. The ANC were furious. The next thing I knew an SABC news team were at my door wanting to interview me on whether the same would now apply to cricket. I said we have great respect for President Mandela but we are not going that route. The Springbok emblem for South African cricket represented a period of our history where only whites could play. For us until today the Protea emblem is not a big thing.

A gesture of greatness

The next morning I received a call from President Mandela at 9am. He told me he had watched my interview. He then went on to invite me to have lunch the following Monday. I took two of my Board members and went along to the Union Buildings. It was the day before his birthday. Even though he did not drink, he insisted on opening a bottle of wine to celebrate with lunch. Then he took us outside and went on to explain why he supported the Springbok emblem. He said he knew how important rugby and the Springbok emblem were to the Afrikaner. His decision was because he wanted to thank them for supporting him as the first black president.

The late Steve Tshwete, who went on to become my great friend and colleague, told that he had also received a phone call from the President that day to tell him to bring a number six jersey to Ellis Park. When he asked why, he was firmly told that it did not matter. Just to bring it. Some of the players then told me the rest of the story. At around half past two that day there was a knock on the change room door and the security guard announced that President Mandela is here and would they mind if he came in. He walked in wearing the number six jersey, and went around the room speaking quietly to each player. As Kobus Wiese later said: "There was no way we weren't going to win for him." And how do you describe the reaction when Mandela walked on to the field? That is a leader that comes along once in a century.

Just a word from Madiba

In 1998 the great West Indies cricketers were due to tour South Africa for the first time. Unfortunately they were having an issue with their Board and had holed up in a hotel in London refusing to budge. Another great South African, Jakes Gerwel, who loved cricket passionately and who was Madiba's right-hand man came to the rescue. I told him that I had to go to England to try and persuade these guys to come and play here. He called me back half an hour later. That night I left South Africa with a letter from Madiba in my back pocket. I waited in London until a journalist tipped me off that the West Indies players were coming out of their room to talk to the media. I rushed over and pulled out the letter: my trump card. Brian Lara later told me they then had a meeting, which lasted a whole two minutes before they agreed to come. That was the power of Mandela.

Getting through the tough times

One of the hardest years of my cricketing career had to be England's 1990 rebel cricket tour to South Africa led by Mike Gatting. As soon as word got out they had arrived we started to hear there was going to be trouble. People were angry. We heard rumours that pitches would be invaded, and worse. Once we arrived in Kimberley we saw these were not empty threats. This was reinforced in Pietermaritzburg where I thought Gatting was going to get killed. So I called our Board together and said we have to call it a day. We will have to negotiate a way out. We cannot go on.

From then on I did not hear another word from a single member of my Board. I felt very much on my own. I found out later that Thabo Mbeki, operating from England at the time, was behind much of the protest action. He then got someone to call Michael Katz, the lawyer, to come and see me. He presented me with a mandate with a couple of options. This saw me negotiating with Krish Mackerdhuj – president of the SA Cricket Board at the time – at Michael Katz's house at 2am on how to go on or get out.

We had played quite well in the first part of the tour. There was supposed to be a second leg but I knew it would be crazy to believe this could happen. The SA Cricket Union guys were after me. Ironically the cricket fans in the township were also after me, but for different reasons. They were so angry I was not allowed back in the townships where we had a flourishing cricket programme going.

Fall out and the way forward

Everyone was angry at me. For the first and only time in my life I found myself leaving work at lunchtime, going home, pulling out the telephone plug and refusing to take any calls. I was absolutely finished. It was only after speaking to Van Zyl Slabbert that I saw some light.

A few years previously he had arranged for me to see Aziz Pahad in London about the situation in South African cricket. This time once again he came to my rescue organising a meeting with the late Steve Tshwete. This was a turning point. From then on Tshwete never stopped helping me. He was so credible amongst the African community and the Black Sports Congress. They knew he was backing me and they said fine. Day by day people who had been my adversaries became my best friends. It just took two allies, namely Van Zyl Slabbert and Steve Tshwete to save me.

Krish Mackurdhuj, who was quite a political animal at the time, said to me that he knew what I had been through but that the tour had to take place because it was a game changer for South African sport. It showed that you could not have sporting bodies come to this country without the majority of people's support.

The turning point

The only reason we were able to return to world cricket in 1991 was because we had the support of the ANC. Thabo Mbeki gave me a letter to go to the black cricketing countries, sending Steve with me to get support for our readmission. This was amazing when you think there was no guarantee that there was going to be a democracy. Or, that the ANC would ever really be in power. But they believed in our programme. And that we were genuinely trying to redress imbalances, giving young black cricketers real opportunities.

This came back to bite us badly when in 1999 with Steve Tshwete at my side, I went to The Wanderers for a test match against the West Indies, where South Africa fielded an entirely white team. This was the only time ever during my time as CEO of SA Cricket when I was forced to step in and ask questions. Even though we had Makhaya Ntini in the squad, I had been told although he was coming along well he was off form. At the time I came out publicly to oppose this policy and say that we must never field an all-white team again. This nearly cost me my lifetime friendship with Peter Pollock, the convenor of selectors, as well as making things very difficult between Hansie Cronje and I.

Tough decisions are not always popular

A week later we had a Board meeting. A policy was put in place that in future there would always be a team of colour. The first casualty of this was my nephew – Adam Bacher – whose place was taken by Herschel Gibbs. For the remainder of the tour – the seven, one day matches – we enlarged the squad from 14 to 17 players, adding three promising young black players. I knew the ANC were putting pressure on Steve Tshwete who had himself on the line for South African cricket since the early nineties. It was time for change. Even if some people were angry.

I had always said if you have a CEO of a company and everybody loves him, he has not done his job. Sometimes you have to make tough decisions and knock a few people off the road.

Let life's lessons guide you

Being a good captain and a leader means drawing on experience and the same goes in sport. I was captain of Transvaal at 21 but by the time I was made captain of South Africa I was 28 with seven years of hard cricket behind me. When Graeme Smith was made captain at just 22 I felt that was much too early. It is a huge responsibility to put on such young shoulders and there is no substitute for experience.

In summary

I believe the key features of a great sports leader are: (i) you have to be a natural (born) leader. You must want it and enjoy the pressures of leading; (ii) lead every player differently according to their specific unique strengths and weaknesses; (iii) strategise and pay attention to detail; (iv) prepare for the challenges of leading, i.e. have good communication and media skills; (v) be accessible to the media and supporters; (vi) where applicable, be inclusive and democratic in your decision making; (vii) be proactive; (viii) confront difficult situations. Bring in additional expertise and value advice; (ix) take calculated risks; (x) stay humble; and (xi) lead through others!

> Aron Bacher, given the nickname 'Ali' at the age of seven after Ali Baba, studied medicine and practised as a GP for a couple of years. He played in 12 Tests for South Africa, and took over the national captaincy in 1969-70, inheriting what was probably South African cricket's greatest side of all times, including Barry Richards, Mike Procter, Eddie Barlow and a pair of Pollocks. He became MD of the SA Cricket Union in the late 1980s. Seeing the democratic change in SA in the offing, he reinvented himself as South Africa's cricket supremo when the previously separate black and white associations combined to set up the United Cricket Board which he headed until the early 2000s.

Creating Team Movement in a Constantly Evolving and Changing Environment

Shameel Joosub

Interview conducted during February 2013 by Adriaan Groenewald of Leadership Platform. Used with permission

In describing myself as a leader and my leadership, it is first and foremost about the team. You need to have the right people around you to be able to deliver. If you have the wrong people, things are not going to happen. So yes, more emphasis on the quality of the team, and making sure we have the right people one level down, two levels down. Our ability to execute really comes down to the quality of the people as far down as possible. And then removing oneself from the detail and rather playing the role of coaching, guiding. You actually do not have the time to get into the detail even if you wanted to.

Also, a big change in the CEO role now is the whole investor relations. So on one side you are operationally involved, guiding, and so on, and then on the other side it is the investor relations, government relations, all the different stakeholder relations. You need to find a happy balance.

Sitting and looking at Vodacom from the CEO chair, firstly and obviously, the competitive environment has changed. I would say that South Africa lags by about 18 months. So having been seconded to Spain as Vodaphone's CEO for 18 month it was very good to see what the trends were, what to do and what not to do. For example, one area we have to improve in would be Customer Value Management. South Africa was quite advanced in what we would call Customer Relationship Management. But the world has moved on into Customer Value Management which is all about the systems and processes that ensure you are managing the value of a customer – one is the loyalty part; how you manage your most valuable customers, all those type of programmes.

I have been in the telecommunications industry already for 20 years. But what keeps me interested about the industry is the beauty that it is constantly evolving, constantly changing. There is always a new trend, there is always something new you are busy with. And that keeps it exciting. The nature of the industry provides so many opportunities as you go forward, and ones we have not even thought of yet.

Just to give one example. Oxford University reckons that the average person will have 16 SIM cards by 2020. All the technology, everything that we need to develop, to evolve, to create the different eco-systems and everything necessary for that to happen. It is going to be the world of connected devices. This puts you into a world where you walk into a store and you swipe your phone to pay for your purchases. All your loyalty cards, everything is in your phone. The reality is the technology is there now. It has already been developed. Now we have to create the eco-systems to take it to its full potential.

To put it in perspective, we have almost 14 million people accessing the internet via their cell phones just in South Africa. When we look at the fixed line penetration to access the internet we have via your desktop computer, this is what's happening on the mobile. It is huge. And every quarter when we look at the numbers, the amount of growth, and how much people are using – data grew by 40% in terms of usage per customer – you are starting to see more and more of that.

As leader it is crucial to be able to absorb intense competition: "The environment is quite competitive so yes, we have to look after our customer base and customers. What's more important is that you don't get fazed by competition no matter where that competition comes from, that you're executing on your own strategy, that's what's important – you have to have your own plan. You can't react to everything that competitors do. There will be times when you will need to react but what's more important is that you have your own plan and strategy that you're executing."

What is essential is to have a clear plan and strategy and everyone knowing exactly what is expected of them, with clear targets that are cascaded down and used to measure people. So they have clearly set targets with five priorities for each person three levels down, to make sure everyone is aligned. Every quarter they review the priorities and set new ones. Joosub believes this "helps to create common goals, common purpose, and common vision. That's extremely important – to know that the different teams within the company are pulling in the same direction."

Leadership is about creating movement. Over the last year, what has positively moved in Vodacom? "Firstly, from an international perspective, we have now cracked the international model – into Africa, and we are doing exceptionally well. Growth is coming from Africa where South Africa started to slow down a bit – that has created some great movement. It's also made us more confident as a team. In coming back one of the things that I've been pushing is a growth agenda. Why? Part of my role is to ensure the future success of the company, not just the current success of the company."

Other things that I think have evolved are our approach to what we are doing with the technology in the different countries. Also our approach to enterprise and the business, and what we started three years ago and how that has evolved. And then trends have changed, and that has forced us to make some evolutions. The other thing is that there has been some movement in people as well – making sure that we have the right skills to be able to deliver. That also plays a big role.

In keeping my mind and awareness sharp and to remain leadership fit as the CEO, a couple of things are important. Firstly, the exposure to Vodaphone as our international majority shareholder and, secondly, the different development programmes that they run. They do not allow you to become leadership-unfit. They run leadership development programmes a couple of times a year to help keep you abreast of trends and so on. Then things like being part of the strategy, being part of the bigger decisions, and playing a role. So you are getting constant feedback and seeing where the world is going and so on. Then I think one needs to stay abreast of technological advancements: what is happening; feedback from your own teams; reading extensively. All of these things I think help you to evolve yourself in terms of making sure you stay leadership fit.

Vodacom's role in making a difference in South Africa is to clearly align ourselves with government in every country in which we operate and help government to achieve its objectives. There is a strong association between access to mobile telecommunications and GDP growth. I think Vodacom has a key role to play in helping deliver those objectives. From a telecoms perspective in South Africa there is a policy that says we want to have access in every home – mobile access – by 2020. So the discussions I have been having with the President, the Deputy President, the Ministers and so on, is to say we can help you to deliver that strategy. We can and we will help you to deliver that strategy.

Shameel has been the Chief Executive Officer of Vodacom Group Limited since September 2012. He also has served as CEO of Vodafone Spain, one of the top 5 companies in the Vodafone Group between April 2011 August 2012. He holds a MBA.

Chapter 14: Leadership stories

Good Leaders Arae Guided by Reality, Not Wishful Thinking

Herman Mashaba

Article published in Sake Beeld on 7 July 2015, translated from Afrikaans, in combination with an interview during April 2012 conducted by Adriaan Groenewald of the Leadership Platform. Used with permission

In South Africa today, we have to focus on political leadership because that is the area where decisions are being taken that are impacting most negatively on the country. We read daily about decisions that appear to be purposely designed to cause harm instead of improve economic conditions for our people. A reality check should be telling the government that decisions they are taking are causing harm. They need to change direction but that is not what is happening. They seem to be determined to keep going in the wrong direction. There are all sorts of international comparisons that can help in making the right decisions to improve South Africa's economic growth but our policy makers seem to be determined to do the opposite of what works in the rest of the world.

You would think that if policymakers wanted to learn something from elsewhere they would choose to look at what the governments of Mauritius or Singapore are doing, not Cuba. As far as healthcare and economic prosperity are concerned there is a great deal to learn from the policies being followed in Singapore. And when it comes to relationships between government, business and the population in general, Mauritius seems to have found a way to utilise the talents of all its people to the best advantage of everyone. Their decisions were based on reality.

In my own business life I made a bad decision in 1997 when I sold a majority share in Black Like Me to a multinational company. My motivation was for our company to benefit from their well-established distribution network and marketing resources. Unfortunately we did not achieve the synergies I expected and the business was sliding backwards. Alien systems and controls were being instituted that added to costs but not to sales. Having done a reality check, I decided to negotiate a termination of the 'marriage', and ended up buying back the business two years later. Reality, not wishful thinking, had to be my guide.

Can our politicians not similarly see where they have made mistakes, do a reality check, and change direction? Do they not realise, for instance, that the talents of all the country's people must be fully utilised to make South Africa a prosperous and peaceful country?

If you look around the world for good leadership of a country you will have difficulty in finding a better example than the late Lee Kuan Yew of Singapore. Lee Kuan Yew became Prime Minister of a poor underdeveloped island of Singapore and turned it into the economic powerhouse it is today. Singapore has an excellent private/public healthcare system and the life expectancy of Singaporeans at birth is 82 years compared to the 53 years of South Africans. Singapore has a GDP per capita of $60,000 compared to South Africa's $11,000, and an unemployment rate of 2% compared to our 36.1%. So what kind of leadership gives you such results?

Would Lee Kuan Yew have introduced a national minimum wage at a time of massive unemployment? Never! Would he have told struggling employers to pay more than the wage they were already paying, which would make them employ less workers? No, he based his policies on reality! Does the government really believe the International Labour Organisation (ILO) representatives who are telling us that establishing a national minimum wage will be good for the economy? Or do they actually know that the ILO is talking rubbish and that if the price of labour increases the buyers will buy less of it and not more and our mass unemployment will increase.

There is no way you can force employers to pay salaries that they cannot afford. So what happens? They will not employ. And when you do employ someone and they do not deliver, you struggle to get rid of them. Why then take that risk. Business on its own is already a risk. We simply need to create a high employment market so that employers know that when they do not pay someone enough they are going to move next door. This is not rocket science, in that employers know they cannot hire and fire randomly after investing in people, because this costs money and time. No employer anywhere in the world would want to employ people just to exploit them. From a logical point of view it does not make sense. Because once you employ someone, for that person to be valuable to you they must be trained, and you do not want to lose people and continually train new people. For you to really stabilise your business, you need loyalty. That is where I believe we make a terrible mistake by ignoring the basic fundamentals of how an economy works. An economy works on the basis of creating entrepreneurs who must be able to employ people where it makes commercial sense. If it does not, then people do not employ.

When I visit less privileged communities I notice the levels of unemployment and the desperation of people, which many of us do. It is actually quite scary. It hurts me that I am unable to assist them. The only way I can assist them is to engage the law makers to understand the devastating effects of our current legislative framework. The responsibility lies with Parliament. They are the ones that developed and approved this legislative framework. They need to understand and appreciate the fact that South Africa is not made out of two million union members. It is made out of fifty million people and all of them are stakeholders. I think that when we come out with legislation, we should make sure we come up with something that is equitable to the fifty million South Africans and not the minority.

As it is, we have 8.7 million unemployed people (36.1% of the potential workforce) in this country. Is the government seriously going to implement a policy that increases that number? Does a reality check not tell them that if you implement the same minimum wage in urban and rural areas, where there is already a low demand for labour, people will definitely lose their jobs? Do they want to cause an 'Arab Spring'? Is that the only kind of reality check that will cause them to change direction? Why consult the ILO? Why not find out from our small and poor employers how many people they will have to fire to stop from going bankrupt themselves? Short-term interventions to create income, like grants, may be necessary. However, it destroys the dignity of our people if we see it as a long-term solution. It can never be a sustainable way of addressing our social issues. Dignity and determining one's own future are principles I believe in passionately.

South Africa's political leaders need to start basing their decisions on reality, and stop basing them on wishful thinking. The survival of the country depends on it!

Herman Mashaba is the Executive Chairperson of Lephatsi Investments; the Founder and CEO of Leswikeng Minerals and Energy; Founder of the beauty products company Black Like Me; and former Chair of the Free Market Foundation. His autobiography entitled *Black Like You* was published in 2013. In his book he shares his growing-up years in Ga-Ramotse, close to Hammanskraal, and how he started selling hair products out of the boot of his car.

Herman was elected executive mayor of Johannesburg in August 2016.

Head In The Clouds and Feet On The Ground

Pfungwa Serima

*Article published in Sake Beeld on 15 October 2016.
Translated from Afrikaans. Used with permission*

Barely two years ago, foreign businesses and analysts were hailing Africa as the world's economic miracle. With economic, political and social reforms sweeping the continent, a burgeoning middle class and growth rates hovering around the 6% mark, people were queuing up for a slice of a $1 trillion opportunity. Today, that picture might appear less appealing to some. Epidemic challenges have swept various countries, especially in West Africa. Across the continent, instability and conflict are either simmering just below the surface. Or worse, bursting out into the open. Between strikes, extremist activities, economic turmoil and political unrest, the African dream might be looking a bit threadbare right now.

Nobody said it would be easy. But for the businesses that are prepared to face the storm and manage the volatility afflicting the continent, there are still huge rewards to be had from doing business in Africa. You just have to be alive to the opportunities and avoid the pitfalls.

As the head of a multinational company that is deeply committed to Africa and its people, I believe firmly that this phase will pass. What is needed at times like this is the ability to manage volatility – something that companies in commodity markets are already familiar with. You do this by having an ear to the ground; have solid relationships with your partners and customers; and as much real-time information as you can get your hands on to make informed predictions and decisions.

The most important component to understanding the continent and its ways is time. When foreign businesses go into a country or a region with preconceived templates and notions, chances are they will miss the opportunity to truly understand how to work and collaborate with governments, potential partners, and potential customers.

Here is the best-kept non-secret to always consider. Africa is a large continent. One size does not fit all. Business is done very differently in Ethiopia than in Nigeria. You will never know Africa based on a PowerPoint presentation. You must immerse yourself into the continent and experience business on the ground, face to face. Choose a few key destinations. Spend time there. Not just for business, but to learn and experience. Engage people in business and on the street. This is the only way to understand the rhythm of the region and understand how business is conducted on the continent.

Of course there are challenges. In many regions, the lack of infrastructure and political instability means that cash is king. This will have a fundamental effect on the way you are paid, or intend to pay, for products and services. You need to stay hands-on. C-suites need to own relationships on the ground. If you're going to try and manage the business by remote control because you think a region is unstable, you are looking at a sure-fire recipe for failure.

I am often asked about the best country on the continent regarding opportunities and stability. There are many options. South Africa will always be right up there, and remains a key launch pad into the continent for many businesses. Angola's a great gateway not only into Lusophone Africa, but into Portugal as well. Nigeria, in spite of its challenges, is the largest economy on the continent and has immense strategic importance to West Africa and the continent as a whole. Ghana is stable, and a relatively easy place to conduct business. While Kenya is experiencing some political unrest, it remains a well-structured country with a strong political agenda. Morocco is emerging strongly as a gateway to West Africa for many European businesses and has created some promising partnerships with English- and French-speaking West African companies. Again, each area has its own regional rhythm of business engagement.

Leadership through volatility requires you to think beyond borders. From an African perspective, we need to drive growth across the continent. We need to start producing home-grown goods and services that our own people will use. We need to think about how we accelerate industries that impact larger geographic areas, thus uplifting more people, communities and smaller businesses that can capitalise on the downstream economic growth. It is Africa doing business with Africa, supported by the many foreign investors who want to contribute to our prosperity.

For us this means delivering a succinct value proposition. And for Africa right now, the Cloud is adding considerably to this task. The Cloud does not require any huge upfront investment. It allows us to be flexible and scalable in what we offer our customers, and what they in turn offer to their customers. It opens doors to locally-relevant, locally-built and locally-developed innovation. Most of all, the Cloud is a great platform to deliver fast, accurate business information and analysis that helps businesses chart their way through unpredictable waters. The Cloud can truly enable Africa to become a connected, networked economy one day.

Feet on the ground, heads in the Cloud. That's the way to do business in Africa right now.

Pfungwa Serima is the Executive Chair of SAP Africa. He is responsible for SAP's strategic direction on the continent. Previously he was the Executive Head of SAP Africa. He holds a degree in business studies and computer science.

SECTION 6
THE FUTURE OF LEADERSHIP

Chapter 15

LOOKING AHEAD

The Future of Leadership

Andrew J Johnson and Theo H Veldsman

In closing our brief excursion into *Leadership in Context* it is worthwhile repeating some key assertions we made in the opening chapter:

- leadership is under severe scrutiny, and;
- leadership is in the overheating crucible of a reframed/reframing world that is in the throes of fundamental and radical transformation, hence; and
- the search is on for better and different leadership, in the present and going into the future.

Going into the future, the need for organisations to have an ongoing, deliberate, comprehensive and in-depth conversation about leadership is an imperative if they want not merely to survive but also to thrive sustainably.

In this chapter we would like to gaze into the crystal ball by posing the question: If there is a need for better and different leadership going into the future, what would it look like with the conditions attached to such future-fit leadership?

To this end we explore the features of the growing crisis around leadership; the unfolding, future contextual leadership challenges; profiling the "context fit" leadership of the future; effective leadership engagement with the future context through Skilful Improvisation; and finally, the implications of Skilful Improvisation for growing and developing future-fit leadership.

Features of the Growing Leadership Crisis

Some of the important features of the growing leadership crisis that will have a significant impact on future leadership are:

- *Leadership no longer has any place to hide*. Leaders are in the public eye and under public scrutiny constantly because of the power of social media, and more stringent and expanding corporate governance requirements and demands.
- *Accelerating mistrust, anger towards, suspicion of, disillusionment in, and sense of alienation from, institutional leadership*, whether in business, the public sector, or in politics. There is a growing general public perception that "they are in it for themselves and their own enrichment. People and institutions are merely the means to satisfy their ego-centric needs, wants and purposes."
- *Greater and unrealistic expectations for "leadership on steroids"*. There is little patience with new leaders taking time to settle into and acclimatise to their new roles. The pressure is for instant delivery from the word "go", often against unreasonable deliverables, goals and standards. In many instances, the leadership role expectations from stakeholders are unclear and ambiguous, resulting in decreasing leadership tenures, and higher frequencies of derailment and burnout.
- The *emergence of more spontaneous leadership* in more places, at more times and by more people, the growing trend of "leaderless revolutions". These revolutions are fuelled

by the multiplication and mobilisation power of social media in the hands of everyone, everywhere, anytime. The spontaneous revolutions are blossoming around issues regarding globalisation, climatic warming, technological innovation, religious "holy wars", and demographic displacements like the European refugee crisis. Recent examples of such "leaderless" movements include the #arabspring movements of the Middle East; the #occupy movements in North America and Europe; and #mustfall movements in the South African higher education sector.

- The *growing cancer of toxic leaders, followers and organisations* because of the fanatical worshipping of unfettered individualism and egocentricity to the detriment of the pursuit common good; the rampant growth in personal self-interest and self-love (in other words, narcissism); putting "Me Pty Ltd" at the centre; the weakening of the overarching authority of commonly accepted ethical values and norms, also because of value clashes resulting from increasing multicultural settings; and weak followers unable and unwilling to challenge toxic leadership courageously and fiercely.

Unfolding Future Leadership Contextual Challenges

Against the backdrop of the above features of the growing leadership crisis, what are the most apparent unfolding future contextual leadership challenges? We would like to explore these challenges in terms of the conceptual framework given in Figure 15.1, constructed around the relationships in which a leader is embedded.

Figure 15.1 Leadership in relationship with the World, Organisation, Others and Self

According to the framework given in Figure 15.1, the leader's success resides in successfully connecting, nurturing and maintaining four interdependent, critical relationships – each with their unique interacting leadership challenges, demands and requirements – with the World; one's Organisation; Others; and Self. Each of the four relationship of leadership will be discussed in turn from a futuristic perspective. Though discussed separately and sequentially, the four relationships form an organic, systemic whole; are in constant reciprocal interaction; and form dynamic patterns, whether vicious or virtuous.

World

Much has been written and spoken about the VUCA World context of Volatility, Uncertainty, Complexity and Ambiguity, expanded here by ourselves to VICCAS: a World of increasing Variety, Interdependence (that is, connectivity), Complexity, Change, Ambiguity, Seamlessness and Sustainability. The counter, "dark" side of the above VICCAS features must also be considered: Over-standardisation, Over-dependency, Over-simplification, Over-formalisation, Over-control, Over-specialisation and Over-concentration. Going forward, the expectation is that the VICCAS Context will intensify.

The key challenges of the VICCAS Context are:

- Pressures arising from *macro destructive and threatening global, socio-economic dynamics invading the global village*, such as wealth concentration in the hands of a few "Haves"; the significantly growing income gap; the relative impoverishment of the middle class; growing structural unemployment because of the Fourth Industrial Revolution (see below); and population displacement because of climatic change and value clashes (see below). The sensitive, interwoven fabric and tapestry of the World – the playing field of leadership – is being torn apart.
- Social media *fragmenting the world into "e-suburbs" of vast global (radicalised) interest groups* talking only to themselves in self-referential ways in self-created echo chambers; radical group recruitment via the Internet; the global tsunami waves of fads and fashions, uninformed opinions and views engulfing the world; the snowballing generation of vast amounts of unvalidated data, information and knowledge feeding and swaying public opinion; parochial, selective views fed by search engines, for example, Google's search engines defining siloed realities for people. Those who have to be led are "disappearing" and becoming faceless in cyberspace through virtualisation and digitisation.
- *Vast technological innovation*, characterised by an exponential rate of change in and merging of multiple technologies across diverse domains such as the physical, digital, and biological manifested in, for example, Artificial Intelligence (AI), robotics, DNA sequencing, the Internet of Things (iot), driverless vehicles, 3D-printing, nanotechnology, biotechnology, big data, materials science, energy storage, and quantum computing. Digitisation and emails are replacing direct face-to-face leadership. It is believed that machines and systems are taking over, replacing people. Against the backdrop of keeping up with technological innovation, future leadership will have to align effectively in real-time technology, people, and working mode continuously relative to the strategic intent they are pursuing.
- Global fundamental *value system clashes and tensions* creating deep fault lines and schisms in communities, organisations and societies. Future leadership will need to build common, shared value spaces enabling diverse people to collaborate for the benefit and common good of all.
- The increasing *untrammelled power of big global corporates* – some bigger than states – leveraged from their control over vast resources globally, pressurising governments, institutions and stakeholders to "toe their line" in order to suit their parochial, narrow, corporate interests. The resources can be moved at the click of a mouse. The challenge to leadership is to move beyond narrow corporate self-interest and adopt a corporate social investment, common good, and a perspective infusing all of the corporate's thinking, decisions and actions.
- The growing *mismatch of global institutions* such as the United Nations (UN), World Bank, IMF, the International Court of Justice, International Criminal Court, and Interpol to

oversee and deal in globally representative ways with the increasing contextual complexity of the World. Increasingly these institutions are becoming too simple for, and too unrepresentative of, the complexifying World. The leadership challenge is the re-creation of the existing, and the setting up of newly conceived, institutions matched to the requisite contextual complexity of the VICCAS Context.

Organisation

Against the features of the VICCAS Context, organisations (including institutions) to be led in the future will be facing at least the following challenges:

- The heightened *vulnerability of the organisation's reputation and brand* to social media used for mobilisation against organisations by lobby/interest/pressure groups. Future leadership will have to be a master of the social media, and dominate this communication in space-time.
- The *disruption of traditional business models* because of virtualisation and digitalisation, for example, Amazon, e-Bay, and the on-demand economy driven by the emergence of applications (apps)-based organisations, for example, Uber and airbnb. Future leadership will have to question their existing business model on a continuous basis from first principles.
- The *deconstruction of big corporates* into smaller, highly autonomous, network-based business units in order to instil corporates with nimbleness, agility, client centricity, and responsiveness. The leadership of the future will have to be a networker and alliance and partner builder. He/she will have to be outstanding at building deep and robust relationships.
- Increasing pressure for *demographic representivity* regarding race, gender and culture at all leadership levels from board-level down the organisation, reflective of the organisation's chosen operating arena. Diversity sensitivity will be essential for future leadership.
- Globalisation, enabled by digitisation and virtualisation, will force organisations and leadership to adopt a *global mindset* manifested in thinking globally but acting locally.
- Organisations and their leadership will need to be *future centric* by visiting the future in order to create previously unimaginable, desirable futures. They will then have to return to the present to realise that future. Merely extrapolating from the present into the future, and applying past success recipes, will be a cause of certain extinction for organisations.
- *Disruptive innovation* because of the Fourth Industrial Revolution will necessitate the ongoing re-invention of organisations in terms of client needs, products/services, markets, and modes of delivery. Organisations will be in a constant state of flux. Future leadership will have to be relentless innovators, entrepreneurs and risk takers.
- The *increasing "algorithmisation" of professional knowledge, expertise and decision-making*, enabling para-professionals and users to take over work previously reserved for and claimed by professionals such as medical doctors, lawyers, chartered accounts, and psychologists.
- The *global demand for talent* appropriate to the VICCAS Context will lead to quicker promotion of leaders, resulting in less "intelligent" and mature leaders (see below) in senior and executive positions.
- The VICCAS Context will impose the imperative to shift from *the all-knowing, all-powerful single leader* to *shared (or distributive) leadership and the creation of leadership communities* in organisations, operating beyond hierarchy and function. This will enable the organisation to address more effectively the "wicked" challenges, problems and issues of the VICCAS Context.

Others

Some of the more important future challenges with respect to others are:

- The *range and diversity of stakeholders* of organisations and leaders will grow by leaps and bounds, also because of some of the above discussed trends and leadership challenges, such as the power of social media. Leadership will have to be knowledgeable about the diverse and conflicting needs of multiple stakeholders, including shareholders, the board, employees, suppliers, customers, regulators, competitors and the communities in which they operate, as well as the dynamics infusing each and among one another.
- In the VICCAS context there will be a *growing sense of disempowerment among stakeholders*, and consequently growing feelings among them of being helpless, threatened, anxious and angry. There will be a fervent, mounting, search for "the leader who can save us", creating the potential for followers to be vulnerable to leader exploitation and toxicity.
- The growing ambiguity with regard to *commonly accepted ethical values and norms*, also because of value clashes arising out of the growth in multicultural settings, giving rise to a greater need for value-based leadership, and to build on the "should" and "right". This leadership will need to focus not only on ethical leadership but also on creating a better society and world for present and future generations. Future leadership will have to be imbued by a moral consciousness, compass and courage leveraged from a transcendental leadership stance, namely "why?" leadership.
- The *growing power of public opinion*, solicited by ongoing surveys and referenda, and resulting in the *rise of opportunistic leadership* playing to the grandstand without a firm point of view, and acting without integrity. The need would be for future leadership acting with integrity from a clearly selected position.
- The employee base of organisations shifting to a *significant number of temporary/part time/contract workers* – many merely linked to the organisation through the Internet or an app – who have no real stake in and long-term commitment to the organisation. The challenge to future leadership would be how to engender high levels of engagement from these employees who in many cases have highly sought-after specialist skills.

Self

The challenges emerging from the above will require the future leader to dig much deeper into him-/herself, even though already being overstretched. Specific to the leader, at least the following major future challenges can be distinguished:

- The *constant onslaught on the leader's identity*: who and what am I?; what do I stand for?; what do I want to achieve?; to what end, and for whose benefit?
- The *rapid unlearning of a fixation on past success recipes*; being seduced by transient fads and fashions, and/or the fervent search for "silver bullets" propagated by snake-oil salespersons.
- More *frequent and widespread leadership transitions* requiring constant transitional adjustments by the leader. Leaders will have to be equipped with strong transition strategies and capabilities.
- A *tuned-in-ness to the vulnerability to succumb to toxic leadership*, arising out of the worshipping of individualism and giving rise to self-love; unclear, ambiguous, and conflicting values; the greying of ethics; and toxic friendly followers.
- Leaders running the risk of falling into the trap of *self-protective, "spin-doctoring" conduct* to protect themselves against relentless, merciless public exposure.

- A significantly greater likelihood and frequency of **burnout and organisational derailment** because of contextual pressures and unclear/unrealistic leadership expectations and demands by stakeholders. Leadership resilience will be a key future capability.

"Context Fit"-Leadership for the Future

A cursory scan of the contextual challenges discussed above, highlights the sizeable and seemingly overwhelming contextual demands on leaders going into the future. Leading in this unfolding new world is somewhat, in the words of Hixonia Nyasulu, Chairman of the women-controlled Ayavuna Women's Investments, "like playing tennis in the dark with unknown opponents, unexpected balls, unclear tennis court lines, and unpredictable weather". Equally, there are the possibly bewildering myriad leadership capabilities seemingly necessary to navigate and lead in the VICCAS Context, as elucidated above.

This situation could potentially leave an existing and/or aspiring leader deeply discouraged, with the natural, spontaneous response to withdraw, succumb or fight, instead of engaging positively. Going into the future, we submit that what is required is not a "silver bullet" set of specific capabilities, all needed at the same time in order to produce the "super" leader, able to be fully in charge at all times and under all circumstances; instead, the need will be rather to appreciate situation-specific leadership requirements and in this way identify, grow and develop context-fit leadership. Additionally, a community of leaders should be established, people who are able to lead effectively in a given/expected context through complementary, shared leadership, supplying collectively all of the necessary capabilities within and across situations.

Furthermore, in going into the future, a long-term, complex, and not short-term, mechanistic, vantage point to leadership should be adopted. Such a vantage point will enable us to re-imagine in a holistic, organic, integrated and dynamic way at a truly deep level a leader as a whole person embedded in his/her fourfold relationships with the World, Organisation, Others and Self, which will have to be dynamically and simultaneously aligned in real time.

Going Wide: Future-fit Leadership Capabilities Domains

Based on the above "design criteria", we would like to submit that contextual future-fit leadership will consist of five interdependent capability domains:
- **Able:** The hard and soft capabilities necessary to perform competently relative to contextual demands. The deployment of the required capabilities needs to be infused with the necessary qualities that will bring about hope, passion, caring, harmony, faith, confidence efficacy, courage and perseverance among followers, the psychosocial capital essential for followers to deal with the VICCAS Context effectively.
- **Intelligent:** Leadership who can observe, think, judge, act, learn and reflect with a growing understanding as they engage – conceptually and practically – with the VICCAS Context through converting experiences into information, information into knowledge, and knowledge into wisdom. The total "intelligence" (or meta-intelligence) of an excellent leader will consist of the five interdependent intelligence modes of Intra- and Interpersonal, Systemic, Ideation, Action, and Contextual Intelligence.
- **Mature:** Leadership able to engage consistently in relevant, productive, meaningful and constructive and uplifting ways with Self, Others, the Organisation, and the World.
- **Ethical:** Leaders and leadership who do the right thing for the right reasons in the right way in the right place and the right time with the right persons, that is, the "Should Do", the "Right thing".

- **Authentic:** Leaders and leadership which nurture and affirm the dignity, worth and efficacy of an individual(s), concurrently creating enabling, empowering, and meaningful work experiences.

Specific Future-fit Leadership Capabilities

Given the need for able, intelligent, mature, ethical and authentic leadership, required by the VICCAS Context, Figure 15.2 provides summarised clusters of suggested, more important capabilities ("Can Dos") for future-fit leadership, as per the leadership relationship dimensions discussed above – World, Organisation, Others, and Self. All of these capabilities are infused by the five capability domains of ability, intelligence, maturity, ethics and authenticity, as outlined above.

Figure 15.2 Clusters of suggested, more important capabilities for future-fit leadership

Effective Leadership Engagement with the Future Context through Skilful Improvisation

It should be clear that even when one distils the future-fit capabilities required by leaders – as per Figure 15.2 – to respond effectively to the VICCAS challenges, the list is daunting and intimidating. Therefore, as suggested earlier, one should rather adopt a situational appreciation for the contextual, relevant application of particular capabilities. Such an approach may then lead one to think of effective leadership as an act of "Skilful Improvisation". Perhaps as the futurist, Alvin Toffler, points out, a "new" type of leader is called for, one who depends less on his/her intellectual and technical skills, and is instead one who is open to learning new things, unlearning old things that no longer serve, and relearning some things of value that have been forgotten. In this case, "effectiveness" can be defined as the extent to which a leader is able to achieve his/her intended consequences in a certain context. If leadership is action, it implies that such action can be effective or ineffective relative to the context concerned. Skilful Improvisation entails enabling and empowering leadership to re-invent him-/herself continuously in real time as contextual leadership challenges, demands and requirements shift, expectedly and unexpectedly.

Conceiving of leadership as Skilful Improvisation accepts certain future-fit capabilities will be required to lead effectively in the unfolding Context. In order to do so, leadership will have to develop – holistically and organically – deep capabilities with regard to all of the relationships he/she is embedded in across the five critical capability domains discussed above: ability, intelligence, maturity, ethics, and authenticity. The development of such deep capabilities will require fundamentally deep self-introspection and reflection because the barriers to true leadership effectiveness, organisational change, and excellence reside fundamentally inside the individual leader.

We contend that the VICCAS Context faced by leadership we have sketched in *Leadership in Context* will only become worse. It is quite possible that by the time we have developed our leaders in what we consider the "necessary" capabilities, they will already have become outdated. Skilful Improvisation appears to be best suited to address the chaotic VICCAS Context adequately: the insight and will to be able to "read" the situation as a leader correctly; to exercise the right judgement; to choose from a set of capabilities such as those given in Figure 15.2 those that are situationally relevant skills as demanded by the task, people, organisational and contextual requirements; reflecting-in-action both on his/her own state of mind and the backtalk[1] of the situation, in order to perform effectively.

Impossible? Then perhaps leadership growth and development should be informed by the approach of artists. The above is precisely what jazz artists do so well.[2] Leaders know very well that life more often than not does not turn out in the way one has planned it. What if our thinking and doing are agile enough to bend with what we get served, analogous to the way in which jazz artists think and act. The jazz band may be playing a piece that they have rehearsed well, then unexpectedly someone makes a mistake. Now what if the thinking in that moment is: "There are no mistakes"; certainly not a "mistake" by someone else. Only the "mistake" of an inadequate in-the-moment response to the backtalk of the situation.[3]

Implications of Skilful Improvisation for Growing and Developing Future-fit Leadership

Skilful improvisation requires very deep personal development. Because leaders have little control over their external (chaotic) context, and quite likely become drained by its demands, it stands to reason that leaders will have to find resources internally in themselves. Such growth and development will include capacity growth and development in respect of the capability range indicated earlier (see Figure 15.2) but first and foremost in his/her relationship to him-/herself.

Going deep

This is essential because there is a blindness in all human beings through years of socialisation that necessitates that such growth and development drill deeper into the deepest layers of leaders' lived world if they are to be capacitated for the intensifying VICCAS Context. Figure 15.3 depicts the respective layers making up the leader's lived world, from "deep" to "shallow".

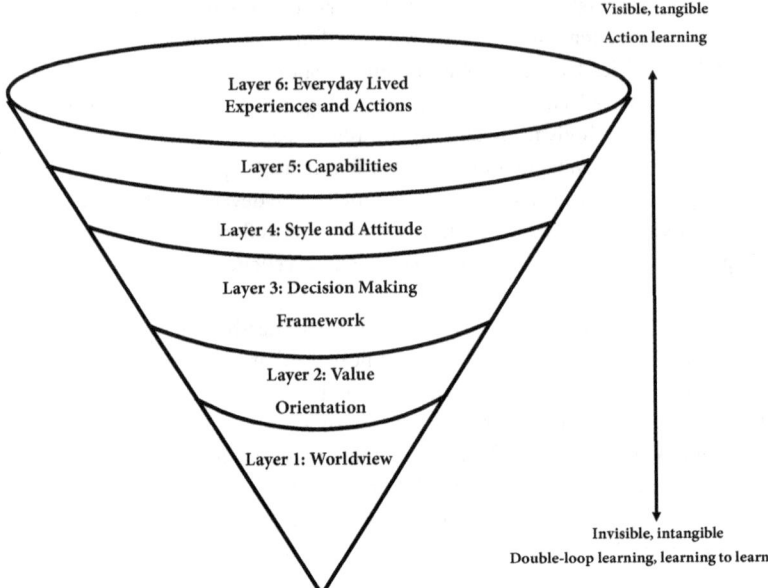

Figure 15.3 Layers making up the leader's lived world

Analogous to the building of a house, future-fit leadership growth and development have to commence with the deep Layer 1: Worldview (or Mental Model), and then proceed progressively to the more shallow layers in a "building onto" manner. Learning in this way will help the leader to bring his socially programmed blindness to conscious reflection, and develop new pathways towards effective leadership, including purposefulness: an authentic balanced disposition to the needs of others (= all stakeholders), the organisation, and the world. Learning approaches and methods will have to be employed by organisations that elicit valid information and knowledge about what individuals think and do at deep layers, because the default pattern of individuals is to employ defensive reasoning. We espouse leadership effectiveness, but as human beings we lack the ability to produce such holistic inside-out development. In addition, we are unaware of this serious, future-compromising limitation.

Bringing about deep learning

How do we effect this deep learning? As indicated earlier, one cannot simply focus on changing Layers 6: Everyday lived experiences and 5: Capabilities (see Figure 15.3). Layers 5 and 6 learning tend to break down when people experience stress because stress triggers default conduct. One has to change the underlying layers, in particular Layers 1 to 3, that drive the conduct, to Layer 6. Skilful improvisation requires drawing on deep, internal personal resources that this type of development endeavours to develop.

The knowledge organisations produce in our leadership growth and development programmes must be in the service of enabling leadership action with regard to Layer 6. Two expressions of such learning are (i) *double-loop learning*, aimed at getting to the mental models comprising underlying beliefs, values and attitudes (Layers 1 to 4) that perpetuate ineffective leadership action, in conjunction with (ii) *action learning*, focusing on conduct change through reflection on real stakeholder and organisational challenges (in other words, Layers 5 and 6) (see Figure 15.3). In the words of Argyris, Putnam, and McLain Smith,[4] methods will have to be employed "to make known what is known so well that we no longer know it, ... so that it might be critiqued, ... and to make known what is unknown, ... the discovery of alternatives so that they too might be critiqued". Skilful improvisation contains such reflexive qualities.

Bridging the science-practice gap

Such leadership growth and development, based on sound scientific principles, will have the potential to respond adequately to bridging the perennial, ongoing science–practice gap. *Leadership in Context* abounds with many such exemplars. In practice, this growth and development in organisations can be self-driven, technology-enabled, classroom- based, experiential and/or coaching, provided it conforms to its purposes: deep, inside-out growth and development from Layer 1 "upwards" towards Layer 6. Then and only then will organisations be preparing and delivering the right leadership in the right numbers at the right time and place, able, willing and empowered to perform effectively within the VICCAS Context.

Fundamental to this leadership growth and learning will be the need for academics and development practitioners to do less "esoteric", practice-estranged work that results in the growing gap between theory – the proverbial ivory tower – and practice. Within the VICCAS Context, real action research partnerships between academic institutions and business/non-governmental institutions/public sector are essential, focusing on leadership growth and development that is useful to leadership in the moment of action where it matters and will make a real difference. In other words, leadership growth and development that is characteristic of reflective practice, reflecting-in- and -on-action. Given financial pressures, organisations need to place a much greater emphasis on evidence-based, actionable knowledge to drive their change efforts. The speed of practice-referenced and -informed research delivery by academics will have to match the speed of change in the practical world. Otherwise, academics and academic institutions will rapidly become irrelevant to a VICCAS Context "running away" from them. They will become the extinct dinosaurs going into the future.

Conclusion

Having explored tomorrow's VICCAS Leadership Context with its features resulting in "wicked" leadership challenges, issues and problem, answering the remaining ultimate question posed in the Introduction is: "Is there a future for leadership?" Yes, there is a future for leadership, but it is conditional on:

- A *deep understanding of the unfolding VICCAS Context* going into the future in terms of leadership's fourfold relationships with the World, Organisation, Others and Self;
- *Adoption of a complexity vantage point* to leadership;
- From this complexity perspective, *re-imagine at a deep level leaders in a holistic, organic, integrated and dynamic way as a whole person,* in terms of their ability, intelligence, maturity, ethics and authenticity, as embedded in their fourfold relationships, all of which have to be dynamically aligned simultaneously in real time;
- Enabling and empowering leaders to engage with the Context through ***Skilful Improvisation***;
- *Growing and developing leadership from the inside-out*, commencing with the deeper layers of leadership's lived world: Layer 1: Worldview through double-loop learning, progressing through action learning towards Layer 6: Everyday Lived Experiences and Actions; and
- *Forming vibrant two-way interactions between the academic and practice worlds,* producing just-in-time, evidence-based, actionable knowledge to drive change efforts to make leaders future-fit.

What a challenge lies ahead of all of us to make it happen in a world that is in desperate need of leadership excellence in order to ensure a sustainable, flourishing future for all.

Endnotes

1. "The situation talks back, the [leader] listens, and as he appreciates what he hears, he reframes the situation once again": *cf.* Schön, DA. 1983. *The reflective practitioner.* New York, NY: Basic Books.
2. *cf.* Also (a) Warren Bennis on jazz and leadership: "I used to think that running an organization was equivalent to conducting a symphony orchestra. But I don't think that's quite it; it's more like jazz. There is more improvisation"; (b) the leadership development training, styled on UK Channel 4s "Whose line is it anyway?", *Workplace IMPROV*, designed by stand-up comedian, Nadiem Solomon. The fundamental rule in this training is "pay attention".
3. Harris, S. 2011. *There are no mistakes on the bandstand.* TEDSalon NY2011.
4. Argyris, C, Putnam, R & McLain Smith, D. 1985. *Action science: concepts, methods, and skills for research and intervention.* San Francisco, CA: Jossey-Bass Inc. 237.

INDEX

A

action intelligence, 27
action lenses, 4
adaptability, 125, 127–128
administrative leadership, 65, 70–71
Affirmative Action (AA), 75
African agentic leadership, 129, 135, 143
African influence, 136
African renaissance, 140, 142–143
agility, ii, 18, 24, 27, 102–103, 110, 117, 119, 121, 123, 125, 127–128, 179, 209, 212
anticipatory thinking, 165–166
archetypical value orientations, 180–181
athletes as investors, 96–97
authentic relationship formation, 18
automated organisations, 20

B

best-fit worldview, 175
breaking down the barriers, 45
bridging the science-practice gap, 215
Broad-Based Black Economic Empowerment (BEE), 75
building human capital, 106
business leadership, 110, 121, 123, 125, 127

C

call to lead, 151
challenges faced by principals, 36
client needs, 106, 114–117, 209
collaboration, viii, 24, 27, 44, 112, 124–125, 165, 212
commercialisation, 93, 95–97, 100, 102, 104
community leader, 80–85, 87–91
community leadership, 79–81, 83, 85, 87, 89, 91
company agility, 121, 123
comparison of expectations, 107
competency-based approach, 73
complexity, 7, 11–14, 16–18, 21–23, 26–29, 35, 56–57, 100, 106, 108–109, 112–113, 169–170, 172–178, 182–184, 208–209

conceptualisation of organisation, 173
conceptual lens, 3–4, 6
conflicting demands, 125, 127
consulting firms, 105–107
contextual change, 11
contextual complexity and stakeholders, 11–12, 28
contextual complexity variables, 13
contextual frames, 11–12
contextual intelligence, 27, 169, 211
contextual vantage point, 11–12, 28, 177
core purpose of principalship, 39
creativity, 18, 41, 62, 157
critical competencies, 57, 165

D

decision-making, 20, 52–53, 123, 151–153, 169–170, 176–179, 182, 209
deep learning, 214
defining leadership, 3, 5
demands, and requirements, 8
demographic shifts, 2, 17, 114–115
differentiation, 93–94, 100, 104
different worldview, 18
digitalised organisations, 20
digital revolution, 119–120, 128
digitised solutions, 115–116
diverse stakeholders, 14–16, 18
DNA of professional firms, 117
dynamics in sport, 93

E

ecologically embedded leadership, 8, 159, 161, 163, 165, 167
ecological stability, 161–162
ecological systems, 163, 166
ecosystem, 16, 113, 115–116, 159–160, 163–164, 167
embedded views of organisations, 163
emerging leadership, 18
emerging world order, 15, 17–18, 20–21, 25–26, 170

engagement mode, 7, 9, 16, 169–170, 182
ethics, iv, 29–30, 95, 100–101, 104,
    121–122, 124, 142, 157, 167,
    184, 210, 212–213, 215
executive leadership, vii, 29, 70–71
experimentation, 18, 176, 179

F

facets of operating arena, 23
facilitating learning and growth, 44
fit-for-purpose alliances, 125, 127
functional leadership, 140
future-fit leadership, 4, 8–9, 11,
    17–18, 20, 26, 206, 211–214
future mega-trends, 114
future of leadership, 8, 205–207,
    209, 211, 213, 215
future perspective, 12, 43, 59, 75, 90,
    93, 103, 114, 125, 139, 154, 165

G

gamification, 96
geopolitical focus, 119–120
globalising organisations, 20
global mindset, 14, 18, 24, 27, 209
global sponsorships, 98
global supporters, 98
governance and responsiveness, 121–122
governance challenges, 71
governance instrument, 138
government schools, 34
growing and developing future-
    fit leadership, 206, 213
growing and developing the organisation's
    leadership talent, 4–5
growing leadership crisis, 206–207

H

headcount enrolment and growth, 54
higher education, iv–v, viii, 8, 34, 41,
    49–53, 55–63, 75, 77, 207
higher education sector, 49, 51, 60–61, 207

I

ideation intelligence, 27
Ignatian spirituality, 145, 150, 153, 156
individual sense-making and
    meaning-giving, 5
inequality of wealth, 121–122
innovation, 17–20, 43, 46, 73–74, 102–103,
    110, 114–115, 117, 121, 125–126,
    152–153, 167, 204, 207–209
innovative solutions, iii, 32, 41, 45
intelligence modes, 26–27, 211
interpersonal relationship, 136
interpretative lens, 4

K

key areas of principalship, 40
key challenges, 36, 65, 81, 208

L

leadership and spirituality, 146
leadership as strategic organisational
    capability, 6
leadership attributes, 23, 25,
    101, 125, 127, 169
leadership brand and profile, 4–5
leadership challenges, 4–9, 11–17, 19,
    21, 23, 25–29, 32–33, 35, 76–77,
    80–81, 93, 206–207, 210, 213, 215
leadership context, ii, 4–8, 11, 16, 215
leadership-context fit, 7, 25, 169, 182
leadership contextual challenges, 207
leadership contextual engagement, 7–8, 168
leadership demands, 7, 16, 18–20,
    23–24, 26–27, 105, 119, 121
leadership dynamics and transitions, 5
leadership engagement, 8, 169, 171, 173,
    175, 177, 179, 181, 183, 206, 212
leadership excellence model, 4–5
leadership for the future, 211
leadership framework, 3–5,
    105–106, 109–110
leadership in practice, 106, 110
leadership outcomes and impact, 5
leadership stories, 5–6, 8, 185–187, 189,
    191, 193, 195, 197, 199, 201, 203

leadership theories, 49
leadership well-being, 2, 5
leading in uncertain times, 61
leading professional firms, 105
levels of work, 22, 30
leverage model, 105–106
lifecycle, 106
listening, 27, 124, 165, 212
looking ahead, 165, 206

M

machine view of organisation, 173
macro, external context, 17
make-up of leadership, 170
managing ethics, 100–101, 104
managing the complexity of sport, 100, 104
Mandela era, 66, 68–69
mass and universal higher education, 52
Mbeki era, 66, 69
merit-based, 75–76
millennials, 115, 125–127
mindset shifts, 19
multidimensional, 129, 131, 133, 176, 186
multiple roles, 106, 108

N

nested dependencies, 162
network, 19–21, 27, 29, 43, 87, 108–109, 136, 146–147, 153, 167, 186, 201, 209
network and hierarchy, 146–147

O

operating arena, 7, 11–14, 16–17, 23–28, 169, 209
opportunistic behaviour, 108–109
organisational action processes, 4
organisational design, 19–21, 30, 117
organisational navigation ability, 18
organisation of the future, 19–21, 183
organised religions, 147
origins of townships, 80

P

Pan-Africanism, 134–135, 139

participatory leadership, 44
Partners for Possibility initiative, 43
partnership model, 106, 112
personal and interpersonal intelligence, 26
planetary boundaries, 160–163, 165–167
political leadership, v, 65–66, 70, 129, 131, 133–135, 137, 139, 141, 143, 201
political savviness, 124
poor education outcomes, 35
pro-actively insights, 9
producing manager, 106–109
professional services, iv, vii–viii, 105–113, 118
profitability drivers, 106
public sector approach, 73
public sector leadership, 65, 67–71, 73–78
purpose and structure, 6

R

radical innovation, 125–126
regions/country features and dynamics, 23
re-inventing business of sport, 100, 104
relevance for higher education, 49
religion, 8, 81, 88, 91, 145–149, 151, 153–157
spirituality and leadership, 145
renaissance decade, 134–135
resilience, 27, 40, 102–103, 125, 127, 161–164, 166, 211–212
resources and education outcomes, 34
responsiveness/agility, 18, 24
risk taking, 18, 124–125, 212

S

school leadership, 32–33, 35, 37–39, 41, 43, 45–47
school leadership challenges, 32, 35
school leadership competency standard, 32, 38
sectorial contexts, 8, 31
sectorial leadership challenges, 7
secularity and spirituality, 149
service delivery, 65, 68–71, 73–74, 76–77, 81, 117
shifting perceptions, 163
skilful improvisation, 206, 212–215
skills versus competencies, 44

social justice, vi, 83, 86, 90–91, 120, 159, 162
socio-economic factors, 119–120
sociopolitical, 66, 77, 119–120, 124, 155
South African school landscape, 32–33
South African standard for principalship, 39, 46
spirited leadership, 153
spirituality, 8, 145–157, 180
sports leadership, 93, 100–101
sports leadership challenges, 93, 100
stakeholders, 11–12, 14–16, 18, 21, 24, 33, 35, 38, 125, 164, 174–176, 178–179, 206, 208, 210–211
state-owned enterprises, 65, 71, 75, 77–78
stewards of social needs, 76
strategic leadership framework, 3–5
strategic leadership value chain perspective, 2–3, 9
strategic postures, 12
sustainability, vii, 2, 14–15, 21, 29, 120, 126–127, 162–165, 167, 208
sustainable performance, 100, 104
systemic, holistic thinking, 18, 20
systemic intelligence, 26
systems thinking, 165–166, 183–184

T

talent grab, 119–120
technological innovation, 17, 114–115, 207–208
theory and practice, 29–30, 41, 154, 163, 184
thinking framework, 3–4, 6, 14
time orientation, 11
training for school principals, 41
transformation, iii, v, viii, 2, 17, 24, 27, 65, 71, 75–76, 93, 99–101, 104, 138, 145
transformational authority, 133

U

uncertainty, 17, 60–62, 75, 112–113, 115, 117, 120, 141, 161, 186, 208
under-resourced schools, 34–37, 40, 42, 45
understanding and sensitivity, 121
unique leadership challenges, 33, 80–81

V

value orientation, 27, 169–170, 179–183
value orientation schemata, 180, 182
virtualised organisations, 20
volatility, 17, 112–113, 119, 203–204, 208

W

world at large, 7, 16–17, 22–23, 169
world of tomorrow, 2, 8–15, 17–19, 21, 23, 25–29, 115, 125, 176

Z

Zuma era, 67–69

www.ingramcontent.com/pod-product-compliance
Lightning Source LLC
Chambersburg PA
CBHW071228170426
43191CB00032B/1128